FLAUBERT'S *SALAMMBÔ*

Currents in Comparative Romance Languages and Literatures

Tamara Alvarez-Detrell and Michael G. Paulson
General Editors

Vol. 107

PETER LANG
New York • Washington, D.C./Baltimore • Bern
Frankfurt am Main • Berlin • Brussels • Vienna • Oxford

Volker Durr

FLAUBERT'S *SALAMMBÔ*

The Ancient Orient as a Political Allegory of Nineteenth-Century France

PETER LANG
New York • Washington, D.C./Baltimore • Bern
Frankfurt am Main • Berlin • Brussels • Vienna • Oxford

Library of Congress Cataloging-in-Publication Data
Durr, Volker.
Flaubert's Salammbô: the ancient Orient as a
political allegory of nineteenth-century France / Volker Durr.
p. cm. — (Currents in comparative Romance languages and literatures; vol. 107)
Includes bibliographical references and index.
1. Flaubert, Gustave, 1821–1880. Salammbā. 2. Carthage
(Extinct city)—In literature. I. Title. II. Series.
PQ2246.S4 D87   843'.8—dc21   2001033165
ISBN 0-8204-5676-4
ISSN 0893-5963

Die Deutsche Bibliothek-CIP-Einheitsaufnahme
Durr, Volker:
Flaubert's Salammbô: the ancient Orient as a
political allegory of nineteenth-century France / Volker Durr.
–New York; Washington, D.C./Baltimore; Bern;
Frankfurt am Main; Berlin; Brussels; Vienna; Oxford: Lang.
(Currents in comparative Romance languages and literatures; Vol. 107)
ISBN 0-8204-5676-4

The paper in this book meets the guidelines for permanence and durability
of the Committee on Production Guidelines for Book Longevity
of the Council of Library Resources.

© 2002 Peter Lang Publishing, Inc., New York

All rights reserved.
Reprint or reproduction, even partially, in all forms such as microfilm,
xerography, microfiche, microcard, and offset strictly prohibited.

Printed in the United States of America

Contents

Preface		vii
Acknowledgments		xiii
Introduction		1
I.	Authorial Motivation, History, and the Orient	13
II.	The Setting of Carthage and the Titular Heroine	39
	Why Carthage?	39
	Salammbô	51
III.	Hamilcar Barca: Revolutionary Chaos and the Charismatic Leader	69
IV.	An Allegory of Bonapartism	87
V.	Making the Old Orient Present	113
	The "écriture" of *Salammbô*	119
	Discourse, Dialogic Practices, and Intratextuality	125
	Aspects of Imagery: Serpents, Snakes, Vipers, and Dragons	134
	Time and Repetition	138
VI.	Epilogue	153
Bibliography		163
Index		177

Preface

With its phantasmagoric setting, extravagant love story, and monstrous events the Afro-Oriental novel *Salammbô* reveals essential traits of Flaubert's self as distinctly as the Egyptian soul drama *La Tentation de Saint Antoine* and the exotic tale "Hérodias." The three Oriental works unabashedly illustrate their author's indulgence in reverie and dreams as an antidote to French contemporaneity represented in his Realist narratives *Madame Bovary, L'Éducation sentimentale,* "Un Coeur simple," and *Bouvard et Pécuchet.* While Saint Antony ultimately resists all seductive apparitions and the setting of "Hérodias" appears as empty at the end of the tale as in the beginning despite the closing promise, "[Jokanaan] has decended to the dead in order to announce the Christ," the foremost characters of *Salammbô* do not shun but eagerly embrace the offerings of the world. In this respect *Salammbô* is unique among Flaubert's creations.

The division of Flaubert's works indicates that the author's personality had two sides. One rejoiced in lavish descriptions of colorful, exotic, and brutal mythical worlds in which the self could live out its primordial instincts such as withdrawal, erotic fulfillment, or will to power, while the other felt the need to confront the prosaic conditions of modern reality with scientific scrupulousness and detachment. To be a saint, a great lover, or a tyrant, these were the alternatives in Flaubert's imaginary life. Although the writer Flaubert opted to live like a hermit, this decision did not prevent him from having occasional mistresses and making sorties to the brothels of Paris; during his journey to the Orient he favored that region's corresponding indigenous establishments. While settling down to the lonely life of a writer, he continued to observe the social and political scene of his present as well as its erotic and sexual mores.

Salammbô is a monument to Flaubert's "true" Orient, that vast region stretching from the Maghreb to the Eastern borders of India, and from

Albania or Bokhara to Yemen and the Sudan. As such, his novel is most likely the best known work of the so-called Oriental Renaissance Raymond Schwab has described with acumen. Whereas Flaubert had been interested in the Orient since adolescence, his journey through the Levant was motivated by Napoleon I's expedition to Egypt and Syria, the travelogues of famous Romantics such as Chateaubriand and Lamartine, and the Oriental poetry of Victor Hugo who had never visited the region. Flaubert wanted to see for himself. The Orient surpassed his expectations and made him appreciative of its imposing landscapes, vegetation, its liquid light, colors, and its people. In many places life had changed little since Biblical times so that actuality had retained its poetic quality: beauty and sordidness, misery and splendor, life and death, existed there side by side. For Flaubert, the Orient constituted the "great synthesis," a seemingly genuine alterity to the compartmentalized social life of modern Europe.

Although the purple lure of the Oriental elements in *Salammbô* initially exerted a strong attraction, in the course of my reading the political events steadily gained significance in its cosmos, as did the perception that the Punic crown and state action was relevant to the political events in nineteenth-century France. What I intend to show, then, is how the Realist writer Flaubert embedded his profound criticism of the revolution of 1848 and the rise of Napoleon III in an allegory of the poetic and brutal ancient Orient. (That Flaubert was deeply affected by the course of the revolution of 1848 is verified by *L'Éducation sentimentale,* just as the event reverberates in *Bouvard et Pécuchet).* Neither Flaubert's contemporaries nor scholars and critics of the twentieth century up to Christa Bevernis and Bosse/Stoll have perceived the relevance of the war between Carthage and its foreign mercenaries (242–237) to the class struggles of revolutionary France in 1789–1804 and 1848–1852. The latter ended with the ruthless subjugation of the working class by the bourgeoisie, Louis Napoleon's coup d'état, and his proclaiming himself emperor. In Carthage, the foreign mercenaries (the lowest class), cheated of the wages due them, rebelled against the avaricious merchant oligarchy which, near perdition, recalled Hamilcar Barca from abroad and granted him sweeping powers to crush the insurgents. Thus, Hamilcar, Salammbô's and Hannibal's father, became tyrant of Carthage and nursed far-reaching plans to make himself king of a Hispanic empire and to found a Barca dynasty.

It is not surprising that the readers of *Salammbô* did not see such political parallels. In the first place, nineteenth-century French readers were unlikely to compare the politics of France, still "la grande nation," with those of a small Oriental people. Was the contemporary Orient not backward and decrepit, unscientific, and languishing in a stupor, as it were, in short, was it not ready to be divided up between France and England? How could the Punic possessions be likened to France since the Carthaginians had been depicted in history, written by their ethnic and cultural enemies, as an abject race: greedy, licentious, perfidious? Around the Mediterranean they had been ubiquitous, but no one knew much about them. The fear and dislike they inspired were due to their uncanny demeanor, their cleverness, and riches, for the Phoenicians, their ancestors, had invented the alphabet, glass-making, and the manufacture of the much sought after color purple, from which they reaped fortunes through the sale of purple textiles. Carthage and its empire were a perpetual danger to every state. On account of its wealth it could raise large armies of mercenaries any time. Yet had the holocaust at the end of the third Punic war not erased it from the face of the earth, and had the Roman victor, Publius Cornelius Scipio Aemilianus not cursed its site by scattering salt over it? In contrast, Paris, "the capital of the world," was becoming ever more grandiose under the aegis of Napoleon III. Moreover, most Frenchmen believed that France was the true heir of Rome which had fought to the death with Carthage, that Afro-Oriental threat to European civilization.

In *Black Athena* Martin Bernal shows that the nineteenth-century French imagination equated the Phoenicians with England: naval powers of shopkeepers and traders with colonies and fortified harbors throughout their worlds. Bernal finds fault with *Salammbô* on two grounds. First, Flaubert supposedly implies that his Carthage of the third century B.C. was typical of ancient Oriental culture, while the novel is a study in decadence depicting "the most decadent aspect (mercenaries) of the most decadent city (Carthage) and the most decadent people (the Phoenicians)." As a result, not only did Carthage deserve "the genocide it received from Rome ninety years later," but as far as the readers were concerned, "there was little moral objection to the colonial destruction of a non-European civilization in the 19th century." Secondly, Flaubert allegedly implied "that Europeans—with the possible exception of the English—were incapable of such things" (utmost cruelty and sadism). However, Bernal's claims are neither supported by Flaubert's texts, nor by historical data. To be sure, Flaubert incorporated many of his observations in the Orient in his novel, but it is by no means certain that he considered Carthage typical of Oriental culture. Whereas in sexual mores, the Phoenicians were similar to other Semitic peoples (e.g. Hebrews and Arabs) before these accepted monotheism (Max Weber), they differed as sea-farers from all other early Orientals. Also, they were more enterprising than their ethnic relatives, and they had drafted one of the best constitutions of antiquity according to Aristotle and Isocrates (this in contradiction to Michelet who accorded the gift of legislation to the Indo-Europeans).

In contrast to Bernal's assertions, Flaubert saw things differently than the representative cultivated Frenchman, for he actually loved the Orient as a place where his dreams had become reality. Not infrequently this love was triggered by what his more conventional contemporaries would have labeled perversions. Thus he was not only attracted by Oriental sexual licentiousness from which the "Victorian" temper throughout Western Europe recoiled, but he actually engaged in some of its practices. In short, he was fascinated by the so-called Phoenician abominations, and he likened the last stage of Carthaginian civilization with its greatest expansion under the Barcas (and its destruction in 146 B.C.) to the fate of France under the Bonapartes, for in the case of his own country, he also feared the end to be near. The great Napoleon had come close to subdoing Europe; his wily nephew entertained even grander visions. After increasing the size of France proper with the acquisition of Savoy and Nice by intervening in Italy, he turned his attention to the Southern shores of the Mediterranean. Indeed, France had occupied Algeria in 1830 and since Napoleon I's defeat of the Mamluks it had maintained a controlling interest in Egypt. French agents and entrepreneurs were beginning to penetrate Tunisia, as Flaubert observed when he travelled there to assess the location of Carthage and its hinterland. The Mediterranean appeared to be on the verge of becoming a French *mare nostrum*. As to the new world, Napoleon III sent an army to Mexico in 1861, set up a puppet emperor, and contemplated a "protectorate" of all Latin nations. The latter project, which comprised Italy and Spain, would simultaneously have given reality to the Mediterranean as a French sea. In the face of such overextension of French resources, Flaubert feared that nothing but a total collapse would ensue since France had progressively lost substance after the middle ages and since the ruling class, the bourgeoisie, was degenerate (see his Realist novels) and ripe for a socio-political revolution. In *Salammbô* he went to great length to demonstrate that the values, social attitudes, and political maneuvers of the Punic oligarchy, which made possible the rise of Hamilcar Barca, closely resembled those of the French bourgeoisie that perverted the revolution of 1848 and abetted the ambitions of Louis Napoleon in exchange for law and order and financial opportunities.

The term "revolution" has a double meaning in *Salammbô*. In the first place it signifies a rebellion of the mercenaries which Hamilcar finally roots out in the penultimate chapter of the novel, and, secondly, a counter-revolution in the sense of a rotation or return to an earlier form of rule. The political changes Flaubert describes in his Carthage are a repetition of changes in tribal government which took place in ancient Canaan-Israel: the passing of power from councils of elders to elected charismatic leaders (the judges or "shofets" of the *Old Testament)* and from them to a popularly acclaimed charismatic king (Saul). The Phoenicians, a subdivision of the Canaanites, had already undergone this development, since they were ruled by kings by the time the linguistically closely related Hebrews arrived on the historical scene. Hence Flaubert reconstructed the political beginnings of the Phoenicians by analogy: knowledge of one people meant knowledge of the other. In turn, the Carthaginians were highly self-conscious of their ethnic, religious, political, and economic heritage. They maintained close ties with Tyre, Sidon, and Byblos, as well as with Phoenician settlements in the Western Mediterranean along the North African coast, in Sicily, Sardinia, and Hispania (Gades). They continued to worship the gods their ancestors had brought with them from the East, and as late as the fourth century B.C. they sent offerings for Melcarth to Tyre. Of course they also owed to their Levantine forefathers their renowned skills and savoir-faire in navigation, the manufacture of commercial goods, and trade. After the Phoenician city-states along the Lebanese shore lost their independence, and all the more after the destruction of Tyre by Alexander the Great in 332 B.C. (who had two thousand surviving men crucified and sold the remaining old people, women, and children into slavery), Carthage assumed suzerainty over all Phoenician settlements in the Western Mediterranean.

As a counterstatement to *Madame Bovary's* prosaic conditions, Flaubert chose not only an Afro-Oriental setting, but he also removed the action in time to antiquity, for there and then, he contended, life was less diluted than in his own present and the historical figures seemed more original since they brought forth everything out of themselves. He even went so far as to call the tyrant of antiquity (e.g. Hamilcar Barca) the most splendid human specimen. Hence *Salammbô* has two heroes: the enchanting titular heroine and her father. The choice of the Oriental setting in antiquity posed a double challenge to the author. He had to present a credible image of the Oriental scenery, and he faced the additional task of finding the right idiom and tone to convey the sensibilities and motivations of Orientals who lived two thousand years ago. On the strengths of his imagination, empathy, vast learning, experiences, and scientific scrupulousness Flaubert decided to enter the realm of the Oriental historical novel.

Acknowledgments

I wish to thank Northwestern University's Research Grants Committe, in particular Dean Michelle Citron and Mrs. Mary Pat Doyle, for co-sponsoring this book with a publication subsidy.

I also wish to acknowledge the kindness of Professor Jeanne-Sarah de Larquier, editor of the *Cincinnati Romance Review,* for granting me permission to reprint much of my article, "Hamilcar Barca and the Emergence of Charismatic Leadership: Flaubert's *Salammbô* and Nineteenth-Century France" [*CRR,* XI (1992), 34-42], in Chapter III of my book.

Last, but by no means least, I express my gratitude to colleagues at Northwestern University who read the manuscript and offered constructive criticism: Kristine Thorsen,

Saul Morson, and Feter Fenves. My special thanks are reserved for my former colleague Kathy Harms who read the manuscript at various stages of its deveopment.

Introduction

Salammbô, Flaubert's only historical novel, was long discreetly ignored by literary criticism but in more recent book-length studies of his oeuvre a number of scholars sought to make amends for past neglect.[1] The same claim can be made by the authors of a host of articles, especially since the early 1970s. Many of them evidently took their cue from R.J. Sherrington's observation that "we have yet to see an adequate treatment of it"[2] and focused their inquiries on formal characteristics of the novel. R.B. Leal, for instance, asks why, up to the present time, no one has taken the trouble "to challenge the assertion of Sainte-Beuve that the work is lacking in formal unity."[3] As a result of recent critical preoccupation with structural and poststructural aspects of narrative, most contemporary readings of *Salammbô* are reductive. One charge that can be levelled against interpretations of these schools is that they disregard the significant political-historical components of *Salammbô* and treat the work not as a novel about events in the capital of an ancient empire, but as if it were indeed the "book about nothing" Flaubert had said he would like to write while laboring on *Madame Bovary*.[4] Of course it would make sense that the scholar or critic concentrate exclusively on formal and narratological elements if *Salammbô* were a work that had nothing to say, yet said what it did not say with intriguing artistry.

Another reason why critical attention was diverted from the substance of the novel can be found in the kinds of success it encountered immediately following publication in 1862. It appealed, for example, to ladies of high society as well as women of the demimonde. Salammbô-costumes, which ladies of fashion and fashionable cocottes wore at great dinners and public balls, were the rage of Paris. Mme. Rimsky-Korsakov stunned the public by showing herself in a transparent "Carthaginian" gown, evoking the "zaïmph," the sacred veil of the goddess Tanit.[5] Moreover,

Salammbô became the artists' novel. While Flaubert denied his publisher Michel Levy the right to have the book illustrated, it subsequently inspired Georges Rochegrosse's commissioned drawings, just as it prompted paintings, etchings, and sculptures. As late as 1927 Alastair contributed his "Salammbô" to Henry Crosby's *Red Skeletons*.[6] The first generation of readers was obviously fascinated by the heroine, and this enthusiastic response engendered echoes reverberating over many decades. The lascivious Oriental virgin Salammbô, femme fatale and precursor of Mallarmé's Hérodiade and the Salome of Flaubert's tale "Herodiade" as well as Oscar Wilde's play and Richard Strauss's one-act opera, became an object of erotic day-dreams. The narrative also promoted the popularity of opulent-exotic interiors. Nadar's photography of Sarah Bernhardt (1887), darling of the Belle Époque, shows how the celebrated actress presented herself as a reincarnation of the Oriental *femme fatale* amidst precious furs, silks, velvets, objets d'art, and exotic greenery, the kind of setting Flaubert's readers encounter in Salammbô's bedchamber.

Just as diverting from the political-historical content of the novel was the attraction its love story exerted on musicians, including Hector Berlioz and Mussorgsky. They welcomed it as suitable material awaiting its transcription into an operatic score. Flaubert actually took a hand in these budding projects by asking his friend Théophile Gautier to mine *Salammbô* for a libretto. Berlioz never wrote the music drama he had envisioned, enchanted though he was with "the mysterious daughter of Hamilcar, this divine virgin," and Mussorgsky never finished his promising enterprise.[7] Aside from a number of completed works by lesser known composers, Ernest Reyer did create a successful lyric opera entitled *Salammbô*, which premiered in 1890 and by 1900 had been performed one hundred times.[8] The very fact that the Oriental narrative was considered appropriate to provide the heroine, the love interest, and plot of a libretto made it suspect to literary critics, for as literary works, libretti had a notoriously poor reputation. By focusing on the heroine's love and passion, the opera *Salammbô* obliterated the main strength of Flaubert's narrative: its "crown and state" action. However, such reductions are characteristic of the relationship between libretti and the literary works on which they draw. Imagine anyone judging Goethe's *Faust* on the basis of Charles Gounod's opera of the same title!

The failure of the reading public to appreciate *Salammbô* is also attributable to the hybrid genre of the historical novel. Every work of this kind consists of imaginative and historical elements. In the "classical" historical novel, as realized by Walter Scott, a historically conditioned individual, a better "everyman," is usually the bearer of the action. Human interest takes up the foreground of Scott's work, whereas the roar of decisive historical forces can be heard like rumblings of a thunderstorm in the distance. The great historical figures embodying these political forces move on the periphery of the protagonist's life. The representativeness and humanity of the average protagonist may occasionally be summoned to mediate between the extreme positions of the powerful. In Scott, the narrative space allotted to the fictional components of his novels exceeds by far the space devoted to strictly historical matters, and the personal and political spheres of life intertwine in a seemingly natural manner. In stark contrast to that, Flaubert created a new kind of historical Oriental novel. For in *Salammbô* the historical events of the Mercenary War take up close to two thirds of the narrative, and the historically verified leaders of the conflict parade and act on center stage. Yet it was the shorter, freely invented component of the novel, the heroine Salammbô and her passion, that intrigued the reading public and inspired painters, sculptors, and musicians. The ease with which musicians and librettists were able to sever the fictive from the historical strains of the novel suggested that the two might not have been sufficiently integrated to form an indivisible aesthetic whole. But can a talented librettist not perform reductive miracles?

In addition, the voices of two outstanding critics have impeded the overall understanding of *Salammbô*. Sainte-Beuve's and Georg Lukács's critiques, seventy-five years apart, are sobering illustrations of how far even erudite minds can stray from a text if they approach it with ideological blinders. Sainte-Beuve judged *Salammbô* by the norms and conventions of the classical historical novel and rejected as irrelevant its Punic setting and events. From his Marxist perspective Lukács reaffirmed Sainte-Beuve's reproach that the laborious "resurrection" of Carthage could not possibly relate to the social and political life of nineteenth century France. He also thought that in Flaubert's African-Oriental novel the Naturalist "principle of the photographic authenticity" could not lead to anything but "archaeology" instead of living history.[9] Flaubert's archaeologism allegedly presents strange and unfamiliar objects, expressed in the jargon of the initiated. This is one of Lukács's main objections to Naturalism, and in Flaubert he saw the fountainhead of the entire movement. In "The Zola Centenary" he asserted that "description and analysis is substituted for epic situations and epic plots," and that the Naturalist does not depict life itself, but only its "outer trappings."[10] Does all or any of this really pertain to *Salammbô*, particularly Lukács's accusation that the novel fails to present a conflict of authentic historical forces and thus resembles

Sainte-Beuve's *Port-Royal* and its "fragmented, eccentric, bagatelle [. . .] picture of history" because the author "[. . .] is reduced to a mere spectator and chronicler of public life"?[11]

Even a first reading of *Salammbô* leaves deep impressions. Foremost among them are the opulence of the settings and the detailed decriptions of beautiful things the text displays over wide expanses of narrative space. Such descriptions are juxtaposed with scenes depicting extreme violence, a combination of seemingly binary opposites characteristic of aestheticism. These interplays of preciosity and violence are shrouded in an aura of smoldering eroticism which the reading public had encountered before only in Charles Baudelaire's poetry. The following questions must be asked. Why did the controversial and highly successful author of the Realist *Madame Bovary* next undertake a historical narrative set in the Carthage of the Mercenary War, provided it was not for the purpose of writing a novel of alterity with respect to subject-matter, color, and mood? Was this project to yield a work about the Orient resembling the phantasmagoric *Tentation de Saint Antoine* though with the author's imagination, leaning towards the exuberant and exotic, bridled by Polybius's transmitted historical outline of the conflict? Would French bourgeois readers recognize themselves in their Punic peers? Were Hamilcar's designs and actions all too transparent to the ever vigilant censors in the aftermath of Napoleons III's rise to absolute power and his subsequent imperial reign? Although Flaubert never indicated such correspondences, they nevertheless are salient in the novelistic text. Was *Salammbô* conceived as a serious joke about the stupidity of his contemporaries, whom he berated forever? Like Stendhal he must have hoped that later generations would understand him.

The novel *Salammbô* gratified not only Flaubert's love of the Orient, but it also accelerated the interest of the reading public in this vast region. Ever since Napoleon I's expedition to Egypt and the accounts and verses of French Romantic travellers, the Oriental theme had found a place in French literature, and Flaubert had paid homage to it with *Smarh* (1837) and the first two versions of *La Tentation de Saint Antoine* (1849 and 1856), while Théophile Gautier published *Le Roman de la Momie* in 1857. The writing of *Salammbô* allowed its author to revive once again his memories of his journey through the Levant and Asia Minor. Although Flaubert presented a more empathetic image of the Orient than his predecessors,[12] it still was not altogether alien from European preconceptions of this heterogeneous and mysterious realm. Thus, it is quite telling that he chose a woman's name as the title of his narrative, for

Europeans were used to ascribe a feminine essence to the Orient. Also, in the nineteenth century, several European powers eyed the domains of the decaying Ottoman Empire like fruits ready to be plucked. Between 1839 and 1841 European politics were preoccupied with an "Oriental crisis" arising from France's intervention in Egyptian affairs. The Suez Canal, the work of a French engineer and diplomat, opened in 1869. Verdi's *Aida* (1871) was commissioned for this event, and Saint-Saëns's *Samson and Delila* (1877) followed in short succession. In between, the third version of *La Tentation de Saint Antoine* was published (1874), and in 1881, one year after Flaubert's death, the Republic of France proclaimed a protectorate over Tunisia whose area formerly constituted the very heartland of Carthaginian power. As a capstone, Ernest Reyer's opera *Salammbô* was performed in the early 1890s to jubilant Parisian audiences.

Yet despite the numerous Franco-Oriental interactions ever since the late eighteenth century, the Afro-Oriental city of Carthage represented the "other" to the reading public largely because it remained quite unknown and had posed the most existential threat to Europe's Graeco-Roman cultural ancestry. This "otherness" was the original reason for Flaubert's turning to the North African capital of antiquity with its strange people, unfathomable gods, wealth, and reputed erotic licentiousness. The image of Carthage evoked in the novel differs sharply from the image of antiquity transmitted by Roman historians and Christian authors after Constantine the Great. For Flaubert presents an important part of the ancient world prior to the so-called *pax romana*.[13] It is a monstrous and colorful picture suggesting the cultural, political, and social diversity of the nations positioned around the Mediterranean, the mythical sea of Odysseus's voyages and clandestine Phoenician trade routes. Regrettably, much of this diversity was lost when Rome absorbed these lands and nations into its empire and turned the Mediterranean into *mare nostrum*. The homogenizing impact of Roman rule was reinforced when Christianity became the state religion and, in due course, most peoples from Armenia in the East to the Pillars of Hercules in the West followed the same creed.

As Michael Butor writes, Flaubert's Carthage represents the reverse side of antiquity, that which has been hidden from us (and our classical education) because of the Roman screen through which we have been accustomed to perceive it.[14] It is, above all, the lust for committing atrocities that purportedly distinguish the army of Barbarians, drawn from all parts of the ancient world, and the reacting Carthaginians, from Roman practices. To these belong the torture of prisoners, the sacrifice of hundreds of children, the crucifixion of rebel chieftains, even lions. In short, the Punics, transplanted Phoenicians who brought with them their Oriental religion, were depicted by Roman historians as utter irrationalists as well as cruel victors and masters. In times of national emergencies the incomprehensible gods had to be placated by human sacrifice. In contrast, the Roman conception of the cosmos, based on Greek thought, was portrayed as more rational, for in its order everyone was said to reap what he/she deserved. However, the Romans certainly comitted their own acts of cruelty of which the utter destruction of the Punic capital and Corinth in 146 B.C. are poignant illustrations. The Punic survivors of this holocaust were sold into slavery. Nine hundred thousand Jews shared the same fate after the conquest of Jerusalem by Titus in 70 A.D. In addition, the Romans all too readily executed "enemies of state." In 132 B.C., for example, they crucified twenty thousand men after the suppression of a slave uprising in Sicily led by the Syrian Eunus. This mass execution took place just fourteen years after the razing of Carthage. Retribution is understandable, but 20,000 crucifixions were hardly a rational application of justice. To this horrendous slaughter must be added the crucifixions of all surviving leaders ending the uprising of Spartacus in 71 B.C. The Romans also crucified Jesus and Peter, and they decapitated Paul, the two apostles being considered dangerous to the empire. Yet Roman propagandists habitually described Punic vengefulness in purple prose. In short, there seems to have been hardly any difference between Punic and Roman cruelty.

Hand in hand with their alleged bloodthirstiness went the Carthaginians' alleged obsession with sexuality and lust. There were "the carnal abominations" practiced in "the lowlands of ancient Phoenicia" (Michelet), as well as the mass copulations staged in Carthage at special occasions. Their sexual customs and cults had earned the Eastern and Western Phoenicians the reputation of maniacal erotomanes. It was this very aspect of Punic life that may very well have induced Flaubert to turn to Carthage in the first place. According to Max Weber, orgiastic rites and temple prostitution were prevalent among early Semitic cultures. *Salammbô* provides several examples of this ancient practice.[15]

With its brutality and sexual licence Flaubert's Carthage diverges from the concept of antiquity held by the eighteenth and much of the nineteenth centuries: the Greek notion of "noble simplicity and quiet grandeur" (Winckelmann). Carthage emerges as an other world from which, according to Sainte-Beuve and Lukács, no bridges lead to modern France that considered itself the principal heir of Graeco-Roman antiquity. A radical Eurocentric perspective, this notion constituted the foremost reason why *Salammbô* was rejected by these noted critics. But, as Eugenio Donato asserts, "what might appear at the outset as a desire for otherness defined as difference is dictated by finding an otherness which would be a form of sameness. What does appear as different is, in fact an effect, an optical illusion, a mirage."[16] Except for this generalization, Donato does not follow up his promising insight by showing parallels between Hamilcar's Punic Republic and nineteenth century France.

The "otherness" of Carthage that really is a kind of "sameness" manifests itself in the crucial political themes of the narrative. Flaubert obviously recognized important features of his own political present in the structure of Carthaginian society, in the politics of the Mercenary War, and the manner in which the latter was conducted. The members of the Punic oligarchy or bourgeoisie may differ markedly in outward appearance from the French bourgeois of the nineteenth century, yet with respect to their mentalities Flaubert perceived them as kindred spirits. It was Punic avarice, the unwillingness to pay the foreign soldiers the wages they had earned with their sacrifices, that caused the Mercenary War, just as the French bourgeoisie robbed the rebellious workers, who had born the brunt of the initial uprising, of their just spoils in the revolution of 1848. The Carthaginian and French upper classes abetted the emergence of a tyrant by handing over power to him in exchange for his guaranteeing them their material possessions and unimpeded "pursuit of happiness."

In his image of Carthage Flaubert perceived in a flash of intuition, much as Walter Benjamin described the phenomenon of historical cognition, the present in the past, and the challenges of the future. An important aspect of Flaubert's novel is the fact that its politics are built on imaginative historical construction and empathy for the Oriental mind, that is, they are not merely contrived as a critique of his own present. Compared with him, most writers of historical novels before the watershed of *Salammbô* appear to be naive fabulists and negligent craftsmen. In short, Flaubert inaugurated a new kind of historical fiction. The "scientific" novelist turns archeologist, erotic dreamer, socio-political critic, and prophet. The Carthage of the Mercenary War and the Second French Empire constituted in Flaubert's view close to final stages in their nations' histories. The decline of Carthage was a historical fact; the possibility that France might have a similar destiny was widely discussed in the author's day and found repeated expression in the somber letters Flaubert wrote immediately prior to, during, and after the Franco-Prussian War. In contrast to Scott's narratives, the primary aim of *Salammbô* is not to show how things "really" were in the Punic metropolis. Quite the contrary, Flaubert employs his Oriental novel as an instrument to make his drowsy compatriots aware of their own situation through a prism displaying an ancient state that had disppeared from history. Thus, *Salammbô* can also be seen as a sobering prophecy concerning France, and as a call for national regeneration.

It is impossible to determine whether the author became aware of these correspondences when he conceived the novel, or at the time he wrote it. However, correspondences are inscribed in the pages of *Salammbô*. These parallels will be brought to light with the help of *L'Éducation sentimentale*, Lukács, Marx, Max Weber, Raymond Schwab, and Edward Said. Concerning the presentation of Carthage (and I write "presentation" instead of "representation," for there was little to re-present), Flaubert recognized that his primary task lay in the depiction of the plausible and the avoidance of absurdities. Since his Carthage could not be directly equated with nineteenth-century France, *Salammbô* must be seen as an allegory. For the purpose of this introduction, "allegory" is defined in general terms as involving "a continuous parallel between two (or more) levels in a story, so that its persons and events correspond to the equivalents in a system of ideas or a chain of events external to the tale."[17] While the characters, events, or settings may be historical or fictitious, such components convey meanings transcending the action of the written narrative. (A more differentiated understanding of allegory will be presented in the Epilogue).

Far from being a book about nothing, *Salammbô* as an Oriental allegory of nineteenth-century France displays an exciting socio-political critique and a highly self-conscious authorial positioning. The resulting *écriture* or narrative text, part retold and invented story, part narratorial discourse, relies on the same devices as *Madame Bovary, L'Éducation sentimentale,* and *Bouvard et Pécuchet*: the laconic manner of narration, the innovative ways of employing free indirect discourse and psycho-narration. These devices contribute to the formation of the "trottoir roulant" of Flaubert's *écriture*. It will be interesting to examine how the characters of the Carthaginian novel are affected by the omnipresence of the narratorial voice and its irony. Other aspects of Flaubert's *écriture* in *Salammbô* are his exacting craftsmanship, including the imagery that contradicts Roland Barthes's assumptions. Consisting primarily of carefully wrought similes relating to the desert and the sea, it adds local color and meaning to the narratorial discourse and invests figures and objects with an African-Oriental ambiance. Deprived of its similes, this historical novel would lose much of its expressiveness and meaning. It is not by chance that Thomas Mann called *Salammbô* "a historical novel of the highest poetic caliber."[18]

One of Flaubert's finest achievements in this narrative of the "timeless" Orient consists in the ways he presents time. Permeated by the historical spirit, his handling of time, an intricate interplay of the epic flow, chronological accounts, lyrical recollections, and elaborate repetitions, undercut by events of subsequent history, constitutes a novelty in historical fiction. Indeed, one might even contend that *Salammbô* is a novel about time. It signals the end of a tradition and the beginning of a new one.

Notes and References

1. Together with the incisive Victor Brombert, there are Maurice Nadeau, Maurice Bardèche, R.J. Sherrington, Jonathan Culler, and Michal Ginsburg, as well as W. Wolfgang Holdheim in *Die Suche nach dem Epos* (1978) and Anne Green with the monograph, *Flaubert and the Historical Novel: "Salammbô" Reassessed* (1982). Except for Green's study, none of these works acknowledges the relevance of Flaubert's historical novel to the author's era.

2. R.J. Sherrington, *Three Novels by Flaubert* (Oxford, U.K.: Clarendon Press, 1970) 231.

3. R.B. Leal, "Salammbô: An Aspect of Structure," In *French Studies*, 27 (1973) 17.

4. Flaubert, Letter to Louise Colet, January 16, 1852.

5. Even the Empress Eugénie asked Flaubert's advice for a "Punic" dress she intended to wear at a masked ball.

6. For illustrations of works of art depicting Salammbô see "Anhang" to Gustave Flaubert, *Salammbô,* transl. G. Brustgi, and commented by Monika Bosse and André Stoll (Frankfurt a.M.: Insel, 1979) 365–400. See also Bram Dijkstra, *Idols of Perversity: Fantasies of Feminine Evil in fin-de-siècle Culture* (New York: Oxford University Press, 1986).

7. The quotation is taken from Hector Berlioz's homage to *Salammbô*. It appeared in *Journal des Debats* (December 23, 1863) and has been reprinted (in German) in "Anhang" to Gustave Flaubert, *Salammbô,* transl. F. von Oppeln-Bronikowski, revised by Franz Cavigelli (Zurich: Diogenes, 1979) 360. Mussorgsky, on the other hand, incorporated substantial parts of the music he had written for "Salammbô" into his *Boris Godunov*.

8. Besides Reyer's successful work, there were short-lived Salammbô-operas by Vincenzo Fornari (*Salammbô e Zuma,* 1881), Nicolò Massa (1886), and Joseph Mathias Hauer (1930). Also see Francis Steegmuller, "*Salammbô:* The Career of an Opera," *Grand Street,* 4 (1984) 103–127.

9. Georg Lukács, *The Historical Novel,* transl. H. and S. Mitchell (Boston: Beacon Press, 1983) 198.

10-11. _____ , *Studies in European Realism,* The Universal Library (New York: Grosset & Dunlap, 1964) 91–92 and 89.

12. Gérard de Nerval is the exception, for he, too, saw the Orient with empathy.

13. In fact, the much acclaimed "pax romana" never really existed, for Roman history appears to have been little more than a succession of wars, rebellions, invasions, etc. Yet Roman rule undoubtedly had a levelling effect on the cultural, social, and

political particularities of its subject peoples. Of course this levelling effect was promoted by the use of Latin as the lingua franca.

14 Michel Butor, *Improvisations sur Flaubert*, Éditions de la différence (Paris: Le Sphinx, 1984) 115–116.

15 In lieu of "prostitution" some critics prefer to see Salammbô's act in the tent as a ritual sacrifice, but the term "prostitution" appears to be more appropriate in the context of Flaubert's other novels.

16 Eugenio Donato, "Flaubert and the question of History: Notes for a Critical Anthology," *MLN*, 91.2 (1976) 869.

17 Chris Baldick, *The Concise Oxford Dictionary of Literary Terms* (Oxford and London: Oxford University Press, 1990) 5.

18 Thomas Mann, "Der alte Fontane" [1910] in *Adel des Geistes* (Stockholm: S. Fischer, 1967) 486.

I

Authorial Motivation, History, and the Orient

"La *Bovary* m'a dégouté pour longtemps des moeurs bourgeoises. Je vais pendant quelques années peut-être vivre dans un sujet splendide et loin du monde moderne dont j'ai plein le dos."
Flaubert to Mlle Leroyer de Chantepie, July 11, 1858.

The vanquished maritime republic of Carthage and its desperate struggle with its mercenaries, this was the exotic and splendid subject to which Flaubert had turned after the completion of his Realist novel about contemporary life in provincial France. He could blame no one but himself and his concept of art for having had to endure for five years the petty milieus of Tostes and Yonville and to enter the mentality of their petit-bourgeoisie whom he utterly despised, for he held that "exterior reality must penetrate us, almost make us cry out with it, if we are to reproduce it well."[1] In reaction to the world of Emma Bovary, the other side of his nature now demanded to write about wondrous things and events: "gigantic battles, sieges, and the fabulous old Orient."[2] In *Madame Bovary* Flaubert had dissected Emma's unbridled eroticism and satirized her penchant for the exotic by revealing her misguided vision of happiness. However, the desires of his heroine also revealed his very own. Writing about and analyzing his feelings and expectations had, contrary to Thomas Mann's claims, neither pacified nor subdued them: they were essential components of his personality. At the age of seventeen he had written the Oriental piece "Smarh," a thematic and formal precursor of *La Tentation de Saint Antoine* (1849/1856/1874). The dates of the three versions of the Egyptian soul-drama suggest that Flaubert remained intrigued by it throughout his life. His journey to the Orient (1849–51) deepened his fascination with the Near East.

At first glance Flaubert's turning to the exotic historical novel after the resounding success of *Madame Bovary* (1856) makes little sense, since its author was well on his way to establish himself as the foremost Realist novelist and critical observer of life in the Second Empire. Even the litigation surrounding *Madame Bovary,* when the state's judicial system aligned its forces against him, had not impaired his status. Its outcome, a "severe reprimand," alienated him neither from the imperial court to whose receptions he was invited, nor from the soirées of the Princess Mathilde. He also had the satisfaction of knowing that numerous French artists had rallied to his support. Having become famous overnight, a legitimate "black artist,"[3] he was lionized by "good society." Why, then, did he risk his reputation in the genre of historical fiction?

Aside from wishing to treat a subject utterly different from French provincial life, he intended, first of all, to create a new kind of narrative independent of "the prose of modern conditions,"[4] which would in no way reflect the constraints, frustrations, and stupidities of bourgeois society. Since the world presented in this new fiction was to be quasi-autonomous with respect to nineteenth century conditions and values, it had to be removed to a distant period in history. As an aesthetic counterstatement to *Madame Bovary,* the new tale was, moreover, to be set in the Orient and give a prominent role to the "Oriental woman." These three subjects had preoccupied Flaubert for quite some time.

With *Salammbô* Flaubert, the scientific novelist, decided to enter the realm of the historical novel and to rescue an Oriental culture from oblivion, drawing on the strength of his memories, imagination, and a huge file of notes. Was he adequately prepared for the challenge? At the Collège de Rouen, his training in history had been thorough, for he had had the good fortune of studying with Gourgand Dugazon and Adolphe Cheruel who was later appointed to a professorship at the École Normale Supérieure in Paris. A student of Michelet, Cheruel taught Flaubert between 1835 and 1839 at school and in private lessons that precision and the uncompromising pursuit of truth were prerequisites in the discipline of history. As a consequence, Flaubert's critical faculties were dramatically sharpened; he won several prizes in history, and as a youth wrote compositions, narratives, and dramatic works on historical subjects (among them "Mort du duc de Guise," "Rome et les Césars," and the five act play "Louis XI"). As M. Jean Bruneau shows in *Les Débuts littéraires de Gustave Flaubert* the people in these adolescent efforts are a stupid herd, despised and deceived by the mighty.[5] About forty years later a number of motifs from his early writings recurred in *Salammbô* and in

"Julien l'Hospitalier." In "Hérodias" (1876) another mature work, he once more took up his adolescent views of the ways of politics. At school he was introduced to Jules Michelet's works of which he savored *Histoire romaine, Histoire de France,* and *Histoire de la Révolution française.* He is said to have known entire pages of *Histoire romaine* by heart, including quite a few describing Carthaginian affairs. What Flaubert admired in Michelet was the clear stance he never failed to take, his emotional involvement with his subject, his vitality, and the brilliance of his style. He appears to have accepted Michelet's assertion in the preface to *Histoire de France* that such personal commitment enables the historian to penetrate to the heart of things and to accomplish a "resurrection of integrated life, not on the surface, but in its inner and profound organism."

Altogether, one must consider it fortunate that it was Michelet's *Histoire romaine* where Flaubert found essential information and a spirited interpretation of Carthaginian events, for Michelet is one of those historians of the nineteenth century whose work can still serve as a paradigm of the distinctly modern historical consciousness. As source and inspiration for a creative writer, three elements of Michelet's narrative defined by Hayden White were most useful. The fact that he emplotted history as romance allowed him to present his account in dualistic terms and sharp contrasts. His narrative depicts a series of struggles between the forces of light and dark, virtue and vice, justice and tyranny. The second element, his "formist" mode of argument, proved to be equally beneficial to the novelist. For this mode of presentation, found in Romantic historians and the great historical narrators such as Michelet's own mentor Niebuhr as well as Theodor Mommsen and George Macaulay Trevelyan, aims primarily at a vivid depiction of the variety and color of past events, not infrequently at the expense of conceptual precision. The concreteness implicit in this approach is reinforced and simultaneously counterbalanced by Michelet's conviction that metaphor is the adequate trope to characterize phenomena of the historical process. The metaphorical mode allows the historian to be concrete, yet the presupposition of the essential sameness of things allows it to transcend Romantic individualism and broach the borders of universality. As Hayden White puts it, for Michelet "a poetic sensibility, critically self-conscious, provided the access to a specifically 'realistic' apprehension of the world."[6] Unquestionably, *Histoire romaine* was a most suitable textual source for a historical novel.

From Michelet's histories Flaubert also learned to consider great historical struggles in racial terms, a favored perspective in the nineteenth century, which Marx subsequently transformed into one of class struggles.

Regarding the wars between Rome and Carthage, Michelet asserts that this "confrontation was not only to decide the fate of the two cities or empires, but it was also a question of determining which of the two races, the Indo-Germanic or Semitic, would dominate the world."[7] He goes on to identify Indians, Persians, Greeks, Romans, and the Germanic tribes as Indo-Germanic peoples, and Arabs, Jews, Phoenicians, and Carthaginians as Semites.[8] Both groups are given distinct characteristics. On the one hand there is innate heroism, as well as genius for art and legislation; on the other the spirit of industry, navigation, and commerce; as well, according to Michelet, "love of gold, blood, and pleasure. The two races encountered each other everywhere, and they attacked each other everywhere"[9] around the Mediterranean, where the confrontations between Greeks and Phoenicians were followed by those between Rome and Carthage, as well as Rome and Israel. The Arab Empire of the Umayyads and Abbesids is seen as the last flourishing of collective Semitic grandeur. However, Flaubert saw the Mercenary War more as a class struggle than a conflict between different races. In this respect he is closer to Marx than one might surmise.

As we will see, Flaubert accepted some of Michelet's views, but ultimately he rejected most by undermining them through irony. He also owed his acquaintance with Vico to Michelet, since he had read and studied *La Scienza nuova* in Michelet's translation of 1827. Two theses of Vico became especially important for Flaubert's understanding of history and his historical fiction. One was the assertion that every people has a characteristic spirit of its own which manifests itself in all expressions of its culture. The historian scrutinizes all aspects of a given culture in order to fathom their common denominator, or the spirit underlying them, a view Flaubert certainly took to heart when he began his research. According to the second thesis the historical process is deterministic, history moves in cycles. Thus nations rise to power, flourish for some time, and then decline, only to be followed by others repeating the cycle. Vico was an early spokesman of "Geschichtsphilosophie" and a forerunner of historicism, two seemingly contradictory conceptions of history refined by Flaubert through his readings. While he embraced Vico's cyclical view of history, he gave it a twist. He, too, thought of history as a series of repetitive movements and recommencements. With respect to his own country's future he believed, despite the notion of "always the same," that in his own time the end was coming. He held that history has no outlet, and that his generation teetered on the brink of collective disaster. "I am disheartened and pained by the stupidity of my compatriots. The incurable barbarism of mankind fills me with black sadness."[10] Also in 1870, prior to the Franco-Prussian War, his pessimism knew no bounds: "I am convinced that we are entering a hideous world in which people of our kind will no longer have reason to live."[11]

Although it is evident that Flaubert was expecting some kind of "Ragnarök" or "Muspilli" for himself and his contemporaries, he nevertheless continued assiduously with his historical research and literary work. Aside from Michelet and Hegel, he studied Guillaume de Barante and Thierry, French historians of the nineteenth century representing the "descriptive school," according to a distinction made by Chateaubriand in the preface to his *Études historiques* (1831). Through the mediation of Victor Cousin and Thierry, he was introduced to the ideas of Herder and their historicist premises. Of equal importance in shaping his understanding of history was his study of French historiography of the eighteenth century, the works of Voltaire and Montesquieu in particular, which stimulated his interest in the comparative aspects of the discipline and confirmed Vico's thesis that there were general laws governing the historical process, for his Oriental novel is, in the wider sense of the term, comparatist. Human behavior followed a universal pattern, and therefore comparable causes effected comparable consequences.

Reverberations of this idea are found not only in *Salammbô*, but also in *L'Éducation sentimentale* where the protagonist's story is presented as a series of repetitions or substitutions, which express the authorial assumption that human nature remains essentially the same. In Nietzsche's terminology one could also say that Frédéric Moreau's life embodies "the eternal recurrence of the same." The biting irony of this case lies in the fact that Frédéric is weak, whereas Nietzsche conceived of the eternal recurrence of the same as a continuous test which only the "overman" would be able to endure. To return to Vico: his essentially mechanistic scheme of things does not allow much room for effective human initiative. It has even been asserted that "it has no room altogether."[12] Although Flaubert accepted these findings as theories, and believed them pertinent to his own present ("comme une fin du temps"), he obviously did not implement them unequivocally in his historical novel. Nevertheless, as the unfolding of *Salammbô* will show, he employed, especially from the retrospective view which is and always must be part of the genre, a mechanistic form of argument, as defined by Hayden White, for the purpose of historical interpretation. The mechanistic principle of his formal argument extends even to his *écriture*, particularly in the braiding of narratorial and free indirect discourse where the automatism of his narrative language is instrumentalized to bridle spontaneous figural speech.

Augustin Thierry must be taken up once more since his writings were crucial in formulating a number of essential issues in *Salammbô*, for Thierry applied the theories of Vico and Herder to his analyses of invasions and revolutions, especially in his histories of England and France. Thierry criticized historians studying political change and the transference of power because they concentrated on the victors to the neglect of the victims. In his effort to redress the balance, he gained insights about the racial element in social structures and the changing of power in the cyclical history of nations. Of special interest to Flaubert and his projected historical novel about Carthage was the relationship between barbarism and civilization which Thierry investigated with respect to the ascendence and decline of a given culture. The barbarian element of this constellation usually consisted in foreign invaders; yet the barbarian could also be seen in the uneducated lower class(es) of a given civilization contesting for power, such as the French workers in 1848. Anne Green notes that Flaubert planned another contemporary narrative which was to explore this very problem openly.[13] The author certainly devoted generous narrative space and empathetic energy to the mercenaries whom he portrayed from within. This stance distinguishes him from the majority of historicists in his own time who, because of their conservatism, would have looked down on the rebels as rabble. In other words, historicists of the nineteenth century showed little genuine interest in social problems, although they were ubiquitous and pressing. Chauvinism prejudiced many of them to emphasize national grandeur at the expense of the underpaid and underprivileged. In *Salammbô*, however, the mercenaries or lowest class in Carthage, come close to wresting power from an established culture.

Obviously, Flaubert was suffiently versed in historical matters to write a historical novel. In several respects he was ahead of contemporary historiography. He made the object of his search live within himself, as Wilhelm Dilthey advocated, and he turned Carthaginian history into contemporary history by making it present (Benedetto Croce).[14] His sources provided him with uncommonly few "fixed points" or facts, and he filled the blank spaces between them, as R.G. Collingwood suggested, by means of "imaginative construction."[15] About certain aspects of history Flaubert was more sophisticated than even renowned nineteenth- and twentieth-century luminaries of the discipline. For instance, his contemporary Leopold von Ranke believed that he was describing events "as they really happened," a formula Collingwood used three quarters of a century later to characterize his own work. This kind of naïveté also underlies his affirmation that the historian's picture of the past "is meant to be true," whereas the novelist simply has to construct one that "makes sense."[16] In contrast to such convictions Flaubert asserted, "Il n'y a pas de Vrai! Il n'y a que des manières de voir" ("There is no Truth! There are only ways of seeing").[17] The fact that he made this statement in one of his letters late at night might explain why he blurred the distinction between "le vrai" and "la vérité" which Vigny had made in the preface to the fourth edition of *Cinq-Mars*.[18] For Flaubert there simply was no Truth, only ways of seeing or perspectives. This is an astounding statement for one of the foremost authors of the so-called Realist school. Herewith the hermit of Croisset anticipates the perspectivism of the hermit of Sils-Maria, the mature Nietzsche. Moreover, *La Tentation de Saint Antoine* can be seen as an orgiastic parade of ancient beliefs or truth-claims. On the other hand, it might seem rather curious that Flaubert decided to hold on to the facts. However, his insistence that knowledge was a matter of perspective gave him sovereignty even concerning historical data and made him an all the more interesting historical novelist.

The Oriental setting of his second novel presented the other major challenge. Did he know enough about the Orient in order to write a credible modern novel? When in his letter to Louise Colet he evoked visions of "gigantic battles, sieges, and the fabulous old Orient," he thought of the region in terms other than those of his friend Théophile Gautier in essays subsumed under the title *L'Orient*,[19] replete with bayaderes, harems, absolute rulers, as well as scimitars, thieves, dancing girls, and adventurers. These were the stock ingredients of the Turkish-Albanian Orient cultivated by Lord Byron. Chateaubriand and Lamartine, in turn, approached the Levant with "idées reçues" and preconceived notions. Mannerists, they expected to replenish their treasury of poetic images and, as a matter of course, reenliven the drowsy region through their poetic imagination. Flaubert's journey to the Orient took over one and a half years and led him to Egypt (including a five-months trip up and down the Nile), Lebanon, the "Holy Land," Syria, Turkey (including Constantinople), and Greece (the planned excursions to the Caucasus and Persia were cancelled due to financial problems). He was well prepared for the adventure. For example, he could fall back on his prodigious studies for *Saint Antony* concerning the religions and heresies of the ancient Orient, for he had read whatever books were available such as Beausabre's *Histoire de Manichée,* Jacques Matter's *Histoire du gnosticisme,* Friedrich Creuzer's *Symbolik und Mythologie der alten Völker, besonders der Griechen* (in translation), and Edgar Quinet's *Le*

Génie des religions. He also perused works like Reuss's *Théologie chrétienne,* Saint Augustin's *Confessions,* and studies of the church fathers. These and additional sources are named in Michel Foucault's introduction to *Saint Antony.* For the journey proper, Flaubert steeped himself in travelogues, Romantic literature about the Orient, and scholarly Orientalist books.

This massive interest of late eighteenth and nineteenth-century scholars, writers, and philosophers constituted for Raymond Schwab an "Oriental Renaissance," a second Renaissance, so to speak, a term he borrowed from a chapter title of Quinet's *Génie des religions.* Like Quinet, Schwab believed that "the Oriental Renaissance marked the close of the neoclassical age, just as the Classical Renaissance had marked the end of the medieval age, and that, in the same way, it promised a new Reformation of the religious and secular world."[20] In other words, European interest in the Greeks was replaced by interest in the Orient. As Victor Hugo states in the preface to *Les Orientales:* "Never before have Oriental studies been explored so deeply. In the century of Louis XIV one was a Hellenist: today one is an Orientalist. This is a great step forward." Yet while Schwab favored the study of Persia and India (e.g. Friedrich Schlegel's "Die Weisheit der Indier"), Flaubert remained committed to the Levant. By the middle of the nineteenth century Orientalism was a firmly established discipline in France, England, and, to a lesser extent, Germany, with a canon of seminal works, conventions, doctrines, and does and don'ts. The concepts of the "Orient" and "Orientalism" are European inventions and served as a means to come to terms with the vast geographical area stretching from the Eastern Mediterranean to present-day Bangladesh. A region much larger and more heterogenous than Europe itself, its only bond consisted for Western beholders in the deviation of every part or unit from European norms. Although the Orient was the source of Europe's religion and culture, it remained throughout history the "other," or Europe's complementary opponent.

There had been considerable interaction between the two since antiquity. With the exception of Greek expansion into Asia Minor that culminated in the conquests of Alexander the Great, and the altogether unsuccessful crusades, Oriental and Asian powers were the aggressors: the Persian attempt under Xerxes to conquer Greece, the Huns' invasion of Central and Western Europe, the Arab foray into the East Roman Empire, their overcoming the Visigoths in Spain, and their advance into the Frankish kingdom, the Mongols' storm into Western Poland and Silesia, and the Ottoman Turks' conquest of Constantinople and traumatic subjugation of the Balkans that reached its apex in their second siege of Vienna (1689). Relations between Europe and the Orient changed drastically in the eighteenth century. While the Ottoman Empire showed unmistakable symptoms of decay, inner disintegration, and outward weakness, Europe made great strides in the natural sciences and military technology. All of a sudden, there was the "sick man of Europe," the "Turkish problem," and the question of what should become of all the lands nominally under Turkish suzerainty? The ultimate possibility of gaining control of new territories and populations catalyzed exploratory and scholarly interests in the Orient. One such example is Comte de Volney's *Voyage en Orient* (1787)[21] that perceives the locales it describes as likely places of French colonial expansion. Indeed, Napoleon had familiarized himself with Volney's work before embarking on his Egyptian expedition in 1801, an undertaking that did more for Orientalism than any other event. Napoleon's magnetism did not only lie in his superior generalship, but equally, if not more so, in the fact that he was a man of revolutionary ideas that initially benefited the majority of the people under his rule as, for instance, the Code Napoléon. Thus he conceived his Egyptian expedition not merely as a military and geopolitical matter, but also as a large-scale cultural and scientific enterprise for which he enlisted an extensive entourage of scholars and scientists. Directly connected with this expedition were his founding of L'Institut d'Égypte and his decree establishing an "École publique" in the Bibliothèque nationale where Arabic, Turkish, and Persian were to be taught. One major achievement of the Egyptian Institute was the publication of *Déscription de l'Égypte* in 23 volumes (1809–1823).

In this Napoleonic venture, the primary goal of which was to disrupt the shortest British route to India, the connection between imperialistic power-politics and Orientalism becomes transparent. Moreover, it engendered Orientalism with new impulses and actually changed the discipline from one of description into one of creation. As Said writes, the "Orient was reconstructed, reassembled, crafted, in short born out of the Orientalist's efforts."[22] The members of the Orientalist school, particularly those belonging to the colonial powers Great Britain and France, saw their principal task in dividing the vast East into manageable and treatable units. To be sure, Orientalists accrued many merits by editing and translating manuscripts, teaching Oriental languages and producing students sympathetic to the region, yet since the earlier Orientalists labored under the eighteenth-century premise that scientific work means the classification of nature and man, their methods were inevitably reductive. Orientalism also projected an unchanging Orient, and for this reason its reductive. Orientalism also projected an unchanging Orient, and for this reason its modern practice includes all traditional attitudes of the discipline. Thus, the Orient of the modern Orientalist "is not the Orient as it is, but the Orient as it has been Orientalized."[23]

Of the renowned Orientalists, Flaubert read above all Silvestre de Sacy, the father of the French Orientalist school, and Edward William Lane. The former's *Chrestomatie arabe,* [24] immersed him in Arabic thought, whereas Lane's *Account of the Manners and Customs of the Modern Egyptians* gave him a good sense of what to expect in the most important country of the Levant outside Turkey proper. In contrast to a traveler like Chateaubriand, who equated the Orient with private fantasies, Lane tried to present an "objective" picture of this strange world, for he believed that general phenomena could be defined. Familiar with the findings, insights, and theses of "Orientalism," Flaubert succeeded nevertheless to remain rather independent of them. I even daresay that it was in the Orient where Flaubert learned to "see."

Four years after his and Du Camp's return from the Levant, another Orientalist work appeared: *Histoire générale et systemème comparé des languages sémitiques* by Ernest Renan. Flaubert and the author were well acquainted personally as both belonged to a group of writers who occasionally met at Magy's, one of the better Parisian restaurants. A man of purpose, Renan decided to do for the Semitic languages what Bopp had achieved for the Indo-European ones. To begin with, he claims to have coined the terms Semite/Semitic. In the course of his studies he must have contracted a deep dislike of the speakers of these languages, their religions, and their cultures, especially of the two great surviving branches, the Arabs and the Hebrews/Jews. Donning the gown of the scientist, he recorded linguistic observations in the "laboratory" in order to generalize about this "race's" intellectual and moral chacteristics. By his procedure Renan presents the disturbing example of a scholar who dislikes the subject to which he devotes his professional life. As a result, his work displays glaring contradictions. He has to raise his subject matter to respectability before he can tear it down thanks to his own "insights." Thus, he states in the opening pages of *Les Langues sémitiques* that although the Semites did not participate in the great conquests of antiquity, he nevertheless finds them distinguished for the role they have played in history. Their superior religious instinct made them the peoples of God which excelled in the religious and moral realms to the extent that "half of the intellectual work of the world must be attributed to them."[25] In contrast to the polytheistic Indo-Europeans who sought a rational explanation of the universe and man's relation to God, this theocratic race expressed its thoughts in enigmatic psalms, prophecies, the pure hymn, and revealed books. Small wonder that three major religions were born from among the Semites.

It comes as a total surprise that after an opening of such massive praise, Renan turns around to affirm: "However I am the first to recognize that compared with the Indo-Europeans, the Semitic race represents an inferior combination of human nature."[26] The alleged Semitic inferiority, which marvellously understands unity, but cannot attain multiplicity, is attributed to monotheism that explains everything: The lack of scientific curiosity since God is the cause of all things, Semitic intolerance, the absence of a scientific and philosophical culture, the absence of a genteel society due to polygamy, the inability to laugh. In addition to these negative characteristics, Renan considers the Semites militarily inferior, for King David, the Phoenicians, Carthaginians, and the Caliphs relied on foreign mercenaries. He also finds the Semite untrustworthy since he has no sense of keeping his word or to render justice in a disinterested way. Such conduct may not seem fitting for a man of God and the Book, yet for the Semite religion constitutes "a special task that has only a dim connection with everyday morals." As if these shortcomings were not enough, Renan summarizes: "Thus, the Semitic race identifies itself uniquely by its negative characteristics. It has no mythology, no epic poetry, no science, no philosophy, no fiction, no plastic arts, no civil life. In everything, there is the absence of complexity, of nuances; the sense of unity reigns exclusively. There is no variety in monotheism."[27] Moreover, he classifies all Semitic peoples as essential shepherds, a finding that allows him to ascribe all Semitic achievements in science, industry, and commerce (e.g. the Babylonians and Phoenicians) to the older indigenous peoples they superseded. Renan reduces the real Semite to the "tribe and the tent."

It is noteworthy that Flaubert read Renan with the same kind of discretion he showed with respect to Michelet's *Roman History*. Concerning specific claims of Renan, he simply knew better: he had seen for himself. For example, Renan's notion of the Semite's inability to "laugh" is plainly contradicted in Flaubert's letter to Jules Cloquet: "In Europe we picture the Arab as very serious. Here he is merry, very articulate in gesticulation and ornamentation. Circumcisions and marriages seem to be nothing but pretexts for rejoicing and music-making" (80). Flaubert's diary is free of disparaging remarks about the people of the Orient. Rather, he looked at them, beheld them, and marveled about how different they were. He had sought the "other" and found it.

Charged with commissions from the French government—Flaubert was to collect agricultural statistics of the Levant while his friend Maxime Du Camp was to take photographs of historical monuments and inscriptions—the two entered the Orient through the port of Alexandria. They were priviliged travelers, for their commissions opened consular French and Egyptian government doors all the more easily since France had maintained a controlling interest in Egypt since the days of Napoleon I. As a result, the powerful viceroy Mohammed Ali, who died a few months before their arrival, had taken many Frenchmen into his service, on quite a few of whom he conferred the titles of Pasha and Bey. One of them, Soliman Pasha, a former French colonel named Sève, according to Flaubert "the most powerful man in Egypt," received them graciously, arranged about their horses for the following day, offered them his personal carriage for their journey to Cairo, and promised them orders to all provincial governors. In addition, they were given soldiers to hold back the crowd when they wanted to take photographs. From Hartim Bey, Minister of Foreign Affairs, they received a *firman* with his seal for the entire journey. In short, they travelled in style, and Flaubert could write to his anxious mother: "It is unbelievable how well we are treated here—it's as though we were princes [. . .]. Sassetti (their servant) keeps saying: 'Whatever happens, I'll be able to say that once in my life I had ten slaves to serve me and one to chase away the flies,' and that is quite true."[28]

Indeed, this was another world, a fact Flaubert had expected and found confirmed at his very arrival in Alexandria:

> Landing took place amid the most deafening uproar imaginable: negroes, negresses, camels, turbans, cudgelings to right and left, and ear-splitting guttural cries. I gulped down a whole bellyful of colors [. . .]. Cudgelings play a great role here; everyone who wears clean clothes beats everyone who wears dirty ones, or rather none at all [. . .]. You see many gentlemen sauntering along the streets with nothing but a shirt and a long pipe. Except in the very lowest classes, all the women are veiled, and in their noses they wear ornaments that hang down and sway from side to side like the facedrops of a horse. On the other hand, if you don't see their faces, you see their entire bosoms. As you change countries, you find that modesty changes its location [. . .]" (29).

The description of disembarking in the "most European city" of Egypt conveys Flaubert's immediate perceptions of Oriental life, several aspects of which will resurface in *Salammbô*. The spectacle in the harbor is nothing short of an uproar of colors and unfamiliar noises which he presents in a tableau of negroes, negresses, camels, turbans (as if the latter walked by themselves), and ubiquitous beatings. Sharp class distinctions are even more obvious than in mid nineteenth-century Europe. The women with swaying rings through their noses remind him of horses (to be ridden), a pre-feminist stance. And finally, there is the relativist remark about "modesty" that "changes location." The women veil their faces but bare their bosoms, while European women observe the opposite convention (except for *L'Éducation sentimentale* where at the great ballroom dances and elite dinners in the Dambreuses' house they also display their breasts). The observation of 1848 about the relativity of modesty points to the aforementioned insight of 1880: "There is no Truth. There are only modes of perception."

It is appropriate to ask what Flaubert gained from this demanding voyage that had the official blessings of two governments. One of his biographers, Jean de la Verande writes, "On his travels the beauty of a landscape excited him less than the sensation of distance and the exotic, also less than the feeling to return into the past when he entered a historical locale."[29] This is not a wholly accurate evaluation. Rather, the Egyptian landscapes conformed to his prescience and expectations, for he had seen many paintings about the subject. Although he wrote soon after reaching Cairo, "very little impressed by nature—i.e. landscape, sky, desert (except the mirages)" (42), he changed his mind after he learned to perceive more discerningly. On the other hand, the countless Egyptian temples soon began to "bore" him "profoundly." It took nothing less than the splendors of Thebes to revive his interest in monuments. Completely new, however, was the experience of the North African light which he appreciated even prior to his landing in Alexandria: "[I] saw the seraglio of Abbas Pasha (ruler of Egypt) like a black dome of the Mediterranean. The sun was beating down on it. I had my first sight of the Orient through, or rather in, a glowing light that was like melted silver on the sea." Indeed, the light of Egypt was a recurrent delight to him, as he records for instance at Esna: "One marvellous thing is the light, which makes everything glitter. We are always dazzled in the towns—it is like the butterfly colors of an immense costume ball; the white, yellow or the blue clothes stand out in the transparent air—blatant tones that would make any painter faint away" (160).

Light and color go together; in some of Flaubert's description, light itself appears colored.[30] In Egypt color and the architecture of the landscape are equally indissoluble. Flaubert enjoyed their combined power after he climbed the Great Pyramid at Gizeh half an hour before sunrise:

> But as the sun climbed behind the Arabian chain the mist was torn into two great shreds of filmy gauze; the meadows, cut by canals, were like green lawns with winding borders. To sum up: three colors—immense green at my feet in the foreground; the sky pale red-worn vermilion; behind and to the right, a rolling expanse looking scorched and iridescent, with the minarets of Cairo, *canges* passing in the distance, clusters of palms (52).

The scene impressed the observer in two principal ways. The first encompasses the landscape as a whole shrouded in mists and, after their tearing apart like the curtain in the temple, revealing a symphony of colors from lush green to pale red to the iridescent brown of the desert. Foreground, middle, and backdrop (the minarets of Cairo and the Nile with canges and palms) are clearly differentiated. Flaubert also noted the landscaping design, i.e., the division of the meadows by numerous canals. On December 11, one day before his 28th birthday, he observed: "Everything in Egypt seems made for architecture—the planes of the fields, the vegetation, the human anatomy, the horizon lines" (58). For him, Egypt embodied monumental grandeur unconscious of itself. It is the characteristic of the pyramids at Gizeh, the vast expanses of the desert, and the Nile which Flaubert repeatedly compares to a lake, more often to an ocean.

Going by sailboat upstream as far as the second cataract, the friends passed through the Thebaid of Saint Antony, where his former studies came to life once more. Frequently, they made excursions on horseback to ancient temples, royal graves, and ruins. Upon mooring at Philae in the evening, Flaubert and their dragoman immediately set out on donkeys for Assuan across the desert in order to inquire about mail. For fear of hyenas they were armed to the teeth; a boy of about twelve, "charming in his grace and nimbleness, ran ahead of them carrying a lantern. "The blue sky is dotted with stars—they are almost like fires—the sky is aflame—a real oriental night" (150). An Arab, riding a camel and singing, crossed their path and completed the picture. Is this not a scene as chthonic as it is enchanting? One strenuous undertaking on camels led them between May 18 and May 27 through the Arabian Desert to the Red Sea and back. They met caravans on their way; "they pass very close to us, no one speaks; it is like a meeting of ghosts amid clouds" (182). His diary also contains descriptions of the approach of caravans to which he resorted in *Salammbô* while describing the closing-in of the enemy host. His growing fondness of the desert is illustrated in the following entry: "Golden clouds like satin sofas. [. . .] the sun is setting in the desert. To the left, the Arabian chain with its indentations; it is flat on top, a plateau in the foreground, palms, and this foreground is bathed in darkness; in the middle ground, beyond the palms, camels pass [. . .]. What silence! Not a sound. Two great strips of sand, and the sun! One sees how awesome it might be here. The Sphinx has something of the same effect" (104). The satin sofas of clouds are a metaphor of wishful thinking; according to Du Camp, Flaubert would have liked nothing better than to be carried on one such sofa through the entire Orient. The image as a whole displays a clear tripartite order. The beholder's comparison of the eerie silence to the effect of the Sphinx may be due to the fact that he let out a loud scream at its sight in Gizeh and that he had sent the monster galloping off in *Saint Antony*.

What also interested Flaubert greatly in the Orient were its people—he actually found them "exciting"—more varied than Europeans, at the same time more mixed and integrated with respect to race or ethnicity despite the sharp class distinctions. As early as Cairo he visited a Coptic church and talked to a bishop of the Copts in a most enjoyable manner, whereby the old man invariably consulted his beard with his right before answering. Later on, up the Nile, he had a conversation with a learned Christian farmer, who took them in when they could not find a commercial place to stay. They discussed St. Antony, Arius, and Athanasius, and Flaubert found this dialogue "marvelous." Also, he attended Armenian and Greek churches, and he witnessed the ceremonies of dancing dervishes. Way up the Nile, he encountered an Abyssinian priest and after listening to him concluded: "As for the common bond of Christianity, it seems to me to be non-existent; the true bond is that of language: this man is more the Moslems' brother than mine" (161). Black Africans interested him in particular, for they constituted a genuine novelty. In a diary entry from Koseir on the Red Sea he noted: "There are, I think, more varieties in the negro race than in the white" (188). From Nubia, he wrote to his friend Bouilhet, "We are now, my dear sir, in a land where women go naked—[. . .], for by way of costume they wear only rings." He also praised their dancing ("Sacré nom de Dieu!") and lay with quite a few Nubian girls. The color of their skin impressed him, for it was exactly like that of their native soil.

At Assiut in Upper Egypt, a place of rendezvous for caravans coming from Darfur, he observed how slave traders dragged in their victims, exhausted by the privations of their long march and parched by the heat of the desert. "Here they stop for quarantine--a compulsory rest, which the *gallabs* (slave traders) take advantage of to mutilate the young negroes, fitting them for service in the harems" (109). On March 19, 1850 on the way up the Nile, he encountered a slave trader in women. "On all these boats among the women, there are old negresses who make and remake the trip continually; they are there to console the new slaves and keep up their spirits; they teach them to resign themselves to their fate and they act as interpreters between them and the trader, an Arab." In Cairo he had attended several slave markets, in Upper Egypt and Nubia he was close to the origin of the victims. It is noteworthy that he does not express outrage about the institution of slavery, but simply records the practice with *impassibilité*.

The slave trade and prostitution go hand in hand. In the Egyptian capital Flaubert had taken the first opportunity to visit a brothel, but he found it second-rate because several years before his arrival Mohammed Ali had outlawed female prostitution and banished all well-known courtesans to Upper Egypt. However, in Kena he deviated from his usual practice when he walked through the whores' quarter where Arab and black women sat bare-breasted in front of their hovels, their loose garments in yellow, white, and red fluttering in hot wind that carried their odors and spices. They induced him by crying, "Cawadja, cawadja." Yet Flaubert only dispensed bakscheesh to all: "I abstained deliberately, in order to preserve the sweet sadness of the scene and engrave it in my memory. [. . .] There is nothing more beautiful than those women calling on you. If I had gone with any of them, a second picture would have been superimposed on the first and dimmed its splendor" (128–129). As he explained, he made this sacrifice for literature, or for his future writings.

At Esna (Esneh) on the Nile, the residence of Kuchuk Hanem, the most famous *almeh* (prostitute) of Egypt, Flaubert did not abstain. He described this woman in the highest accolades as "a tall, splendid creature" from Damascus with a skin lightly coffee-colored, dark and enormous eyes, heavy shoulders and apple-shaped breasts." Her dance, meant as prelude to their sexual union, was of distinct hieratic character. It harnessed its sensual appeal in the measure of prescribed steps and poses and combined in the Oriental manner a lascivious eroticism with the religious. The transparency of the spiritual in the sensually real, which Flaubert perceived, was an experience of which the consciousness of the nineteenth-century European no longer had any concrete knowledge. For this consciousness suffered, as Hegel had shown in his discussion of "Romantic poetry," from the incompatibility of the European sensibility with European actuality: the depreciated empirical world could no longer gratify the expectations of the modern mind. Richard Wagner's music dramas and Nietzsche's *The Birth of Tragedy* (1872) constitute serious efforts to fuse once again the spiritual and the sensual, and Thomas Mann, heir to both, provides a sparkling illustration of the theme, albeit undermined by narratorial irony. In *Death in Venice* (1910), Socrates tells the object of his desire, "For beauty, my Phaedrus, beauty alone, is lovely and visible at once. For, mark you, it is the sole aspect of the spiritual which we can perceive through our senses, or bear so to perceive."[31] In contrast to the agitated self-containment of the Orient and its immanent transcendence Flaubert witnessed at the first cataract of the Nile in the dance of the Nubian woman Azizeh the stark sensuality of black Africa. "This is no longer Egypt; it is negro, African, savage—as wild as the other was formal" (121). Yet this kind of self-abandonment and openness to frantic excess also seized his imagination, for on his journey back from the Orient he wrote from Rome on April 9, 1851 to Louis Bouilhet that he was dreaming of bayaderes, frenzied dances, and the whole "tumult of colors." After his return home he would "close the shutters and live in the light."

As early as January 5, 1850 he could affirm in a letter to his mother: "You ask me whether the Orient is up to what I imagine it to be. Yes, it is; and more than that, it extends far beyond the narrow idea I had of it. I have found clearly delineated everything that was hazy in my mind. Facts have taken the place of suppositions—so excellently so that it is often as if I were suddenly coming upon old forgotten dreams" (75). Indeed, this is an intriguing statement, for on the one hand he acknowledges that his experiences at this early stage of the journey exceeded his expectations and that facts have taken the place of suppositions, and yet he affirms on the other that Oriental reality evoked and confirmed forgotten dreams. In the Orient Flaubert's dreams and reality coalesced. In many ways, however, things were to become even better when the friends reached Beirut by ship and entered the Turkish province of "Syria" which included Lebanon, present-day Syria, Palestine (except for Jerusalem), and ancient Mesopotamia (Iraq).

Near the port of Tyre, Flaubert beheld a shipwreck on the beach, which over ten years later he turned into one of the most important similes of *Salammbô*. The Republic of Carthage itself is compared to a ship of the seafaring Phoenicians grounded in the sands of North Africa. However, just as in Egypt it was the women in whom he showed the greatest interest, especially since he found those of Tyre "very beautiful." At the sight of a matron, sitting immobile across from him, with her deep, dark eyes, an aquiline nose, and a face as if cut in marble, he "thought of the races of antiquity and that she could have been the wife of a patrician of Tyre."[32] In Galilee, the Northern province of ancient Israel, he found women unchanged since the days of the Old Testament as they were drawing water at the fountain; several of them were blonde, and as they walked, the sash gathered around their waist lifted their hips in a Biblical manner. Such vistas enticed Flaubert to dreaming of the Song of Songs, as the women of Nazareth paraded by with their prominent hips and buttocks.[33] In contrast to these women he found those of modern Europe bigoted, limited and unnatural.

"Syria" impressed him as enchanting, colorful, and wild, a real contrast to the regularity of Egypt. For the Turkish province of Syria was, above all, the land of ancient religions and the Bible, which he had internalized for the sake of *Saint Antony*. Riding from Caiffu to Mount Carmel, he noted on account of the enormous olive trees, hollow inside, that he had reached the "Holy Land." To him, the olive trees were for the Holy Land what the palm trees were for Egypt. He scrutinized them closely and resurrected them in his Carthaginian novel. However, his stay in Jerusalem turned out to be utterly disillusioning. Everything struck him as false; everything was dirty except the Armenian quarter. "There are ruins everywhere that reek of the grave and desolation; the malediction of God seems to weigh down the city, the holy city of three religions [. . .]."[34] The jealousies and mutual hatreds of the various Christian sects repelled him, for they necessitated that the Turks kept the keys to the holy sepulchre. Flaubert left with the observation that "Luther returned as a protestant from the Italy of Leo X,"[35] suggesting that he departed from Jerusalem as an agnostic. Outside Jerusalem he was recompensed by the "immense and magnificent plane," known as the "Campagne of Israel" with a view of Mount Tabor in the distance.

Damascus, the next major destination, residence of the Umayyad caliphs, proved to be a more enjoyable experience. It rose like a shimmering mirage of minarets and white copulas before the travelers' eyes. Later on, Flaubert described its location from an elevated position: "in the midst of immense green, surrounded by desert, surrounded by mountains." This perception reminds of his panoramic description of the landscape of lower Egypt he saw from the Great Pyramid. In the city of Damascus itself, Flaubert was impressed by the superb bazaars, the colorful dresses of the women, the beauty of its young men between the ages of eighteen and twenty, and the politeness of the people in general. He interpreted the latter observation that the Moslems were becoming more tolerant. This insight led to another reflection: "Mohammed is also falling, even though he did not have his Voltaire, the great Voltaire is nothing else but time, the general consumer of everything."[36] (This insight was to become the great theme of *L'Éducation Sentimentale*). While tolerance might signify progress from a European perspective, it nevertheless constituted a softening of the Orient, if not its Europeanization. In Egypt, Flaubert had already noticed such signs, particularly at the tomb of Mohammed Ali's family. He found its style deplorably Euro-Oriental, painted and festooned like cabarets, with little ballroom chandeliers." (64) Moreover, in Damascus he witnessed Turks in European suits playing billiards and believed that whatever the essence of the old Orient might have been, it could be regenerated only by the uncorrupted bedouin. As a matter of fact, the entire Levant was decaying, if not disintegrating as a consequence of all-invading Europeanization. "It dismayed Flaubert thus to observe the rotting of a civilization he had dreamed of and its conquest by a world he had fled."[37]

It is only appropriate that Flaubert and Du Camp concluded their Oriental journey proper at Constantinople, capital of the waning Ottoman Empire. Yet he made it clear that he was less captivated by Turkey than by Egypt and "Syria": "Passing Abydos, I thought of Byron. This is his Orient, the Turkish Orient, the Orient of the curved sword, the Albanian costume, and the grilled window looking out on the blue sea. I prefer the baked Orient of the bedouin and the desert."[38] What the Orient really signified to him, he explained in a letter to Louise Colet of March 27, 1853:

> This is the true and, consequently, poetic Orient. Villains in rags with tresses and covered by vermin. But let the vermin be, it forms golden arabesques in the sun. [. . .] This reminds me of Jaffa, where at the same time I inhaled the fragrance of lemon trees and the smell of corpses; in the torn up cemetery one recognized rotting skeletons while green bushes swayed their golden fruits above our heads. Don't you feel how complete this poetry is, [. . .] the great synthesis? It satisfies all desires of the imagination and the mind; it does not exclude anything.[39]

The juxtaposition and intertwining of the beautiful and the ugly, growth and disintegration, life and death expresses much like Baudelaire's *Les Fleurs du mal* (1857) a holistic conception of reality enfolding seemingly irreconcilable opposites. *Les Fleurs du mal* were a tour de force, a series of provocative visions of a genius who lived against the grain of his time. Baudelaire revolted against established norms of taste by reuniting disparate things neatly separated by conventional propriety into startling images and tableaux. In contrast to this strained accomplishment, Flaubert believed to have found in the Orient a synthesis of all forms of being as the foundation of cultural actuality and the true poetry of life. Flaubert's image of the Orient is, on account of his modern aesthetics, essentially different from that of his predecessors.

If one tries to assess Flaubert's sojourn in the Orient, two major results come to mind: his new understanding of those parts of the region he had seen and his development as a writer. How and as what he learned to perceive the Orient has been sufficiently discussed, yet before turning to the second result a few words about his relationship with Du Camp are in order. Prone to lengthy depressions and essentially inactive, Flaubert was neither an easy nor obliging traveling companion. While Du Camp climbed the Great Pyramid like a weasel, Flaubert had to be pushed and pulled by several Arabs, paused five or six times, and was totally exhausted when he reached the top. Along the Nile, he would sit for hours in the shade of palm groves and drink coffee, whereas Maxime was measuring and photographing ancient monuments. At one point Du Camp, annoyed by his friend's "lassitude and boredom" (140), suggested that he return to France accompanied by his (Du Camp's) servant. Here it must be added that Maxime had also to watch over him with respect to his medical problems arising from chronic syphilis and his epileptic attacks. Nevertheless, Flaubert's travel notes display a condescending attitude towards his companion to whom he repeatedly refers as "young Du Camp." From Constantinople he related with some glee to Bouilhet that his guardian had caught a chancre for the third time, whereas his more discerning self got away with contracting just one at Beirut: "I suspect a Maronite—or was it a little Turkish girl?—of having given me this present" (215). He had to undergo mercury treatment for the rest of his life. Boredom was another cross Flaubert had to bear, for he recorded: "Deianira's tunic was no less completely welded to Hercules's back than boredom to my life! It eats into it more slowly, that's all" (151). However, his moods could change quickly, for occasionally he also experienced moments of genuine bliss: Thus after a stunning sunset over Medinet Habu on the Nile and music making and dancing by the sailors of their cange, he affirmed:

> It was then, as I was enjoying those things, and just as I was watching three wave-crests bending under the wind behind us, that I felt a surge of solemn Happiness that reached out towards what I was seeing, and I thanked God in my heart for having made me capable of such joy: I felt fortunate at the thought, and yet it seemed to me I was thinking of nothing: it was a sensuous pleasure that pervaded my entire being. (112)

This prayer, in which Flaubert thanks the Lord for bestowing extraordinary sensitivity and perceptiveness upon him, stands in sharp contrast to the depressions he suffered in Egypt. Many of the latter issued from the disaster of the first version of *Saint Antony,* which he had read to Louis

Bouilhet and Maxime Du Camp just before departing from France. They were unable to approve of it. The question whether he really was a writer haunted him. Hence he was "full of doubts and indecision" and asked himself, "What shall I do when I return?" And the question recurred over and over, "Is *Saint Antony* good or bad? [. . .] Who is mistaken, I or the others?" (74). Uncertainty about his own abilities in conjunction with daily confrontations with another culture turned Flaubert's journey through the Orient into a series of self-encounters. Yet Egypt was hardly the place to encourage an aspiring writer, for "the Orient [. . .] flattens out all worldly vanities. The sight of so many ruins [makes] one indifferent to fame" (96). At the same time, he had considerable confidence in his abilities. Although he was still an unpublished author, he decided not to publish anything about the Orient for quite a while. Hence he declined Lavallée's offer to write articles or submit parts of his letters to the *Revue de l'Orient et d'Algérie*. Instead of seeking public recognition he believed that one's own satisfaction with one's work was what really mattered.[40] As to Du Camp's assumption that Flaubert was not sufficiently interested in his Oriental surroundings, he recanted in 1864 when he wrote: "the impressions of that journey that he seemed to disdain returned to him in totality and in full force when he wrote *Salammbô*. But then Balzac was the same: he looked at nothing and remembered everything" (163).

By and large, Flaubert was a quiet and highly perceptive observer, although occasionally he could display a boisterous enthusiasm to the annoyance of his urbane friends (e.g. the brothers Goncourt): "I cannot admire in silence. I need to shout, to gesticulate, to expand; I have to bellow, smash chairs—in other words I want others to share in my pleasures" (176). It was on this journey that Flaubert realized that the modern artist "must cultivate exaggeration"[41] in order to rise above the vortex of impressions overwhelming the modern reader. There is the example of taking leave from his mother. He was not merely sad as a normal son would be, but wept for hours in the carriage. His letters to her from the Orient sound like those of a lover to his muse; the apostrophe "my darling" occurs throughout. The notion of exaggeration is inseparable from Flaubert's conception of the artist who stands high above human normalcy. He saw more perceptively and felt more deeply than others. The intimate relationship with his mother led to another decision. When she asked in one of her letters if upon his return he might not get a job, even if only a small one, he retorted that there was not a single one he was capable of filling. Those "bastard existences where you sell suet all day and write poetry at night are made for mediocre minds [. . .]: When one does something, one must do it wholly and well" (107). This was the point when he committed himself to being a writer. The suggestion that there was no other occupation that would keep them as close together, finally appeased her.

Although Flaubert sounded assured about his vocation in this letter, doubts continued to plague him, for he believed he belonged to a "weak" generation. He wrote to Bouilhet: "what we lack is the intrinsic principle, the soul of the thing, the very idea of the subject. We take notes, we make journeys: emptiness! emptiness! We become scholars, archeologists, historians [. . .]. What is the good of it all? Where is the heart, the verve, the sap?" (198–199) At this instance Flaubert was thinking of his own time as an analogue to the learned and overwrought Alexandrians of the Ptolemaic era, who knew everything but were not distinguished for their creativity. A bit later he elaborated on this perception to the same addressee by pointing out that their generation, profoundly historical as it was, had taste, admitted everything, and adopted the view of everything it was confronting. "But have we as much inner strength as we have of understanding others? Is fierce originality compatible with so much breadth of mind. . .?" (212).

The problem to which Flaubert alludes is one of the great challenges a writer and, for that matter, a historian must solve. For if they empathize completely with their subject, which may be a historical period or a historical figure, and look at it only from within, how can they judge it? This has been one of the characteristic weaknesses of historicism, say, in contrast to teleological historians and creative writers with an ideological basis. In the second half of the nineteenth century, there obviously existed a discrepancy between the historicist approach of Flaubert and the impulse to judge of literary historians such as Ferdinand Brunetière ("il faut juger"). Flaubert's observations also imply that too much knowledge stifles creativity, a foreshadowing of Nietzsche's essay, "On the Use and Disadvantage of History for Life," which appeared roughly twenty years after Flaubert's missives. Both were highly sceptical about the emotional and creative abilities of their present; yet while Flaubert restricted himself to describing what he saw, Nietzsche proposed questionable remedies such as the "overman" and the "eternal recurrence of the same."

This, then, is how his sojourn in the Orient contributed to Flaubert's development as a writer. First of all, it was there that he decided to devote his life to writing at the exclusion of any other occupation. He also learned that whatever reality he was going to present in his future narratives was to be all-inclusive, for in Egypt and "Syria" he had perceived the great synthesis. Besides *Saint Antony,* the Orient was to be the setting of two narratives: *Salammbô* and "Hérodias." The encounter with this other world sharpened Flaubert's perception and broadened his horizons. He learned to "see" and make fine distinctions between individuals and between the nuances of natural phenomena such as light and colors. Through the continuous practice of transcribing his impressions, he developed the art of presenting architectural landscapes and tableaux. Last but not least, he realized that the modern writer must exaggerate and that his work cannot be anything but a tour-de-force.

In Cairo Flaubert also arrived at an important geopolitical insight. Although France seemed to be the dominant European presence throughout Egypt with consuls in all important cities and Frenchmen in high positions in the Egyptian government, he wrote two months after his arrival to Jules Cloquet that it "seems almost impossible that within a short time England won't become mistress of Egypt. She already keeps Aden full of her troops, the crossing of Suez will make it very easy for the redcoats to arrive in Cairo one fine morning [. . .]. Remember my prediction: at the first sign of trouble in Europe, England will take Egypt" (81). This is remarkable clairvoyance occuring even before the building of the Suez Canal (1859–69) under the direction of Ferdinand de Lesseps, a French engeneer, with mainly French money and Egyptian labor. Indeed, England did occupy Egypt in 1882. Flaubert displayed comparable insight concerning the Revolution of 1848 in *Salammbô* and *L'Éducation sentimentale.*

Notes and References

1-2 Flaubert, Letters to Louise Colet, July 7, 1853 and January 2, 1854.

3 For Flaubert's relations with members of the imperial family see also Henri Troyat, *Flaubert,* transl. J. Pinkham (New York: Viking Penguin, 1992) 189 and 193-196.

The designation "black artist" is used by Jean-Paul Sartre in his monumental study *L'Idiot de la famille,* 3 vols. (Paris: Gallimard, 1971-72); the term reflects to no small degree the influence the Marquis de Sade had on Flaubert's thought.

4 I am referring here to Hegel's assessment of "modernity" as a "prosaically ordered reality." See G.W.F. Hegel, "Vorlesungen über die Ästhetik," *Theorie-Werkausgabe in zwanzig Bänden* (Frankfurt a.M.: Suhrkamp, 1970) III, 392.

5 M. Jean Bruneau, *Les Débuts littéraires de Gustave Flaubert 1831–1845* (Paris: Armand Collin, 1962) especially 79–108.

6 Hayden White, *Metahistory: The Historical Imagination in Nineteenth-Century Europe* (Baltimore: The Johns Hopkins University Press, 1973) 150.

7 Jules Michelet, *Histoire romaine, Oeuvres complètes,* ed. P. Viallaneix (Paris: Flammarion, 1972) XI, 440.

8 The struggle for supremacy in the Mediterranean was perceived differently from the besieged Greek position of 480 B.C.: The Orient [Persians, an Indogermanic people, Phoenicians, Carthaginians] versus the Greeks as representatives of the Occident.

9 Michelet, *Histoire romaine,* II, 440.

10 Flaubert, Letter to George Sand, Wednesday evening between July 8 and August 3, 1870.

11 Flaubert, Letter to Claudius Popelin, Thursday evening between August 3 and September 21, 1870.

12 Jean-Pierre Duquette, "Flaubert, l'histoire et le roman historique, *Revue d'histoire littéraire de la France,* LXXV (1975) 344.

13 Anne Green, *Flaubert and the Historical Novel: Salammbô Reassessed* (Cambridge, etc.: Cambridge University Press, 1982) 26.

14 Benedetto Croce, *Zur Theorie und Geschichte der Historiographie,* transl. E. Pizzo (Tübingen: J.C.B. Mohr, 1915) 2-3 (my translation). Compare to Croce, *Theory and Historiography,* transl. Douglas Ainslie (New York: Harcourt, Brace and Co., 1921) 13

(I think my translation is more accurate).

15–16   R.G. Collingwood, *The Idea of History* (1946), (London, Oxford, New York: Oxford University Press, 1968) 242 and 246.

17   Flaubert, Letter to Léon Hennique, February 2–3, 1880.

18   Alfred de Vigny, *Le Journal d'un poète, Oeuvres complètes*, ed. F. Baldensperger (Paris: Gallimard, 1948) XI, 888.

19   Théophile Gautier, *L'Orient* (Paris: Charpentier, 1877) 29–30 and 37–38.

20   Raymond Schwab, *The Oriental Renaissance—Europe's Rediscovery of India and the East, 1680–1880* [1950], transl. G. Patterson-Blackard and V. Reinking (New York: Columbia UP, 1984) 11.

21   Constantin-François Comte de Volney, *Voyage en Egypte et en Syrie* (Paris: Bossange, 1821).

22–23 Edward Said, *Orientalism* (New York: Pantheon Books, 1978) 87 and 104.

24   Silvestre de Sacy, *Chrestomatie arabe, ou Extraits de divers écrivains arabes, tant en prose qu'en vers, avec une traduction et des notes* [1826], reprinted (Osnabrück: Biblio Verlag, 1973).

25–27 Ernest Renan, *Histoire générale et système comparé des langues sémitiques* (Paris: Calmann–Lévy: 1855) 144, 145–146, 155.

28   Gustave Flaubert, *Flaubert in Egypt*, transl. and ed. Francis Steegmuller (New York: Penguin, 1996). Herewith all citations from this work will be followed by the page number(s) in parentheses.

29   Jean de La Verande, *Gustave Flaubert* (Hamburg: Rowohlt, 1986) 32. (My translation).

30   See Anne-Sophie Hendrycks's article "Flaubert et le paysage oriental," *Revue d'Histoire littéraire de la France,* 6 (1994) 999: "Cette lumière est coloré: elle est "d'argent' et, plus souvent, "d'or, d'une grande intensité, elle peut, paradoxalement virer au noir [. . .]."

31   Thomas Mann, *Death in Venice and Seven Other Stories*, Vintage (New York: Random House, n.d.) 45.

32–36 Flaubert, *Voyage en Orient, Oeuvres complètes* (Paris: Club de l'Honnête Homme, 1973) X, 554, 582, 563, 564, 590–91.

37   Benjamin Bart, *Flaubert* (Syracuse, N.Y: Syracuse University Press, 1967) 204.

38   Flaubert, Letter to Louis Bouilhet, November 14, 1850.

39   Flaubert, Letter to Louise Colet, March 27, 1853.

40   Flaubert, Letter to Louis Bouilhet, June 2, 1850.

41   Benjamin Bart, *Flaubert*, 233.

Chapter II

The Setting of Carthage and the Titular Heroine

> "J'ai des besoins d'orgies poétiques. Ce que j'ai vu m'a rendu exigeant."
> Flaubert to Louis Bouilhet, April 9,1851

Why Carthage?

As a counterstatement to *Madame Bovary* Flaubert's new novel had not only to be removed in time from his own bourgeois present, but it was to have also another setting. One of his favorite epochs was the Hellenistic era (fourth to the second centuries B.C.). During this time decisive political changes took place among the peoples and states around the Mediterranean. There and then, the individual found unprecedented opportunities for self-realization. "What makes the figures from antiquity so beautiful," Flaubert wrote, "is the fact that they were original: Everything is there, brought forth out of the self."[1] The Greek conception of individuality enabled strong characters to liberate themselves from religious orthodoxy, the tribe, and the polis in order to transform the world and themselves. They founded new kingdoms and dynasties, transplanted entire nations, destroyed old cities and built new ones until the grandiose "tumult of colors" fell piece by piece under the hegemony of Rome and, finally, came to rest in the frail pax romana.

Since the Orient was the only exotic region Flaubert had seen for himself, the choice of setting was a given. But why Carthage of all possible places? There were several reasons that made him decide for the capital of the Punic empire. Indeed, his interest in the maritime republic reached back to his youth, for as early as 1838 he had noted that Carthage was "monstruous and wild [. . .], full of terrors and arrogant cynicism."[2] As their corrupted name indicates, the Punics belonged to the Phoenician people of Canaanite stock who had founded Carthage, "Kart hadascht," the new city, near present-day Tunis in the late ninth century B.C. A seafaring Oriental people inhabiting the African coast, they fought first with the Greeks and later with the Romans for domination of the ancient world. Did such confrontations not harbor sufficient tensions and causes of conflict for a novelist who wished to write about "gigantic battles, sieges, and the fabulous old Orient"? A peculiar attraction of Carthage consisted in the fusion of African and Oriental components in the Carthaginians themselves and in Punic culture, the complimentariness of which had excited Flaubert when he compared the ritualistic dance of Kuchuk Hanem[3] with the wild frenzy of the Nubian Azizeh. Moreover, the Punics had a complex mythology that made their lives more "poetic." Renan's *The Life of Jesus,* which appeared after *Salammbô,* describes the aesthetic charms of polytheism with which Westerners are familiar through Homer's epics and Germanic mythology. The author relates a journey of Jesus in the direction of Sidon and Tyre, where he found himself in the midst of paganism. On the road he encountered such sites as the grotto of Panium (which was thought to be the source of the river Jordan), the marble temple erected by Herod near there in honor of Augustus, as well as the votive statues to Pan and to the Nymph of the grotto:

> A rationalistic Jew, accustomed to take strange gods for deified men or for demons, would consider all these figurative representations as idols. The seductions of the naturalistic worships, which intoxicated the more sensitive nations, never affected him. He was doubtless ignorant of what the ancient sanctuary of Melcarth, at Tyre, might still contain of a primitive worship more or less analogous to that of the Jews. The Paganism which, in Phoenicia, had raised a temple and a sacred grove on every hill, all this aspect of great industry and profane riches, interested him but little. Monotheism takes away all aptitude for comprehending the pagan religion; [. . .] Jesus assuredly learned nothing in these journeys.[4]

On February 1853, only ten days after his acquittal in the trial concerning *Madame Bovary,* Flaubert inquired as to what was known about Punic Carthage. Although the maritime republic had played a important role in the affairs of antiquity, it was almost inaccessible to modern scientific historiography, not only because of its remoteness in time and "foreignness" to the European sensibility, but also because of the holocaust with which its Roman conquerors had terminated its existence. The destruction of Carthage in 146 B.C. almost obliterated it from historical consciousness. Its libraries had been burned, and the survivors of the three-year-siege were sold into slavery. However, these measures seem to have been insufficient to set the Roman mind to rest about Carthage. Since there definitely existed a "Carthaginian problem" (i.e. Roman sense of guilt), Roman historians either mentioned the vanquished enemy as little as possible, or they gave it negative press. Whatever was handed down to posterity about Carthage was the work of Romans, or of historians on Roman payrolls including Polybius, a Greek.

For all these reasons, a fictional "reconstruction" of Carthage proved much more difficult than Flaubert had assumed. Aside from accounts of the Phoenicians in general, random traces of Carthaginian customs, plastic descriptions of the Punic hinterland in Diodorus Siculus, or occasional remarks in Polybius's *Histories,* there were no noteworthy sources which provided a reliable picture of this metropolis of antiquity and its daily life. In the face of this lack of primary information Flaubert had no choice but to immerse himself in a sea of books. He studied the historians of antiquity and made use of every single fact and hint insofar as it related in some way to his subject. He combed the Bible for references about the Phoenicians and Canaanites. And he read an immense number of archeological, cultural, religious, and scientific publications in addition to those he had perused for *Saint Antoine* and his journey to the Orient. Flaubert's approach was based on two theses: that of ethnic-cultural correspondences and that of the ahistorical Orient. His premise was the close ethnic kinship of Phoenicians and Hebrews; he deduced that the way of life of one people would also provide knowledge of the other's. Moreover, during his journey to the Orient he had become quite sure that much remained essentially unchanged since the days of the kings Solomon of Israel and Hiram of Tyre, and that the Bible was almost the equivalent of a description of Oriental life in his own century (e.g. the sight of Jewish women at the fountain in Nazareth). In addition to primary works and scientific literature concerning later Carthaginian history, as well as the method of analogy, there was a third factor which made Flaubert confident of coming to terms with the challenging project of Carthage; his gift of extraordinary empathy. It rested on the belief, or wishful thinking, that he had lived at different times under the most varied circumstances.[5] His trip to Tunisia in the spring of 1858 gave further impetus to such notions. After he had visited the site of Carthage and undertaken several excursions into its vicinity, he believed that he possessed sufficient understanding of life in the ancient city.

In his endeavor to evoke Carthage as an image Flaubert was less concerned with the absolute precision of the archeology than with its probability and the avoidance of absurdities. He conceived of the whole as a mixture of "soap-bubbles and the real,"[6] as a "fixed fata morgana." This artificial paradise, which has its analogy in Baudelaire's poem "Paysage," was expected to reward the author for the time he had spent on researching the topic. In *Salammbô* he found occasion to amass "brutal effects," and he was able to fill the novel with "screams of horror and mystic pleasure" (298) under the golden cupolas, coral roofs of temples, and emerald obelisks of a mysterious people. The intertwining of precious objects and irrational brutality in an eroticized atmosphere is characteristic of an aestheticism whose representatives loved to depict the sudden change from overrefinement and opulence to barbarism. The setting thus gathers a force of its own as a scene of wild splendor iridescent with the spectrum of colors, particularly purple, a Phoenician invention obtained from the secretions of small mollusks and ranging in hue from crimson, the color of kings and emperors, to blue.

Flaubert's image of Carthage builds on the documented commercial and military harbors, the Byrsa or ancient citadel, a few transmitted names of urban districts, suburbs, and streets, and a number of impressionistically described temples, palaces, statues, interiors, and utensils. He also drew on natural givens he had observed in the Orient: the light, the gradations of light, and the colors it discloses. He mustered his literary energies, he wrote to Ernest and Jules Duplan, and left everything in a "state of uncertainty" in order that the dream-like image of the metropolis would not be destroyed. Regarding the latter, Flaubert was also concerned about the reader. He resisted all attempts by his publisher to commission illustrations for the novel, for he did not wish to have his fata morgana pinpointed. Instead, he expected readers to approximate objects they encountered in the exotic narrative with things they had seen themselves.[7] Thus, in spite of occasionally precise details, the three extensive descriptions of the city do not add up to a graphic panorama. They are not "objective" descriptions, but impressions of the metropolis rendered from three different perspectives: those of Mâtho and Spendius, the Barbarian army, and Hamilcar Barca. The first description is the most encompassing:

> But a bar of light rose up in the East. On the left, right below the canals of Megara began to wind their white coils across the greenery of the gardens. The conical roofs of the heptagonal temples, the stairs, terraces, ramparts, gradually took shape against the pale dawn; and all around the Carthaginian peninsula pulsed a girdle of white foam while the emerald-colored sea seemed frozen. [. . .] Then as the rosy sun spread wider, the tall houses tilted on the slopes of the ground grew taller and massed together like a flock of black goats coming from the mountains. The empty streets lengthened out; palm-trees, rising out of walls here and there, did not stir; the full water-tanks looked like silver shields abandoned in the courtyards, the lighthouses on the Hermaeum promontory began to pale. On the very top of the Acropolis, in the cypress wood, Eschmoûn's horses, feeling the ap-

proach of day, put their hoofs on the marble parapet and whinnied towards the sun (29–30).

High up on a terrace, Mâtho and Spendius do not perceive a static tableau but an action. Dawn is a favorite time of Flaubert's landscape descriptions. The first light of day is just a bright bar that spreads until the rosy sun itself rises and aspects of the city appear. This image of awakening Carthage is a composite of the novelist's experiences during his Oriental journey, his brief visit to Tunisia in 1858, and his empathetic imagination. The presentation as a whole displays striking parallels to what he beheld from atop the Great Pyramid at Gizeh composed of foreground (the canals cutting through the green meadows), middle (the iridescent brown desert), and the Nile, palm-trees, and the minarets of Cairo in the distance as backdrop. For Carthage he offers a similar foreground of green gardens through which canals meander not along the straight lines of Egypt, but coil-like, a tribute to the fetish of the House of Barca and the Punic national symbol, the serpent. The middle is here taken up by the temples of the Acropolis on the Byrsa, and the background displays the emerald-colored Mediterranean. It is another ethnically pertinent touch that he describes the "white foam" of the breakers hugging the peninsula as pulsing, for the sea was the Phoenicians elixir of life.

The description focuses on the middle of the image, and aside from the temples refers to terraces, stairs, and ramparts, all unspecific architectural terms, for no one knows what the Punic capital looked like. Yet the "tall houses" that emerge with the advancing light from the slopes near the ground, have been confirmed by several antique historians. Since the Phoenicians founded their settlements on narrow peninsulas whenever possible, protected from the mainland by strong fortifications across the isthmus, space in such communities was precious. Hence they became the first builders of highrises, as for instance in Tyre, Lilybaeum (Sicily), Gades, and Carthage. While the sun continues to rise, it throws its magical light over all things: the spurs of ships in the commercial and military harbors and the golden roof of Khamon's temple which seems ablaze.

According to Lukács, the precious and exotic objects which are assembled, named, and described appear to exist only for their own sake.[8] Yet a closer look at such passages of the text reveals that the objects have definite functions within the fictional cosmos, which makes *Salammbô* a work of art instead of a collection of bibelots. Three extensive descriptions are particularly impressive on account of their Oriental opulence. First of all, there is the tableau of the feast of the mercenaries. This celebration, which functions as an overture to the action of the novel, is given by the Carthaginian state in honor of the rescued soldiers in the gardens of the absent Hamilcar, their former commander and maritime suffete. The enumeration of the menu's exotic courses provides the narrator with the opportunity to introduce the ethnic contingents of the Punic army by letting them react one after another to the foreign dishes.[9] The Greek and Italic wines soon drive the mercenaries into decrying the avarice of Carthage. The ensuing carouse reveals how undisciplined the mercenaries are and how irreverent toward higher sentiments. For in the midst of gastronomic abundance they catch the sacred fish of the Barcas and fry them alive. By doing this, they introduce themselves with a heinous deed. Their total disregard for the sacred and their hedonistic excesses bode ill for future negotiations with Carthage regarding payments due them from the war in Sicily.

The second example, Salammbô's chamber, constitutes an anticipation of art nouveau interiors. With its painted panels, a ceiling of beams decorated with amethyst and topaz, tiles ornamented with gold, mother of pearl, and colored glass, a bathing basin made of solid onyx, and the bric-à-brac of flamingo wings mounted on black-coral branches, purple cushions, tortoise shell combs, and ivory spatulas, the opulent interior might well have been designed by the studios of William Morris, Émile Gallé, or L.C. Tiffany. Flaubert describes the world of Hamilcar's daughter from the perspective of Mâtho, leader of the mercenaries, who violently intrudes into her precious realm. This confrontation between brute strength and the exquisite luxury of an old culture accentuates the opposing forces in the conflict of Carthage with its mercenaries.

Hamilcar's treasure vault is the third example of the world of objects and their functions in *Salammbô*. He inspects it after his return from abroad, for he has been recalled in order to resume command of the Carthaginian forces:

> There were callais torn from the mountains by slingshots, carbuncle formed by lynx's urine, glossopetri fallen from the moon, tyanos, diamonds, sandastrum, beryls, the three kinds of rubies, four kinds of sapphire, and twelve kinds of emeralds. They flashed, like splashes of milk, blue icicles, silver dust, and shed their light in sheets, rays, stars. Ceraunites engendered by thunder twinkle near chalcedonies, which are a cure for poisons. There were topaz from Mount Zabarca to ward off terrors, opals from Bactria that prevent miscarriages, and horns of Ammon which can be put under the bed to inspire dreams. (129)

The explanations relating the origins of the precious stones and their healing powers read like a breviary of superstition and encourage conjectures about the Carthaginians' image of the world which was neither empirical nor rational. They believed in the arbitrary ways of their gods. On the other hand, Hamilcar's treasures also permit the reader to fathom the extent of Punic trade routes, which led to all ends of the known world, and beyond. "Money," Michelet writes, "was the king and god of Carthage."[10] The Greek slave Spendius pointed out this fact in the first chapter of the novel by comparing the maritime republic to those Punic wretches "bent down on the edge of the oceans, [plunging their] arms greedily into every shore" (30). As a nation of traders and the only Oriental people in the Western Mediterranean, the Carthaginians were looked upon and treated as outsiders by the canny Greeks and martial Romans. Thus, the Punic merchant, whom Plautus presents in *Poenulus* dressed in a caftan as a vendor of pitchforks, shoe laces, shovels, nuts, and herring, was not only met with derision by the Roman theater audience, but also with apprehension since his wealth enabled Carthage to raise formidable armies at any time by hiring mercenaries.[11]

Appropriately, Flaubert shows that the power of Carthage emanated from the Syssitia, societies of traders, who elected the inspector of finances. They also chose the one hundred members of the Council of Elders. In addition there was the General Assembly, a gathering of the Rich. The two suffetes were comparable to Roman consuls, though less powerful and usually came from rival families of distinction. Hence any attempts to overthrow the republican form of government seemed to be forestalled. In public affairs Carthage maintained a prudent system of checks and balances, and hence Aristotle called its constitution one of the very best in antiquity.

One should not assume that such a well-ordered state of affairs and the dedicated pursuit of wealth infringed upon the "joie de vivre" of the Carthaginians. Quite the contrary, for the rich at least life was not only relatively free of cares, but enjoyable. According to Flaubert, three times a month, members of the Syssitia met in a large courtyard of the harbor district Malqua, on the site where the first Phoenician sailor from Tyre had landed, in order to discuss business and politics: "[. . .] and from below one could see them at open air tables, without boots and cloaks, with diamonds on their fingers as they prodded the food and their great earrings leaning against the pitchers—all big and fat, half-naked, happy, laughing and eating under the blue sky, like great sharks playing in the sea" (92). This sumptuous image of Carthaginian life makes up for the more somber traits of the Punic character. Altogether, the protean beauty of the sea enlivens the phantasmagorical images of Carthage.[12]

Since Carthage is inconceivable without the Mediterranean, the mythical sea, it became the element from which Flaubert created his most successful metaphors and similes. For instance, he expressed the origin of Carthage, its essence, and its position in world politics in an image indebted to the sea: "A galley anchored on the Libyan sand, [Carthage] maintained its position by sheer hard work. Nations, like waves, roared round it, and the slightest storm rocked the formidable craft" (91). The ship recalls the distant origin of the Carthaginians and their ancestors' tradition as a sea-faring people. The image, a composite of metaphor and simile, also reveals the frightful weakness of the Punic state in Africa. Instead of civilizing the indigenous tribes of the hinterland by creating an integrated Punic-Libyan cultural and political realm, or a multicultural society,[13] they exploited and brutalized them: Carthage was bleeding these peoples, even allied Phoenician cities like Utica and Hippo-Zarytos. During the first war with Rome (264–241), the republic had doubled the contributions of the allied cities and requested one half of the harvest of the rustic population. It punished failure to comply with stiff increases in the cities' contributions, whereas the chieftains of the ethnically unrelated tribes were crucified or thrown to the lions. Such practices earned the Carthaginians the reputation of cruelty. In *Salammbô* even the rough mercenaries are moved by an incident of Punic cruelty. For instance, they see a number of lions nailed on crosses: "What sort people are these," they thought, "who amuse themselves by crucifying lions!" (38) To the alleged national characteristics of cruelty, avarice, and vindictiveness, Roman authors added that of perfidy and raised the concept of "perfida Carthago" to a literary topos, e.g. Virgil's expression of the "forked-tongued Tyrians."[14] Flaubert translated this concept into action by describing an event related to the departure of the mercenaries after their feast of welcome. While the Carthaginians loudly bestow the blessings of Melcarth upon them, under their breath they mutter his curse and thereafter massacre three hundred unarmed Balearic slingers who overslept the exodus of their comrades.

What compelled the Carthaginians to commit such acts of faithlessness and cruelty is an open question, but Flaubert alleged that they lacked political genius and that their "concern for profit prevented [them] from having that prudence which goes with higher ambition" (91). As a consequence, "the slightest storm" was capable of shaking the Punic ship of state. As soon as a hostile army landed in North Africa, the realm of

Carthage shrank to its city walls, since the exploited towns, tribes, and peoples inevitably deserted the oppressor and, Michelet notes, joined the invader as did, for instance, the older Phoenician city of Tunis (89). The Carthaginians were not only racists, but they also practiced a brutal form of colonialism. In times of national emergencies as that of the Mercenary War, Carthage, well knowing it was surrounded by deadly enemies, "clutched to its heart its money and its gods" and marshalled its old virtues of courage and self-sacrifice. In the case of the Punics' harsh treatment of their subject peoples, Flaubert seems to have greatly exaggerated this tendency for political reasons, i.e., mindful of French colonial practices in Algeria.

The Punic gods and their religious ceremonies, which had essentially remained similar to those of their Phoenician ancestors, captivated Flaubert. For their religion displayed not only the Oriental ability to accommodate contrary forces in one all-encompassing view, but it had also constructed its "Olympus" and interpretation of the world on the premise of "mystic" causality. The famous tablets of Ugarit, which were discovered long after the completion of *Salammbô*, confirmed that Flaubert had grasped the essential ideas of Canaanite mythology by representing the fortunes of the Carthaginian world as reverberations of the continuous struggle of two deities or principles.[15] In arid Canaan and in Phoenicia/Lebanon these had been Aleyan Baal, the god of moisture and vegetation, and Moth (Moloch), the god of heat and summer drought. The Carthaginians had made the Canaanite-Phoenician conception of a dualistic world order even more pronounced, and more interesting to Flaubert, by replacing Aleyan Baal with Tanit, the goddess of the moon, akin to the Near Eastern Astarte. The confrontation of the two deities could therefore be seen as a struggle between the male (Moloch) and female (Tanit) principles. During the religious reforms following the military disaster of Himera (480 B.C.), Carthage had proclaimed Tanit tutelary goddess of the city so that Punic culture, whose origins retraced to the Tyrian princess Elissa, displayed strong feminine traits. This situation found expression in the fertility rites surrounding the cult of Tanit. As a matter of fact, many Europeans writing about the Orient equated the region with woman, as Said points out. Also, Lisa Lowe entitles Chapter 3 of her *Critical Terrains: French and British Orientalisms,* "Orient as Woman, Orientalism as Sentimentalism: Flaubert."[16]

The reverse of the Punics' strict obedience to religious laws was an utter lack of restraint in certain cultist ceremonies which constituted precisely what Flaubert had observed in the Orient as the intertwining of sexuality and religion. The "Book of Judges" and the two "Books of Kings" of the *Old Testament* provide eloquent testimony of the excesses enacted by the followers of Baal and Astarte (Tanit), which Max Weber graphically summarized:

> The cults of the baalim, like most agricultural cults, were and remained throughout orgiastic, especially with respect to alcohol and sexuality. The ritualist copulation on the field as homeopathic magic of fertility, orgies of alcohol and dancing with sexual promiscuity inevitably ensuing, which in subsequent times were modified into sacrificial offerings, dance, and song, as well as temple prostitution, were in all certainty also components of Israelite agricultural cults. [. . .] To serve the baalim meant, once and for all, to "whore after them."[17]

As to the Phoenicians in particular, Michelet describes their nocturnal rituals as a sequence of "wailings, tears, and shameless pleasures," and he finds no other comparison for their perversions than the indecencies of modern Malabar.[18] Concerning the Punic dominion Flaubert found evidence of temple prostitution and sacred promiscuity which he incorporated in his novel. Sicca, about one hundred and thirty miles from Carthage is introduced as the center of temple prostitution. Also, during the celebration of their victory over the mercenaries, the Carthaginians plan to serve the baalim in the time-honored Canaanite manner: "[. . .] torches were already being lit in the sacred woods; during the night there was to be massive prostitution; three ships had brought harlots from Sicily and some had come from the desert" (277). The cosmic struggle of the male and female principles, orgiastic cults, and prostitution as religious acts filled Carthage with an atmosphere of pan-eroticism inviting the hermit of Croisset to indulge his imagination.

Aside from the city of Carthage proper, its monstrous lure, power, as well as the religion, customs, and commercial achievements of its people, the novel also discloses vistas of the Punic hinterland. For the Carthaginians were for a long time not only the finest sailors of antiquity, but they also excelled as exemplary agriculturalists. Just as in the descriptions of the city, the novelist-narrator does not present the countryside from an omniscient point of view but through the eyes of the mercenaries. The scene I have chosen shows the Barbarians on their way to Sicca traversing an intensively cultivated area with prosperous farms lining the road, and irrigation trenches flowing through palm-groves that border on olive plantations and vineyards. As in his descriptions of Egyptian landscapes, the novelist divides the image into three sections, for behind the cultivated land the soldiers perceive pink mists hovering in the gorge of the hills, followed by blue mountains. In contrast to scenes along the upper Nile, the foreground is richer in implied gradations of green, from the dark hues of the vineyards to the greenish silver of the olive trees; and whereas in the Nilotic depictions the middle is dominated by the brown of the desert, here it is replaced by the pink of the gorge. Yet in either case blue mountains form the horizon.

What amazes the soldiers most are "the artificially twisted horns of the oxen, the ewes dressed in skin to protect their wool, the lozenge patterns of criss-cross furrows," and "the pomegranate trees sprayed with silphium. Such fertile land and such ingenious inventions dazzled them" (35). The care with which Punic farmers husbanded their plants and animals underlines the remarkable age of their culture reaching back to Canaan. As a matter of fact, a book about agriculture is the most extensive text that survived the holocaust of Carthaginian libraries. Cato the Elder, who clamored in Rome for the destruction of the rival empire after Hannibal's war, advocated at the same time that his countrymen adopt Punic agricultural practices.

This, then, was the Afro-Oriental setting of Carthage Flaubert had created for his historical novel. The analysis in the preceding pages is not complete, but it does show that what Flaubert presents as his image of the Punic capital is quite plausible, even in the light of archeological discoveries since the publication of *Salammbô*.[19] This achievement must be ascribed to his prodigious research, his Oriental experience, and his empathetic imagination. This is all the more astounding since Flaubert's attitude towards the Carthaginians was ambivalent. He despised the Punics for lacking imagination as artists, a deficiency he believed to be bound up with their practicality and success in commerce.[20] Yet he admired the vitality of Phoenician-Punic culture, that of a tiny people, which lasted for well over two and one half thousand years around the politically volatile basin of the Mediterranean.[21] He also appreciated the poetically useful tensions in their mythology affecting their daily life. While he assiduously consulted Michelet, he evidently did not accept his disparaging evaluation of the maritime republic and its people. Flaubert neither shared Michelet's democratic ideals nor his racial prejudices. As an artist of the "decadent" second half of the nineteenth century and aficionado of the Orient, he was appreciative of the wayward aspects of Punic life, such as the carnal excesses in religious celebrations. Had he not indulged in all kind of copulations along the Nile and in "Syria"?

It is probable that Flaubert's success in his evocation of the maritime republic was to a large extent due to his ability of making the forgotten

Carthaginian past present, by revivifying that which seemingly had been lost forever. Lukács errs when he claims that in contrast to Scott, in whose works supposedly exists complete agreement between material things described and the lives of the protagonists, "there is no such connection between the outside world and the psychology of the main characters" in *Salammbô*. The same can be said about the critical reservations of the archeologist Guillaume Froehner and a good many modern critics who have claimed that the archeology in *Salammbô* is not worth a farthing. Flaubert's detractors question the novelist's ability to relate the setting, i.e. his image of Carthage, to the thoughts and lives of his characters. Since the vitality of the historical novel depends on the interplay of the depicted past and the present, a given specimen of the genre cannot be "good," if the setting is not "right." If the setting is not right, the protagonists and minor characters cannot be right, and if both of these are not right, the entire novel cannot be right. In addition, the image of the past as an allegory or critique of the present would necessarily lose significance.

However, the preceding discussion of the novel's setting has shown that Flaubert succeeded in breathing life into the geographical and social background by means of images. A case in point is that of the Phoenician galley anchored on Libyan sand which contains the idea underlying the narrative as a whole. This point must be emphasized, for in his study of Flaubert's novels, Victor Brombert sees the settings in close proximity to the works of the Parnasse. He even goes so far as to call *Salammbô* a "Parnassian epic." The elements of the novel named in support of this classification are, above all, Flaubert's "architectural obsession" in the descriptions of the city, which "suggest a real choreography of geometric figures and patterns,"[22] and in the imagery of the novel. Here, organic phenomena are frequently related to precious stones, whereas inanimate objects often appear to assume a life of their own. The result of such poetic practices is, according to Brombert, an "uncanny sense of immobility," the very quality characteristic of a Parnassian tableau in the style of Leconte de Lisle.

In support of his thesis Brombert quotes a literary bon mot from Harry Levin's *The Gates of Horn,* according to which imagery seems deprived of "perspective in a land where metaphors come true."[23] This keen insight may apply to the poetry of the Parnassians and to Symbolist narratives such as Huysmans's *À Rebours* because they are largely self-referential and where a thing is no more, no less, and no other than the absolute image suggested by the linguistic sign. Due to their severance from empirical reality, such artifacts do not open themselves to perspectivist approaches of interpretation. Yet do these criteria also pertain to *Salammbô?* There is, to be sure, a tradition of reading Flaubert's historical novel as a Symbolist work that reaches from Gautier's exalted review of the narrative to the renowned twentieth-century literary historian Albert Thibaudet. In his study *Gustave Flaubert* the latter describes the novel as "a block of pure past, a kind of dead star like the moon under the influence of which Salammbô stands."[24] Comparable views are held by W. Wolfgang Holdheim who perceives Flaubert's narrative devices conspiring to "abstract what appears to be solid into the unreality of a radical otherness,"[25] and Lawrence Schehr who reads *Salammbô* as the novel of alterity: "[It] is ergon without parergon, text without frame."[26]

Is *Salammbô* indeed a dead star, divorced from the world and the life of the author? Rather, it would appear that Flaubert wrote his Oriental novel as a critique of his own time by resurrecting a forgotten past. In his effort to make it present, which according to Dilthey and Croce is accomplished in the act of thinking the thoughts of the past once again, Flaubert relied (for the purpose of enlivening the setting) on the participation of the reader. The great majority of his imagery does not consist of metaphors but similes, i.e., rhetorical figures that are coordinated with allegory. The comparison made in a simile, particularly an epic simile, is evaluated by the readers against the experiences of their own lived and imagined lives. Together with the suggestively presented objects, which the readers complete and specify in their imagination, the imagery of *Salammbô* is instrumental in enlivening the historical milieu.

"Carthage," "Les Mercenaires," and "La Fille d'Hamilcar" were titles Flaubert considered for his historical novel before he found the magic name, "Salammbô." The titles refer to utterly different subjects: the capital of an empire, a group of soldiers, a princess. This suggests that the author found it difficult to direct his narrative and attempted to accomplish too many things at once. He wanted to present a vanquished civilization by describing one of its most dreadful military conflicts. He also wished to create a work of beauty, centered around an attractive figure. Finally, he sought to endow the genre of the exotic historical novel with new aesthetic qualities and socio-political dimensions. As a result, the narrative has several foci.

Salammbô

The preceding pages explained Flaubert's reasons for choosing Carthage as setting. The next question is why did he select the Mercenary War as the historical element of his novel? One explanation is analogous to his decision to set the novel in Carthage. In comparison to its confrontations with Rome, the "truceless" war of the Punic republic with its mercenaries was shrouded in obscurity. Historiography has neglected it; the only extensive treatment is found in Polybius's Histories on which Michelet based his account. Martin Bernal suggests that the "Indian Mutiny," better known as the "Sepoy Mutiny," which broke out in February 1857, may have "caused Flaubert to choose his new topic."[27] Following the massacre of most of the English at Delhi, the gravest incident occured at Cawnpore on the Ganges where sepoys (Indian mercenaries in British service) hacked to pieces four hundred Englishmen and eighty "loyal" natives plus two hundred women and children. After the collapse of the rebellion, British retributions were horrendous. "Thousands were hanged, and many were blown to bits from the mouths of cannons—a particularly terrible punishment, as the Hindus believed that the bodies could never be reassembled for the future life."[28] The gore of the war of Carthage with its mercenaries was comparable.

The ubiquitous atrocities form a sharp contrast to the intriguing figure of the heroine, the incarnation of the author's dreams of woman and eros. It was the sketchiness of Polybius's work, the blank areas of Carthaginian life during the Mercenary War, which gave Flaubert the opportunity to introduce his protagonist. Polybius mentions a daughter of Hamilcar to be wedded to the king of Numidia, and no more. As to the title, the heroine's name had the advantage of emphasizing Flaubert's creative contribution to the narrative, while "Carthage" would have stressed the painstaking archeology, and "The Mercenaries" the transmitted historical material. Regarding appeal, there can be no doubt that the mysterious name of a woman was more alluring than a forgotten civilization or a troop of soldiers. And did the name of Salammbô with its phonetic affinity to the biblical Salome not promise something Oriental and extravagant, qualities to which the aesthetic elite of the second half of the nineteenth century was particularly receptive?

Flaubert's struggles with the title accentuate the basic design of his historical novel. Against the physical, social, and political background of Carthage, a series of personal, diplomatic and military actions is set in motion. Aside from the breath-taking location of the city on a peninsula jutting into the Mediterranean, there is, first of all, the realm of love, the imagination, and Punic mythology. The non-historical chapters devoted to the heroine—"Salammbô," "Tanit," "The Serpent," and "In the Tent"— take up little more than a third of the novel, even if one adds parts of the

The Setting of Carthage and the Titular Heroine 53

opening and concluding chapters where she plays important roles. Almost twice as much narrative space, however, is given to the historically transmitted actions from the soldiers' return to their final defeat under the walls of the city, and to political events. The allocation of narrative space should be a clue to the author's ultimate intentions. Are the two strains of the narrative integrated? According to Lukács this is not the case: "This lack of relation between the human tragedy, which is what kindles the reader's interest, and the political action clearly shows the change already undergone by historical feeling in this age."[29] What Lukács believes to have perceived in *Salammbô* is the bourgeois severance of personal from public life so that personal life has become private life. Hence the human motivations "do not spring organically out of a concrete socio-historical basis," but are grafted onto essentially isolated and lonely protagonists by modern psychologizing. However, the question of whether the two strains of the narrative are sufficiently intertwined is considerably more complex than Lukács acknowledges. It remains to be seen whether he is justified in his dismissal of Salammbô's intervention in the affairs of state as purely external. Characteristically, he does not trouble himself with reflecting on the nature of Punic mythology and its function in the novel, although the firmament of Tanit, Moloch, Melcarth, and lesser Canaanite-Phoenician gods looms over the North-African metropolis. Salammbô is not only a lay-priestess of Tanit, but she is also described in terms of the tutelary goddess of the thriving city. At the conclusion of the novel she is clearly identified with the spirit of her people, just as she is inseparably linked to the mythological machinery that reflects the fate of Carthage. Thus, one should assume that the success or failure of her role in the novel depends in large measure on whether the reader is able to accept the Carthaginian gods as credible powers according to whose wishes the citizens of the maritime republic conduct their lives. In *The Uses of Uncertainty* Jonathan Culler classifies all critical attempts to make light of the mythology, like that of R.J. Sherrington, as reductive readings.[30]

Salammbô is above all an alluring maiden, a configuration of Élisa Schlesinger, the married woman Flaubert had adored in his adolescence and as a young man, and Kuchuk Hanem, the famous Egyptian almeh he encountered and savored at the first cataract of the Nile. Théophile Gautier has glorified Salammbô as a "chaste creature submerged in perfumes, sacred rites, and ecstasies, around whom the halo of the moon seems to form."[31] The two foremost traits of the heroine, her innocence and her ecstatic nature, are named in this accolade, as well as her public function as priestess of Tanit (i.e. the trope of "the halo of the moon"). Indeed, the text reveals the dual aspect of Salammbô's nature and public role during her first appearance at the mercenaries' feast. Her religious and patriotic chants reconcile the disgruntled soldiers with Carthage. In this precarious situation Salammbô triumphs on the strength of her virginal beauty and enthusiasm. She also displays unconscious erotic impulses, for suddenly her "ardor rose to the gleam of the naked swords; she cried out with open arms. Her lyre dropped, she fell silent—and pressing both hands to her heart, she stayed for some moments with her eyes closed, savoring the excitement of these men" (28). Her gestures speak for themselves. What is important is that her first appearance exerts a decisive influence on future events. Mâtho, the gigantic Libyan, falls in love with her and thereby enters into deadly rivalry with the Numidian king Narr'havas. At the very opening of the narrative, Salammbô is thus presented as a "femme fatale" whose irresistibility resides in the fact that she is not fully aware of the effect she has on men. Her encounter with Mâtho amid the raucous gathering marks the beginning of the novel's love interest and sets a tone characterized as "sex and violence off the battlefield" and a "personalized version of the military conflict."[32] Indeed, all her meetings with Mâtho (and there are only four) take place under the auspices of individual, public, and cosmic violence. As lay-priestess of Tanit and daughter of Hamilcar, Salammbô embodies for Mâtho the genius of Carthage. In his imagination she converges with Tanit and the moon, whereas from her perspective he takes on the aura of the sun god Moloch: "[. . .] with the zaïmph enfolding him he looked like a star god surrounded by the firmament" (84).

Such identification of the self with a deity was not an infrequent phenomenon in antiquity, especially in its "poetic" age, as Herder and Goethe called it,[33] at the dawn of culture when myth and reality were indistinguishable. In that era the histories of peoples were formulated as poetry narrating the fates of entire nations and the intervention of the gods in human affairs: in the Mesopotamian epic *Gilgamesh* from the end of the second millennium B.C., the myths and legends of Ugarit, the *Old Testament,* the *Iliad* and *Odyssey*. It was the time when the pharaohs were considered divine, the magi of Babylonia produced ominous writings of God on palace walls, and the Olympians sat in council over the Trojan War. There and then the God of Israel gave verbal directions to the leaders of his people, and exalted Canaanite- Phoenician names were coined: Hamilcar (son of Melcarth), Hannibal (son of Baal), Hasdurbal, Bomilcar, and Jezebel (wife of king Ahab of Israel and daughter of the Sidonian king Ethbaal). They signified either the bearer's direct descent from a god or an intimate relationship; hence an identification with the deity after whom a man or woman had been named was plausible.

Although in historical times a more rational view of the universe based on Babylonian science, supported by the codification of laws and the politics of consensus, was less conducive to personal identification with a deity, it nevertheless remained possible. In 480 B.C., for instance, Xerxes, who claimed divine powers and rights, had the waters of the Hellespont lashed because they behaved contrary to his wishes. Alexander the Great proclaimed himself a god, and long after the demise of Carthage, the Roman caesars and augusti declared themselves deities. It is against this spiritual background that Salammbô's and Mâtho's respective identification with Tanit and Moloch must be seen. However, only the lovers viewed each other in these roles. For the Punic people Salammbô embodied Carthage. The dual aspects of her status in the cosmos of the novel are also objectifications of her personality and of her allure. A virgin awakening to love, she is invulnerable, in a mythical sense. For to the ancients, the purity of a virgin constituted something irretrievable, endowed with extraordinary powers. Salammbô's, which come close to being magical, manifest themselves in her ritual with the python, a "national and private fetish" (166), and in Mâtho's tent.

Before an interpretation of these events can be attempted, one must consider her first encounter with her father after his return from exile. As an avant-propos to this meeting, Flaubert informs the reader that Salammbô had been an unwanted child because Hamilcar "had had her after the death of several male children," and because "the birth of daughters was regarded as a calamity in the sun religions" (121). Although Hamilcar had pronounced a curse on her at birth, the reader learns that "meanwhile Salammbô continued on her way" (122). This statement can be taken literally, i.e. she proceeds step by step toward her father, but it may also be read figuratively in the sense that she continues her chosen or fated path independent of Hamilcar's wishes. In the ensuing confrontation father and daughter misunderstand one another completely. The expected dialogue turns out to be an utter failure. Whereas Hamilcar suspects that the rumored violence of the soldiers against Carthage meant the violation of his daughter, she is thinking of the sacrilegious theft of the zaïmph by Mâtho, of which she is innocent. As Flaubert suggests, their misunderstanding transcends the scope of a family quarrel. Salammbô embodies patriotism, while her father appears to be speaking for family pride and his own interests. Further actions by the heroine must therefore be seen as efforts to win back her father's favor and to vindicate herself in public opinion.

Chapters X and XI, "The Serpent" and "In the Tent," constitute the climax of the love episode. They relate the heroine's preparations for her encounter with Mâtho and their union. Prior to these events she had seen him at the feast of the mercenaries, where a special relationship was established between them,[34] and in her chamber after he made off with the zaïmph. The two climactic chapters are directly connected with the theft of the sacred symbol since they give account of Salammbô's retrieval of it. By this time the narrator has shown the heroine to be incomparable among the women of Carthage: "young, beautiful, virgin, of ancient lineage, descended from the Gods, a human star" (165). In the plot of the novel, Chapter X is preparatory to her confrontation with Mâtho (XI), in Flaubert's words, "dirty, chaste, mystical, and realistic. A slime as one has never seen, yet actually beholds with one's own eyes."[35]

In the 1860s the depiction of the ritual with the naked Salammbô and the serpent was a daring act. One must only recall that Edouard Manet's painting "Breakfast on the Grass" (1863), showing a nude woman in the company of two men in modern suits, caused a scandal one year after the publication of Flaubert's Oriental novel. To be sure, in European art nudes had been the subjects of paintings (and sculptures) since the Renaissance, yet they customarily represented figures from mythology, history, or exotic lands. As the works of Delacroix, Chasseriau, Corot, and Ingres document, this convention was observed up to the middle of the nineteenth century. Hence the scandal over Manet's nude and her dressed male companions. Flaubert's description had a classical subject, and an exotic one at that, but while staying within the limits of contemporary propriety in these respects, he violated it in others. In Chapter X, Salammbô is first portrayed in a mood of despondency and helplessness, mirrored in the listlessness of her pet serpent. In her distress the heroine calls for Schahabarim, high priest of Tanit and sage of Carthage. Dressed in the white robes of the priests of the goddess, he instructs her how to cope with the situation. Salammbô must travel to Mâtho who is encamped amidst his Barbarians and bring back the sacred veil. In order to be successful in this adventure, the heroine is to perform a number of minutely prescribed rituals, including that with the serpent. As has been stated in connection with the author's resistance to permit illustrations for the novel, much of *Salammbô* remains unspecified and imprecise, yet suggestive to a high degree. The text makes constant appeals to the imagination of the reader in whose mind a given scene is filled in and made complete. Another characteristic of the scene consists in its intimacy. The attendants have been sent away, "no one could know the mystery that was being prepared," and within the room the ritual area is shielded with Babylonian tapestries hung from cords, "for Salammbô did not want to be seen, even by the walls" (173). Yet the solitary reader "sees" and observes her every gesture and motion. The ritual is not a tableau, the conventional form of presenting mythological or historical nudes, but an action, a mythologized striptease, in which nineteenth-century prudishness may even perceive hints of sodomy. In French the python is a male creature, and while shedding its old skin, its glistening body is compared to "a sword half out of its sheath" (171).

Flaubert buttressed Salammbô's ritual with a variety of strong causes and motivations. Foremost among them is a mythological imperative, which makes the ceremony an offering to the goddess of the Moon. The serpent, this national and dynastic fetish, is associated with Tanit and thus confirms the hermaphrodite nature of the goddess and Punic mythology as a whole. It reminds one of the depths of the earth and the primordial darkness of fertility, from where it was said to have emerged; its fine skin covered with golden spots is reminiscent of the starred firmament, and the intelligence of Eschmôun, the Punic Aesculapius. Schahabarim, a complex individual, has his own reasons for prompting Salammbô into action. A priest tormented by doubts about the goddess he serves, he is preoccupied with the question whether Moloch is not stronger than Tanit. In order to resolve his doubts, he decides to use Salammbô as his instrument to test the power of his goddess. Although he regards Salammbô "like a flower growing from the crack of [his] tomb," he is willing to sacrifice her. If Tanit triumphed and Carthage was saved, "what did a woman's life matter?" (170).

The real force motivating the heroine is her patriotism and her fear for and of her father. For Salammbô these two impulses are indistinguishable, since in her eyes, Hamilcar embodies Carthage. She is disturbed that he and many other Carthaginians hold her partly responsible for the loss of the sacred veil, a serious blow to the prestige of the empire. When Schahabarim entreats her to retrieve it, Hamilcar, whose superior strategy and tactics have beaten the rebellious soldiers at the battle of the Macar, has been encircled by the mercenary forces. Her father and his army are in peril: the very existence of the state is at stake. This, then, is the background of Salammbô's audacious journey to the mercenaries' camp. The scene with the serpent has three functions. Aside from imploring the aid of the goddess, it serves as a sexual initiation rite for the heroine. Also, in the structure of the novel it is "a kind of oratory measure of precaution for the purpose of toning down the chapter taking place in the tent."[36]

Salammbô travels there in order to commit an act of sacred prostitution, although she does not quite know what it entails. Her mentor has given her only vague instructions such as, "whatever he tries, do not call out! You will be humble, do you understand, and submit to his desire, which is the order of heaven!" (172). Moreover, Salammbô goes to Mâtho dressed with the magnificence of a bride.

In Chapter XI the narrative's language and imagery, as well as the perception and imagination of the protagonists conspire to elevate them to the stature of the two deities ruling Carthaginian life. For quite some time Salammbô's image has merged in Mâtho's mind with that of Tanit, whereas Schahabarim's insinuations confirm her intuition that the leader of the mercenaries is an incarnation of Moloch. Appropriately, they face each other under the light of the moon, with Moloch's thunder rolling in the distance. Salammbô and Mâtho have become the rival and complementary deities. Their erotic attraction is conceived in terms of the struggle between the male and female principles: "Are you not omnipotent, immaculate, radiant, and beautiful like Tanit? [. . .] Unless, perhaps, you are Tanit?" and, reciprocally, "Moloch, you are burning me!" (184–187).

With their embrace Flaubert has finally realized the representation of perfect love, an ambition he had nursed for over a decade: the fusion of the carnal and religious. It is only fitting that he conceived of the subject during his journey through the Orient.[37] In probing the representational dimensions of the subject, Flaubert must have come to the conclusion, especially after his labors on *Madame Bovary,* that a convincing treatment of perfect love required a setting far removed from the bourgeois conventions of nineteenth-century Europe. Richard Wagner, who staged *Tristan and Isolde* (1859), a music drama about love as passion, in the Celtic mists of prehistory, certainly did so for the same reasons."[38] What motivated Flaubert to decide that the Orient with its peculiar commingling of sexuality and religion would best serve his purpose, has been explained. As the parallel of Wagner's opera demonstrates, Flaubert's wish to portray perfect love was by no means unique in his time. Rather, as an outcry against bourgeois-capitalist civilization, which echoed the Parnassians' and Symbolists' revolt against the mechanization of social life, and Dostoevsky's invectives against the triumph of rationality and the facile belief in progress symbolized by the Crystal Palace,[39] *Salammbô* is an attempt to present love in all its irrationality as an absolute.

What adds an additional dimension to the narrative is the fact that in Chapter XI Salammbô is given the opportunity to emulate the biblical story of Judith and Holofernes. When she enters Mâtho's tent, a "naked sword leaned against a stool, beside a shield" (182). After their union and Mâtho's falling asleep, she does not emulate her Israelite precursor because in his trance her ravisher beckons her with a loving gesture. That she does not counter his love with cold-blooded murder reveals an important trait of her character. Salammbô acts instinctively and on impulses, which are never ungenerous. Although she possesses some of the qualities to become another "virgin in arms" like the titular heroines of Friedrich Schiller's *Jungfrau von Orleans* (1801), Heinrich von Kleist's *Penthesilea* (1808), Balzac's Marie de Verneuil from *Les Chouans,* and Friedrich Hebbel's *Judith* (1841),[40] she does not opt for this resolution. Flaubert's main reason for restraining Salammbô was undoubtedly the fear that such a deed would have destroyed the image of the heroine he had created in the preceding pages. Just as important must have been his realization that cold-blooded homicide perpetrated in the interest of the state would have contradicted her nature and role as woman, as the nineteenth century conceived of them. In ethics, the woman embodied subjective substantiality, inwardness, and spontaneity, qualities which predestined her to be the center of family life and to cultivate relationships, while the man represented the "objective" values of the state.[41] Deviations from these norms were considered unnatural. Hebbel, for instance, characterized the biblical Judith who kills Holofernes without having been violated, as "a fanatic-cunning monster,"[42] and intended to make his Judith more human by showing her to be the instrument and victim of God.[43] In her role as virgin in arms manquée, Salammbô remains true to herself, her femininity, and the image of the Oriental woman for the sake of which, as the title of the novel suggests, the author may initially have undertaken the novel.

Ironically, there is no causal relationship between Salammbô's submission to Mâtho's desire and her recovery of the zaïmph. In the fictitious parts of the narrative, which follow the laws of "mystical causality," no exchange of goods is transacted. Instead, Mâtho is summoned away, and Salammbô escapes with the veil. Thus, she had paid the price for what she sought, but received what she had come for without striking a bargain. For if Mâtho had had his way, he would have kept the zaïmph and her as well, as captive, slave, lover—his woman. He might even end the war; for had he not been set on conquering Carthage for the sole purpose of winning Salammbô? Flaubert seems to be touching here, if ever so lightly, on the theme of Helen of Troy: a war of nations to the death over a woman.

The heroine's appearance with the symbol of Carthaginian splendor in the Punic camp affects her countrymen like an elixir, and she savors this moment of personal triumph and adulation. When her father notices that the golden chain Carthaginian maidens wear on their ankles is broken, he promises her on the spot to Narr'havas, the slippery king of the Numidians who just deserted the mercenaries. It is ironical that on the very day Salammbô loses her virginity and experiences perfect love, she is promised in marriage to another man so that he may never again betray the republic. In her quest to retrieve the zaïmph, Salammbô has broken several taboos of Punic culture. She has touched the sacred veil of Tanit, a transgression that warrants the perpetrator's death. In addition she has violated Carthaginian customs concerning the chastity of maidens, perhaps not a religious law, but a cultural convention nevertheless. And she has consorted with the enemy, thereby trespassing against patriotism, so dear to the Carthaginians, surrounded as they were by a hostile world. The text foreshadows the consequences of these transgressions in imagery and provides direct commentary. Here are three illustrations. At the occasion of Mâtho's theft of the zaïmph, Salammbô curses the robber, while the narrator laconically states: "Just to look at it [the veil] was a crime: it partook of the God's nature and contact with it caused death" (85). Of course the heroine herself becomes a victim of its deadly properties in the end, for in its retrieval she cannot help touching it. Another instance of foreshadowing occurs at the end of Chapter X when her servant observes her setting out for the mercenaries' camp: "[. . .] in the moonlight, she made out, in the cypress avenue, a gigantic shadow walking diagonally on Salammbô's left, which was an omen of death" (176). The third illustration occurs at a narrative juncture. Salammbô has regained the zaïmph in Mâtho's tent and the leader of the rebels is absent. At the moment of finding herself in limbo between the mercenary and Carthaginian armies, she encounters Gisco, one of the few honest Carthaginians and emissary of the republic, whom the barbarians had taken prisoner. Gisco has witnessed part of her dialogue and her sexual union with Mâtho. Since he does not know why Salammbô traveled to the camp of the rebels, he who had never doubted Carthage and had believed in its eternal existence is outraged by the heroine's behavior and, hence, condemns her with a triple curse.

Such portents, broken taboos, and curses make it a narrative necessity that, with the restoration of the sacred veil to Carthage and her betrothal, Salammbô's active role in the novel comes to an end. She disappears for about one hundred pages from the action, only to resurface once more in the large colorful tableau at the end of the last chapter. After the destruction of the enemies of the republic, two events are to be related: Mâtho's running the gauntlet and Salammbô's wedding to Narr'havas. For the benefit of both occurrences Flaubert arranged the scene in the form of a triangle or a pyramid, the sign of Tanit engraved on numerous Punic steles.[44] The Carthaginians filling the square before the Khamon temple represent the base of the pyramid; midway up, on the terrace of the temple the priests, the Elders, and the Rich occupy three long tables; and above them another table has been placed for Narr'havas, Hamilcar, and his daughter who sits slightly elevated above her two companions on a throne, thereby forming the tip of the pyramid. Thus, the closure opens with a panoramic view of Carthaginian society, including those who hold religious, political and economic power. Most major characters reappear so that the dominant events of the novel are evoked once more in the reader's memory.

The last chapter of *Salammbô* seems designed to emulate the conclusion of a primary epic such as the *Odyssey* since it also presents an apparent return to normalcy: "[. . .] everywhere was a sense of order restored, a new existence beginning, immense happiness spread far and wide" (275). Yet appearances are deceptive. The Punics display a feverish excitement that does not fit the blessings of normalcy regained; neither does it constitute a trustworthy foundation for a better future. At the conclusion of the *Odyssey,* in contrast, the presumptuous suitors of Penelope are killed by the returning lord of Ithaca, and there is good reason to assume that with the elimination of all troublesome elements, Odysseus's proven wisdom will henceforth rule the island. At the end of Flaubert's novel the divisive forces have not disappeared with the defeat of the mercenaries. Rather, the cruelties perpetrated by man on man, the selfishness of individuals displayed in this "truceless war", and treachery or lack of faith as shown by Narr'havas, Schahabarim, and Hamilcar are carried over into the "new" Carthage.

There remains, of course, the figure of Salammbô. The people of Carthage view her as savior of the republic, but they have no inkling that her recovery of the veil was preceded by her lustful outcries in Mâtho's tent. If the future of Carthage were to depend on the titular heroine of the novel, its chances of survival, or new grandeur, would be slight. For Flaubert, she is the embodiment of the Oriental woman: instinctive, sensual, alluring, patriotic, but apolitical. Her sure instinctiveness is revealed again when Mâtho has to begin running the gauntlet: it is she who senses the moment. She follows the horrific progress of her lover to the plaza in front of the Khamon temple when, against all ceremonial instructions and political prudence, she forsakes her high seat to be near him. Her memory of their night of love, conveyed in the form of free indirect discourse,[45] draws her irresistibly to Mâtho. At the moment when the eyes of Carthage focus on her, she is only a loving woman who shares his passion. In what way could the opinions of "others" matter since "the outside world was blotted out and she saw only [him]" (281). Flaubert is kind in letting her sink into unconsciousness and thus sparing her from witnessing how her mentor Schahabarim, who has donned the red mantle of the priests of Moloch, cuts Mâtho's heart from his chest and offers it to the setting sun. What follows can only be explained in terms of the author's irony. While the people regard all of this as Salammbô's work and howl her name, she dies when Narr'havas symbolically takes possession of her. She died, the text states, "for touching Tanit's veil" (282).

Is this explanation to be accepted at face value? Is it trustworthy and if so, does it reveal the whole truth? If one takes the novel seriously, one must also accept its mythological machinery and not regard it as a delusion of the protagonists. The fact that the Carthaginians sacrificed four hundred of their children to placate the gods leaves no doubt as to how real their deities were to them. Hence Salammbô's violation of the taboo of the zaïmph may outwardly explain her death, perhaps even the day it occurred, for Carthage then stood once more under the sign of Tanit. And what about Gisco's threefold curse, which carries all the more weight since it was uttered by a dying man. And there is the inescapable bond to Mâtho. After having experienced perfect love, the logic of Flaubert's novel makes it inconceivable that Salammbô would go on living in a political marriage with the slick Narr'havas. Her wedding took place in Mâtho's tent, and her death, then, is as much a love-death in the spirit of Wagner's *Tristan and Isolde,* as it is a consequence of the broken taboo of Tanit and Gisco's curses in a world of mystic causality.

Responding to Sainte-Beuve's critique of his historical novel, Flaubert mustered sufficient magnanimity to point out a shortcoming of his work: "The pedestal is too large for the statue," he writes. "Salammbô alone would have required another hundred pages, for one never sins by [doing] too much, but by [giving] too little."[46] This assessment seems correct, as it should be detrimental to a novel if the titular heroine is absent from the narrative space of its last third only to reemerge in the coda. To put it differently, the narratological deficiency derives from the preponderance of historical material in proportion to Flaubert's fictive contribution. An acknowledgment of this "flaw" in *Salammbô* is not tantamount to an acceptance of Lukács's view that the "crown and state" conflict and the love interest are but externally connected. For Hamilcar's daughter has crucial functions in the cosmos of the novel. Besides being the focus of aesthetic interest, she breathes life into the otherwise quite inaccessible mythology of Carthage, and she is the only figure who personally encounters Schahabarim, Hamilcar, and Mâtho. She is the pivotal figure of the work, and the leaders of the adversaries are partially evaluated by their behavior toward her. Viewed from this perspective, her father does not measure up. Evaluating Hamilcar's encounter with Salammbô after his return, Flaubert described him as an "enraged bourgeois father"[47] fearing that Salammbô's blemished reputation will diminish her usefulness for his ambitious plans. On the basis of his attitudes and gestures toward Salammbô, Mâtho clearly is the more amiable man. In contrast to the politician and statesman Hamilcar, he pursues no grand scheme of his own, but simply reacts to people and situations. Like Salammbô he lives and acts according to his feelings and impulses. After their first encounter in Hamilcar's gardens, where his love of her strikes him like a thunderbolt, Mâtho is obsessed with the idea of winning her even if this means the destruction of the North African world in which he had grown up. His love of Salammbô is as monomaniacal as her idée fixe; he resembles Marc Antony who lost an empire for his love of Cleopatra.

Salammbô follows the star of her mystical destiny. Together with her beauty and lascivious eroticism, her purity and devotion to a single cause inspired artists of the later nineteenth century to present their visions of her. Of course it did not matter to them that the narrative space allocated to the heroine was relatively circumscribed and unevenly distributed. Flaubert's depiction was suggestive enough to stimulate their imaginations. Could she not be a figure out of the *Arabian Nights,* alluring and mysterious, whose dominant character trait explains her course of action?[48] For her, cause and effect are tightly joined. Salammbô's lure makes it understandable that artists saw the tragic titular heroine as the main focus of the novel. However, the narrative space left blank by the long absence of the heroine is taken up by a foil figure: Hamilcar Barca, the other hero of this Oriental novel.

Notes and References

1. Flaubert to Louise Colet, May 8–9, 1852.

2. Quoted in Benjamin F. Bart, *Flaubert* (Syracuse: Syracuse UP, 1967) 396.

3. The name Kuchuk Hanem is spelled differently in various references to her, which is most likely due to the transcription from Arabic to the Latin alphabet. Besides Kuchuk Hanem, it also appears as Kuchiuk Hanem, Kuchiuck Hanem, and Ruchuk, as well as Ruchiuck Hanem. In his letters Flaubert hyphenated the name.

4. Ernest Renan, *The Life of Jesus,* intr. J.H. Holmes, The Modern Library (New York: Random House, 1955) 171.

5. Flaubert, Letter to George Sand, September 29, 1866: "I was a boatman on the Nile, a dealer in women in Rome at the time of the Carthaginian Wars, a Greek rhetorician in Subarra [. . .]. Perhaps also emperor of the Orient."

6. Flaubert, Letter to Ernest Feydeau, middle of October, 1858.

7. Flaubert, Letter to Jules and Ernest Duplan, June 10 and June 12, 1862.

8. Georg Lukács, *The Historical Novel,* transl. H. and S. Mitchell (Boston: Beacon Press, 1962) 189.

9. In Chapter II of her study *Description and Meaning in Three Novels by Gustave Flaubert* (New York, Washington D.C., Baltimore, Bern, etc.: Peter Lang, 1994), Corrada Biazzo Curry argues that in *Salammbô* the author introduces too many elements the reader does not understand as, for example, the strange foods served at the feast of the mercenaries in the opening chapter. This seems to be a questionable objection, for when a novelist describes exotic peoples who lived over 2000 years ago, he cannot have them devour nineteenth-century French dishes.

10. Michelet, *Histoire romaine,* II, 447.

11. Plautus's hostility to everything Punic is understandable, for he lived during the second Punic war (Hannibal's war), and for twenty years after its conclusion.

12. Flaubert, Letter to Alfred Le Poittevin, May 13, 1845.

13. Although there was a good measure of cultural penetration throughout North Africa outside Egypt, as seen, for example, in the names of the royal house of Numidia such as Mastanabal and Adherbal, the emulation of Carthaginian customs did not entail political loyalty. For these names see Sallust, *The Jugurthine War,* transl. and introd. S.A. Handford (Harmondsworth: Penguin, 1977) 39.

14. This expression occurs in the first canto of the *Aeneid;* other Roman authors, including Sallust, have used comparable derogatory terms.

15 The tablets were found in 1931 at the site of the vanished capital of the mysterious kingdom of Ugarit, near modern Latakia in Western Syria. Between 3000 and 2000 B.C. important ethnic changes evidently took place in Ugarit as the original population was gradually superseded by Amorites and Canaanites migrating northward. The tablets were inscribed in the 14th century B.C. in a cuneiform script which represented a hitherto unknown language. They were the first authentic specimens of pagan Canaanite literature and related poetry and myths of the ancient Canaanites.

16 Lisa Lowe, *Critical Terrains: French and British Orientalism* (Ithaka and London: Cornell UP, 1991) 75–101. It should be noted, however, that Lowe bases her equation of Orient and woman only on Flaubert's portrayal of Kuchuk Hanem in the famous letter of 1853 to Louise Colet and on the titular heroine Salammbô of his Carthaginian narrative.

17 Max Weber, *Gesammelte Aufsätze zur Religionssoziologie* (Tübingen: J.C.B. Mohr, 1923) III, 202 (my translation).

18 Michelet, *Histoire romaine*, II, 441.

19 The general correctness of Flaubert's presentation of Carthage is confirmed by Gilbert and Colette Charles-Picard, *Daily Life in Carthage at the Time of Hannibal*, transl. A.E. Foster (New York: The Macmillan Company, 1961) and Gilbert Picard, *Carthage*, transl. M. and L. Kochan (London: Elek Books, 1964). Both studies find that the Carthaginians were unartistic and that even their manufactured goods were of shoddy quality. Only their metal work and textiles were renowned for their beauty.

20 Concerning this point it should be noted that the beleaguered Punics were a very small nation and required all men to do their duty in industry, agriculture, commerce, the army (as officers), and the navy.

21 This is all the more remarkable when one considers the comparably short histories of the Philistines, Moabites, and Amorites. In North Africa the Punic language (Neo-Phoenician) survived the destruction of Carthage for centuries until the Arab conquest.

22 Victor Brombert, *The Novels of Flaubert* (Princeton: Princeton University Press, 1966) 106.

23 Harry Levin, *The Gates of Horn: A Study of Five French Realists* (New York: Oxford University Press, 1963) 277.

24 Albert Thibaudet, *Gustave Flaubert*, 6th ed. (Paris: Librairie Plon, 1922) 156.

25 W. Wolfgang Holdheim, *Die Suche nach dem Epos* (Heidelberg: Carl Winter, 1978) 138.

26 Lawrence R. Schehr, "Salammbô as the Novel of Alterity," *Nineteenth-Century French Studies*, 17 (1989) 339. Two additional French critics should be mentioned who arrive at similar readings of the work. In *Gustave Flaubert, écrivain* (Paris: Les Lettres Nouvelles, 1969/80), Maurice Nadeau follows Gautier in

labelling *Salammbô* an epic. Nadeau claims that its characters are "arbitrary," "loaded," ("chargés," 159) and remain unsubstantiated. According to Nadeau, the work owes much to the Marquis de Sade, and it expresses Flaubert's personality better than any other of his novels. Maurice Bardèche also considers *Salammbô* an epic, "at least a barbarian palace aspiring to resemble an epic" because of "les gueulades," "the beautiful sonorous phrases, the color, the grandiose tableaux." Other epic elements Bardèche mentions include the numerous gorish battles as well as the "ornamental" descriptions of nature and the war machines. Bardèche, *L'Oeuvre de Flaubert* (Paris: Les Sept Couleurs, 1974) 252 and 239. See also Laurent Adert, "*Salammbô* ou le roman barbare," in *Poétiques barbares/Poetische barbare*, ed. Juan Riglio and Carlo Caruso (Ravenna: Longo, 1998) 47–64. This essay differs in nuances from Bardèche's work.

27   Martin Bernal, *Black Athena*, eighth paperback printing (New Brunswick: Rutgers UP, 1994) 356.

28   Walter P. Hall, Robert G. Albion, Jennie B. Pope, A *History of England and the Empire-Commonwealth*, fourth ed. (Boston, New York, etc.: Ginn and Co., 1961) 454.

29   Georg Lukács, *The Historical Novel*, 190.

30   Jonathan Culler, *The Uses of Uncertainty*, revised edition (Ithaca and London: Cornell University Press, 1985) 213–226.

31   Theophile Gautier, "Salammbô par Gustave Flaubert," *Le Moniteur universel*, December 22, 1862, 2–3.

32   A.J. Krailsheimer, "Introduction" to Gustave Flaubert, *Salammbô* (Harmondsworth: Penguin, 1977) 12.

33   Herder had made this point a cornerstone of his theory of poetry. Goethe, who accepted many of Herder's speculations during his studies at the University of Strasbourg, restated the theory of pre-history as the "poetic age" in "Geistesepochen nach Hermanns neusten Mitteilungen," *Werke*, Hamburger Ausgabe, ed. E. Trunz, 6th ed. (Hamburg: Wegner, 1965ff.) X (my translation).

34   This is at least true from Mâtho's point of view, for the Gaul Autharite tells him—after Salammbô offered Mâtho a cup of wine—"[. . .] with us when a woman gives a soldier a drink, [. . .] she is offering him her bed" (28).

35   Flaubert, Letter to Ernest Feydeau, October 21, 1860.

36   Flaubert, Letter to Sainte-Beuve, December 23–24, 1862.

37   For the execution of this theme Flaubert had three projects in mind, "Une nuit de Don Juan," "L'Histoire d'Anubis," and "roman flamand," the outlines of which were, for all practical purposes, too similar to yield three independent narratives (See his letter to Louis Bouilhet of November 14, 1850). All of them were to depict the desire to fuse carnal and religious love. In "Anubis," a story of a woman who sleeps with a god, this human dream was to be fulfilled. From the project of

The Setting of Carthage and the Titular Heroine 67

"Anubis" a line of development leads to *Salammbô* (Flaubert mentions the project of his "Egyptian tale" in letters to Louise Colet of May 23 and June 6–7, 1852).

38 On account of his expansive personality, Richard Wagner found nineteenth-century conventions particularly restrictive (as his problems with financial creditors and scandals resulting from his love affairs show). Thus, most of his music dramas are set in mythical times, but they also have a modern component, psychology. The terms "myth and psychology" (Thomas Mann) have therefore been used to characterize his oeuvre.

39 I am referring to Dostoevsky's *Notes from the Underground,* a short novel from the 1860s, which was a prophetic attempt to defend human freedom by means of stressing man's basic irrationality against the levelling onslaught of modern technology.

40 See Helmut Kreuzer, "Die Jungfrau in Waffen. Hebbels Judith und ihre Geschwister von Schiller bis Sartre," in *Untersuchungen zur Literatur als Geschichte–Festschrift für Benno von Wiese,* ed. V.J. Gunter, H. Koopmann, P. Pütz, H.J. Schrimpf (Berlin: Erich Schmidt Verlag, 1973) 363–384.

41 Although the formulation of this separation of supposed natural characteristics and appropriate realms of responsibility of man and woman was the work of Hegel, its convention was observed throughout nineteenth-century Europe. The distinction of female and male qualities can be found throughout Hegel's voluminous writings, though with greatest explicitness in his *Philospy of Right,* the *Phenomenology of Mind,* and in the last chapter of his *Aesthetics* entitled "Die konkrete Entwicklung der dramatischen Poesie und ihrer Arten."

42–43 Friedrich Hebbel, *Sämtliche Werke,* historisch-kritische Ausgabe, ed. Richard M. Werner, Second Edition (Berlin: Behr, 1904) I, 80.

44 Artists who illustrated *Salammbô* or who were inspired by the novel to represent scenes from it, took their cue from Punic steles, as for instance Rochegrosse and Theodore Rivière. Both artifacts—one has Tanit and Salammbô as its subject, the other, as expressed in the sculpture's title, "Salammbô and Mâtho"—display the artists' knowledge of the high position the goddess Tanit held in the imperial realm of Carthage. Hence the triangular or pyramidal designs of their pictures and sculptures.

45 In this instance of "discours indirect libre" there is an unbridgeable discrepancy between Salammbô's public and private life. Since it constitutes the only occasion when her public and private functions in the novel diverge, the incident must be ascribed to Flaubert's narrative irony.

46 Flaubert, Letter to Sainte-Beuve, December 23–24, 1862.

47 This characterization occurs several times in Flaubert's notes for his novel. See Anne Green, *Flaubert and the Historical Novel: Salammbô Reassessed,* 28–57, in which she reprints and comments the different folio manuscripts.

48 See Tzvetan Todorov, *The Politics of Prose,* transl. R. Howard, Fourth Printing (Ithaca and New York: Cornell UP, 1987) 67–69.

Chapter III

Hamilcar Barca: Revolutionary Chaos and the Charismatic Leader

"Je déteste assez la tyrannie moderne parce qu'elle me paraît bête, faible et timide d'elle-même, mais j'ai un culte profond pour la tyrannie antique que je regarde comme la plus belle manifestation de l'homme qui ait été."
Flaubert to Louise Colet, August 6 or 7, 1846

In *Salammbô* Flaubert might initially have intended to reflect history in the fate of a "non-historical" heroine.[1] This had been Scott's practice. To be sure, Salammbô is not a representative of the "people" as, for instance, Jeanie Deans of *The Heart of Midlothian* (an ideological premise of the classical form of the historical novel according to Lukács's anatomy of the genre). While creating his heroine, Flaubert was, as has been shown, -motivated by interests other than those of Scott. For the figure of Salammbô was conceived not only to enliven and reanimate the mythology of Carthage through her identification with Tanit and her relationship with Mâtho/Moloch, but she was also to experience perfect love, an idea with which the author was veritably obsessed. In order to make her convincing, Flaubert endowed her with the salient qualities of both the courtesan Kuchuk Hanem and Élisa Schlesinger. The heroine Salammbô was to embody smoldering sensuality and chaste sublimity.

The principal flaw of *Salammbô* may lie in the fact that because of her personality and the circumscribed role of women in Carthaginian society, the titular heroine is not capable of exerting a continuous influence on the "historical" events of the novel. Her glory arising from the recovering of the zaïmph is rather brief. Nevertheless, aside from giving the Punics a psychological lift, her courageous deed contributes to saving her father and his trapped army and, thus, to the existential deliverance of Carthage from its foes. After the retrieval of the veil, the republic suffers serious reverses, including the siege of the city and the cutting of the aqueduct.

On the very account of her overt erotic gestures at the opening feast, Salammbô has to be described as innocent. This innocence is reinforced by her indeterminacy as a character, which is at least partially the result of the limited narrative space devoted to her. Regarding the structure of the narrative, such a heroine is incapable of influencing the "crown and state" action in a ubiquitous manner, particularly since politics lie outside the sphere of her being.

However, the historical Oriental novel *Salammbô* does have a forceful hero in Hamilcar Barca. It is he who determines the military and political actions in the novel, and he appears as the very embodiment of intelligence, resourcefulness, and awesome will power. In all of literature no one but Homer's Odysseus is his equal in effective versatility. Hamilcar's character traits and abilities give him the dimensions of a highly complex individual. Gautier found him to be almost divine, while George Sand was shocked to discover that the great Hamilcar was a "villain."[2] He seems "round" (according to E.M. Forster's definition) and true-to-life because, like Odysseus, he is presented from different perspectives and shown in the most varied activities. Hamilcar is the undefeated military leader, strategist, and tactician; the eminent speaker in the Carthaginian Council of Elders; and the farsighted Oriental merchant whose ships and caravans travel to the ends of the earth. He is depicted loving his son with a mother's fervor; at the same time he treats his daughter with callous indifference. Hamilcar also is the manufacturer of forged goods, and he defrauds Tanit of her due share of his revenues. He is the cruel lord of his slave-masters, whom he has whipped till they are no longer recognizable as human beings, and he is the negotiator of the republic who does not keep his word to the mercenaries and their leaders. He acts like a theatrical deceiver, yet he is also a man who ruthlessly avenges a personal insult and savors the taste of revenge. The fact that he is a truly mixed character makes him all the more convincing. What distinguishes him from all the Carthaginians, however, is his unconditional will to power and greatness.

Flaubert has done his utmost to give Hamilcar the semblance of a heroic, if not superhuman figure. He shrouds him in an atmosphere of the uncanny, Freud's "Unheimliches," i.e. that with which we were but are no longer familiar. Thus, to the mercenaries, whom he commanded for years in Sicily, his face appears "solemn and impenetrable," his military decisions are "incomprehensible." During the campaign he consistently rides at the head of his troops on a horse "covered in yellow spots like a dragon, and throwing up spray all round him" (142). After the Carthaginian victory in the battle of the Macar, Spendius, the evil genius of the rebels, compares him to an "eagle" flying on the cohorts' flanks and signalling them with his head. When Spendius is asked why he did not cut him down with his sword during their negotiation, he stammers: "'Him! Him!' as if this were something impossible and Hamilcar someone immortal" (255).

Hamilcar Barca radiates charisma, and this is in evidence the moment he enters the novel. His trireme, carrying him home to Carthage after a long absence, is reminiscent of a large bird skimming along the surface of the sea with its long wings. Of course it is also significant that he enters the narrative aboard a ship, the symbol of the maritime republic's former might.

> [. . .] the sail fell, and beside the pilot a man could be seen standing, bare headed: it was he, the Suffete Hamilcar! Around his waist he wore plates of glittering steel; a red cloak fastened to his shoulders revealed his arms; two very long pearls hung from his ears, and his black, bushy beard pressed against his chest as he bent his head. Meanwhile the galley tossing among the rocks came alongside the mole, and the crowd followed it along the stone slabs, crying: "Hail! Blessings! Eye of Khamon! Oh, deliver us! It is the fault of the Rich! They want to bring about your death! Take care, Barca!" (105)

Only a hero makes such an entrance; an Oriental hero at that, dressed in colorful splendor. The enthusiastic crowd, which testifies to his popularity by celebrating him as liberator from the misrule of the Rich, apostrophizes him "eye of Khamon," an address suggesting the almost divine stature Hamilcar enjoys among the people. As the text reveals, Hamilcar's mythical attributes are bestowed on him by the clear-sighted Greek Spendius, the inimical mercenary, and the populace of Carthage, but not, as in the case of Salammbô and Mâtho, by an enamored and subjective Thou. As far as dramatic effect is concerned, the narrative preparations of Hamilcar's entry into the novel could hardly be more effective. Although he does not make his appearance prior to Chapter VII, i.e., in the harbor scene, his presence is, nevertheless, strongly felt throughout the first six chapters. Because of his initial absence, various interest groups within the Afro-Oriental republic repeatedly refer to him in conversations, so that he is there as a hovering presence. His appearance becomes a question of intense expectation. Close to the end of Chapter VI the reader is alerted by the emphatic declaration: "[. . .] one man, one alone, was able to save the republic. They regretted not having recognized him, and the peace party itself voted holocausts for Hamilcar's return" (103).

The assumption that Hamilcar possesses the qualities of charismatic leadership finds confirmation in Max Weber's essay, "The Three Forms of Legitimate Rule." As characteristics of such leadership, Weber names "dedication to the person of the master and his 'miraculous gift' (charisma)—such as magic abilities, revelations or heroism, as well as intellectual acumen, and the power of speech—offering the promise of novelty and the transformation of everyday life [. . .]. These are the sources of personal devotion. The purest types of charismatic rule are those of the prophet, the war hero, the great demagogue."[3] In Weber's words, the conditions for charismatic leadership exist whenever national, social, or economic security is threatened, traditional authority finds itself unable to resolve the crisis, and an individual with obviously extraordinary abilities offers itself as savior. The greater the danger to the security of the nation, the higher the "charismatic receptiveness" of a people. His special gifts ("Gnadengaben") assure the charismatic leader of divine support, which finds expression in figures of speech such as "it is written," "but I say onto you," and in the quite recent past, "providence has chosen me [. . .]."

Applying Max Weber's definition of charismatic leadership to the "Book of Judges" of the *Old Testament,* Abraham Malamat provides significant insights about Flaubert's Carthage.[4] For at the time of its territorial conquests from the thirteenth to the eleventh centuries B.C., the Israelites' political structures and military challenges were analogous to those of the Punic republic in the centuries of its conflicts with Rome and the mercenaries. During their wars with the Canaanites, Edomites, Moabites, Ammonites, Amorites, and Philistines, the Hebrews were ruled by councils of elders who seemed, however, no longer capable of coping with the challenges of rapidly changing situations. The persistent threat to the very existence of the entire people and alternating defensive wars and wars of conquest demanded a strong central authority capable both of organizing national infrastructures and of protecting the people from acute danger. Situations of collective crises and the appearance of charismatic leaders determine the rhythm of the "Book of Judges."[5] Ehud, Deborah, Barak, Gideon, and Jephtah were not only judges and military saviors, but according to the etymology of the Hebrew word "schofet," also "rulers" and "governors." The "First Book of Samuel" tells of the Israelites' desire to institutionalize charismatic leadership which had been bound up with the person of the individual judge, by giving it the permanent form of a hereditary monarchy. As exemplified by Saul, the first king of Israel, who was overcome by the spirit of the Lord before his election, charismatic leadership was to become a feature of everyday life. The "Book of Judges" and the "First Book of Samuel" describe the evolution of political rule in Israel from the council of elders via the office of judge and charismatic leadership to its institutionalization in the popularly acclaimed, hereditary monarch.

Of Phoenician-Canaanite provenance, the Punics were as conscious of their ancestors' political traditions as they were of their religious customs, for as late as the third century B.C. they still sent yearly sacrificial offerings to Melcarth, patron god of Tyre. In *Salammbô* Flaubert suggests that the Carthaginians reenacted the socio-political development of ancient Israel around a thousand years later. This thesis is impaired neither by the myth that the city had been founded by a Tyrian princess, nor by historical evidence that until the catastrophe of Himera, Carthage was ruled by kings, foremost among them the Magonides. Their military defeat in 480 B.C. engendered religious and political reforms which decisively changed the distribution of power in the Punic capital and the constellations of its pantheon. Carthage evidently remembered the pre-monarchic forms of political leadership in Phoenicia and Canaan, which corresponded to, but predated, those of Israel. By following a backward cyclical pattern, Cathaginian political institutions had once more returned to their origins. To put it differently, the Punic oligarchy constantly dreaded a return to monarchic rule. In *Salammbô,* for instance, the Council of the Elders dislikes old Gisco because of his popularity: "[. . .] they feared the risk of a master, and out of terror for monarchy tried to attenuate what remained of one or might bring it back" (61). The oligarchy's fear of the royal ruler had also prompted the religious reorientation after Himera, for in their course Melcarth was replaced by Tanit as tutelary deity of the city since Melcarth was identified with the monarchy.

The key institutions of the Carthaginian constitution and the distribution of political power presented in *Salammbô* had been stable for well over two hundred years prior to the Mercenary War and were severely tested by this conflict, above all the relationship between the councils and the suffetes. Since Flaubert used the Latinized form "suffete" instead of the Phoenician-Punic "schofet," which is identical with the Hebrew designation "schofet" of the "Book of Judges," literary critics and scholars have not perceived this parallel. This is all the more puzzling since Flaubert knew a number of key Hebrew terms and combed the bilingual Hebrew-French *Old Testament* as one of his principal sources for things "Canaanite and Phoenician." As Hebrew and Phoenician are closely related, many other key words are the same in both languages such as "baal/baalim" (god, ruler), "cohen/cohanim" (priest), or "schekel/schekalim" (coin, weight).[6] Renan, moreover, has shown how closely related the two ancient languages were, whereby Western Phoenician (Punic) had remained closer to the ancestral idiom than the Eastern variation.[7]

The brief survey of the political history of Carthage and the listing of a few key words that are identical in Phoenician and Hebrew demonstrate that Flaubert, who relied on ethnic and cultural analogies, was historically justified in developing the phenomenon of the charismatic leader in his Carthage out of the office of the Hebrew "schofet" (the charismatic leader), from where it led directly to the charismatic "king." In his Punic novel Flaubert not only created the political, social, and emotional preconditions for the emergence of the charismatic leader but also endowed Hamilcar Barca with the required charismatic gifts and ambitions. On the basis of Max Weber's typology of charismatic leadership, Hamilcar clearly embodies that of the war hero, while he also displays characteristics of the prophet and the demagogue. He can certainly claim the gifts of divine grace Max Weber considered prerequisites of charismatic leadership. His name "Hamilcar"—"gift of Melcarth"—has charismatic connotations and connects him with a powerfull god, patron of trade and protector of the monarchy. The apostrophe "Eye of Khamon" recognizes him as the highest subsolar representative of the foremost ancient Phoenician deity. Finally, his family name "Barca" (Lightning) denotes ties to Moloch (Molk) and suggests that its bearer is able to translate his gifts of divine grace into deeds. His return to Carthage has been prepared by holocausts in the besieged city, and it is illuminated by the rising sun to which Hamilcar is linked through his name and the color symbolism of his red cloak. As maritime suffete, he stands under the sun's protection and is supposedly "inviolable."

When Hamilcar contemplates his treasures, which are "inaccessible, inexhaustible, infinite," the author makes the point that Barca does "not so much delight in the sight as in awareness of his wealth." And so it is with religion and the signs of divine grace. For him everything is a means to an end, an instrument to attain power. Whereas his peers and his daughter "accepted pure symbols as true in themselves" (169), Hamilcar banished from his thoughts "every form, every symbol and name of the gods, the better to grasp the unchanging spirit hidden behind appearances" (107). He is not only free from religious coercion, but "he felt stronger than the baalim and full of scorn for them." He provides the most salient proof that he alone stands above religious convention when, in Carthage's darkest hour, the Council of Elders votes to sacrifice over four hundred children from the best families.[8] For the gods, as Flaubert writes, "were looked on as cruel masters, to be appeased with supplications and bribed by presents" (230). Although Hamilcar publicly agrees to the resolution and promises to offer his son Hannibal, he nevertheless subverts the council, and Punic belief, by handing over a slave's child dressed in royal purple. Barca not only deceives the priests, but is also devious enough to exploit the extreme situation for his political goals. When his "son" is thrown into the flames, Barca's theatrical gestures of horror and grief earn him the sympathy and admiration of the crowd.[9]

His thoughts and deeds demonstrate that he is not likely to content himself with the office of a suffete appointed by the Council of Elders. Quite the contrary, the text furnishes ample evidence that Hamilcar intends to build an incontestable basis of power for himself, relying on his wealth, charisma, cunning, and vision. The circumspection he uses in pursuit of his goal is without parallel in Carthage. Since he had proven his ability as military leader during five years of war with the Romans in Sicily, he is accepted as such by the vast majority of Carthaginians, rich and poor. On the day of his return to Carthage he orders his steward to buy up all available grain and to import additional shipments from Bruttium and Etruria. When famine breaks out in the city, Hamilcar alone possesses large supplies of corn which he distributes among the masses. He proceeds with comparable prescience to raise the means and men for a new army. By making a large donation of his own, he forces the Rich to follow his example. As to recruitment, he does not hesitate to reject unfit sons of the oligarchy but instead accepts men in disgrace, the scum of Malqua, and freedmen alike to whom he promises full citizenship as a reward. With such measures Barca wins the affection and support of the common people, a policy his son-in-law Hasdrubal and Hannibal were to continue. Such deeds make the Barcas the undisputed popular leaders in Carthage. Against these political realities the shouts of the people at the occasion of Hamilcar's return gain momentum: "Oh, deliver us! It is the fault of the Rich! They want to bring about your death. Take care, Barca!" (105)

Hamilcar's profound knowledge of politics and his skills of manipulation are most convincingly depicted in the dramatic meeting of the Council of Elders. His confrontation with this body of seasoned politicians also gives him the opportunity to display his "secondary" charismatic gifts: Oriental prophecy and demagogic genius. The meeting, which has been called one of the most perceptive descriptions of political assembly, takes place in the somber temple of Moloch. The enormous lions in its courtyard foreshadow the violent mood of the meeting, which the Elders of mixed Phoenician and African descent create through their sheer presence and their excitement about the agenda:

> These old pirates ploughed up the countryside, these profiteers fitted out ships, these landowners supported slaves who practised crafts. They were all versed in religious discipline, skilled in stratagems, ruthless and rich. They looked tired through long anxiety. Their flashing eyes had a wary look, habitual experience of travel and lies, trade and command, gave their whole person an air of cunning and violence, a sort of veiled and cunning brutality (111).

The devious and ruthless physiognomies of many even appear grotesque since they wear their beards enclosed in little mauve leather bags fastened around their ears, a sign of mourning for their sons killed in military confrontations with the mercenaries. They have recalled Hamilcar because they need him ("one man, one man alone, could save the republic"), yet their hatred of him is as intense as their fear for their own safety. They also display legitimate anxiety about the survival of republican government. Hamilcar could indeed stage a coup d'état and, emulating the example of the tyrants of Greek city states such as Peisistratus of Athens or Hiero of Syracuse, seize all power for himself.

The initally congenial atmosphere of the meeting quickly turns poisonous when Hamilcar places a statuette in front of himself, "an image of truth" (113).[10] In return, his peers level several charges at him. For instance, they accuse him of treason (of making common cause with the mercenaries). Additional charges and counter-charges fly, revealing the bitter divisiveness of Carthaginian politics. The party of aristocrats rallying around the decrepit and incompetent commander Hanno resents the constant demands of the people's party led by Barca, which it considers infringements on their traditional rights and privileges. The reproaches of the Elders, the great majority of whom belong to the aristocratic party, culminate in the accusation that Salammbô has taken a lover from among the rebellious soldiers. After having twice put down his accusers, Hamilcar, the "enraged bourgeois father,"[11] musters all his grandeur and climbs the stairs to Moloch's altar. Customarily this move meant nothing short of offering himself for sacrifice, but the suffete merely swears an oath that he would not even deign to question his daughter about such outrageous allegations.

Politically, however, another accusation is even more significant. It does not concern Hamilcar as pater familias, but the politician Hamilcar who is suspected of scheming to reinstitute the monarchy. "He wants to make himself king" (117), Hanno howls, whereupon all of them rush toward Barca waving daggers. This occurrence illustrates how corrupt Carthaginian politics have become, for even though it is forbidden under penalty of death to attend a meeting bearing a weapon of any kind, the

Elders soon feel reassured by the scene. Although they are all guilty, Hamilcar is no better, for he answers their move by drawing two broad cutlasses from his sleeves. There is, consequently, no one to hurl the stone of righteousness. Instead, we have tort against tort, or the squaring of faithlessness, a characteristic of Punic political ethics during the last century of the republic's existence. Barca is well justified in his wrath against his peers who welcomed him "like brothers meeting their brother again," but when they were kissing his hands, had to make "an effort to keep [themselves] from biting them" (111 and 117).

Where could such a state of political life lead but to perdition? Hamilcar assesses the geopolitical situation of Carthage accurately when he blames the Elders and the Rich for being cowardly, miserly, ungrateful, and without any real political sense. Their schemes have, for instance, failed to assure Carthage of a firm grip on North Africa. Beginning with this pointed observation (which, by the way, is shared by only a few of those assembled), Hamilcar's speech rises to a crescendo of indictment that equals the verbal power and strength of conviction evinced in the tirades of *Old Testament* prophets:

> [. . .] when the Libyans in the east come to an understanding with the Numidians in the west, when the Nomads come from the south and the Romans from the north [. . .], you will beat your breasts, you will roll in the dust and tear your garments! No matter! You will have to go and turn the mill in Subarra and harvest the grapes on the hills of Latium. [. . .] You will lose your ships, your lands, your chariots, your hanging beds, the slaves who rub your feet. Jackals will lie down in your places, the plough will turn up your graves. Nothing will remain but the eagles' cry and heaps of ruins. You will fall, Carthage!" (115)

Hamilcar's prophecy does come true; not in his own time, but a hundred years later. At present, the suffete is capable and willing to defend Carthage, and in spite of mutual distrust and hatred he accepts command of the Punic forces. This is what he had wanted from the beginning. Would he have returned otherwise? After assuming command, Hamilcar once more proves his qualities of leadership. There is no problem, no obstacle he does not overcome. When all things seem to flounder, even the foundations of the state, he unfailingly finds a counter-measure, a solution. In the worst conceivable peril he is unshakable, resourceful, ingenious. When the mercenaries blockade Carthage from the sea, he breeches the outer walls of the military harbor and gains a direct outlet; when they destroy the aqueduct and thereby cut off the water supply, he himself discovers untapped springs. He also raises new revenues by taxing the Rich and the colleges of priests, and he appoints his own lieutenants, a privilege of the Grand Council he blatantly usurps. "All bent before the force of his spirit. He took charge of war, government, and finances; and to forestall any accusations he asked Hanno to inspect his accounts. [. . .] Hamilcar's spirit filled the republic" (138).

From Flaubert's nineteenth-century perspective, Hamilcar must have presented the image of a superb military and political leader. This overwhelming personality not only possesses genius and willpower, but also the means of realizing his conceptions. Coupled with favoring the lower social classes are his reassuring presence and the military successes that make him the hero of the people, all the more so since his actions promise the salvation of the Punic state. As his charisma lends his victories an aura of the miraculous, he can rely on the blind trust and unconditional support of the masses. In the meeting of the Council of Elders, Hanno pronounces Hamilcar's ulterior motive with the accusation, "He wants to make himself 'king'!" Ironically enough, this is the only time in the course of the novel that Hanno is right. Indeed, classical historiography and archeology support his view. In any case, these sources must have given Flaubert sufficient hints about Hamilcar's position within Carthage and his ultimate ambitions. Diodorus Siculus, for instance, writes:

> Even before his appointment as military commander, Hamilcar had already given distinct proof of his splendid qualities. After he assumed the leadership of his country, he showed himself worthy of it, for he used every opportunity to increase his fame, and he did not fear any danger. He possessed extraordinary intelligence and bold courage, and no one was more adept at waging war so that he was both, a good king and a formidable fighter in war.[12]

Obviously this ancient historian upheld values rather different from those of modernity. To name just one instance, Hamilcar would most likely be accused of self-aggrandizement today if he used every opportunity to increase his fame. Equally remarkable, however, is the fact that Diodorus, a contemporary of Julius Caesar and Augustus, already mythifies the Carthaginian Barca by characterizing him with a quotation from the *Iliad*, i.e., Helen's words about Agamemnon: "Both, a good king and a formidable fighter in war." Although Diodorus well knew that Hamilcar held the office of suffete (at best, that of a vestigial king), he wanted to indicate Hamilcar's power in Carthage and his renown in the world of antiquity. For Flaubert, however, the key word "king" may have been the inspiration to instil *his* Hamilcar with the goal of transforming the vestigial kingship into a charismatic monarchy and of institutionalizing it dynastically. Moreover, the archeological discovery that Hamilcar, his son-in-law Hasdrubal, and Hannibal had coins struck with their image in Spain, an exclusive royal privilege, supported Flaubert's intent of describing the genesis of charismatic leadership in *Salammbô*.

Immediately after his arrival in Carthage, the author lets Hamilcar enter the Admiralty in the military harbor, the geographical focal point of Punic naval and world power. There the Carthaginian leader remembers what he had experienced and accomplished, especially during the five years of war over Sicily where he had held his own against the superior forces of Rome, only to lose everything in the end; for Carthage had withdrawn its support and preferred an unfavorable, if not dishonorable, peace to continued military expenditures. "Then he saw again the lemon groves, goat-herds on the grey mountains; and his heart leaped at the idea of another Carthage established there" (107). The object of Hamilcar's vision of the future was the Hispanic peninsula. There he had evidently been on reconnaissance during his long absence from the capital, for at the beginning of Chapter VII the text explicitly states that Hamilcar's trireme approached Carthage from the West. There he intended to more than compensate for the loss of Sicily by founding a new empire; and there his son-in-law Hasdrubal was to build Carthago Nova, which exists still today under the name of Cartagena. The significance Hamilcar attaches to the idea of this new empire is suggested once more in the form of free indirect discourse before the final battle with the mercenaries:

> He had, though, never felt such anxiety; if he succumbed it meant the destruction of the republic and he would perish on the cross; if on the other hand, he won, by the way of the Pyrenees, Gaul, and the Alps he would reach Italy and the Barcas' empire would be eternal (269).

We know from history that accidental death prevented Hamilcar from invading Italy by crossing the Alps. This feat was accomplished by his even more celebrated son. For any such operation against Rome an Iberian power base was indispensible. In Hamilcar's vision Hispania is not conceived as a colony of the maritime republic, but as an empire of the Barcas, a dynastic dominion. Such far-reaching plans explain his love of his son, his protectiveness, and the care with which he has him educated. For Hannibal, whom Flaubert makes Hamilcar's only heir (the historical Hamilcar had two additional younger sons) is groomed to assure the survival not only of the dynasty, but also of Hamilcar's ideology: The father regards the son as a projection of himself and his charismatic leadership. This is why the suffete is deeply gratified upon learning that the ten year old Hannibal has already committed a heroic deed by killing an eagle with his bare hands. "[. . .] everything about [Hannibal] displayed the indefinable splendor of those destined for great enterprises" (221). As has been shown, Salammbô also plays an important, though mediate, role in the political plans of her father. The titular heroine becomes the means to enlarge and safeguard the power of his house. Through her arranged betrothal and impending marriage with Narr'havas, Hamilcar hopes to tie the Numidians forever to the cause of the Barcas. While Polybius mentioned the planned political marriage of Hamilcar's daughter and Narr'havas, king of Numidia, Flaubert undoubtedly also thought of another Carthaginian marriage. It was that of the tragic Carthaginian woman Sophonisbe, a descendent of another Gisco, with the Numidian ruler Syphax during the time of the third Punic war with Rome. Does this not emphasize the political importance of the heroine's marriage and constitute additional proof of Hamilcar's dynastic ambitions?

Toward the end of the narrative the suffete Barca is about to realize all his goals. The endeavors of the Elders to weaken him by refusing adequate support of his campaigns and eliminating some of his followers have been ineffective. Prior to the decisive campaign they made a last effort to diminish his merits and those of his ally Narr'havas: "[. . .] if Hamilcar and the Numidian king vanquished the mercenaries alone it would be impossible to resist them. So they resolved, in order to weaken Barca, to give a share in delivering the republic to the one they favored, old Hanno" (261). This measure proves to be a deadly blunder, for even before Hamilcar has the chance to beat the rebels, they defeat Hanno, take him prisoner, and crucify him. Hence Hamilcar and Narr'havas earn the glory of victory by themselves, and from then on there is no internal opponent left with whom they might have to contend.

The aforementioned tableau concluding the novel presents the complete triumph of the Barcas. On the terrace of the Khamon temple, high above the ecstatic crowd, Salammbô is enthroned as Narr'havas's bride, and below her Hamilcar and the Numidian preside over the Elders and the Rich. The raising of the Barcas above all others is the result of the historical and fictional events of the narrative. Thus, the image appears to be an appropriate visualization of the political thrust of the novel. Or, isn't it? While Salammbô assumes the rigid posture of a statue and Narr'havas bears the rock salt crown of a groom, Hamilcar is shown in a violet tunic with golden vine leaves, and his battle-sword. The color of his raiment is, of course, a gradation of the Phoenician purple, the national color. The golden vine leaves represent wealth, vigor, and life. The battle-sword he displays even on this festive day is the instrument and symbol of his power.

Hence it is Hamilcar who embodies the restored might of Carthage and, together with his absent son Hannibal, its future. He is the "boundless hope" of the Punic people who, having been destabilized and disoriented by the gruesome years of war and their sudden deliverance, seek the taming hand of the charismatic leader whose sword, as Kafka wrote with respect to Alexander, will give new directions to their energies.

From the perspective of the later nineteenth century, things appear to be too good to be true; or, at least, to remain so for long. Hence the author resorts to irony in order to undermine the moment of the Barcas' triumph by letting Salammbô succumb on the dais (explanations of her death have been provided in the previous chapter). With her demise, one pillar of Hamilcar's dynastic policy, a permanent alliance with the Numidians, is lost before it has been cemented. On the other hand, the plot of the novel has shown that Salammbô's contribution to the deliverance of Carthage is not quite comparable to the deeds of her father who inspired and organized the Carthaginian war effort and defeated the mercenaries on three occasions: at the Macar river, in the Defile of the Axe, and under the walls of the city. His strategic masterpiece was setting the trap at the Defile of the Axe, a narrow valley in the mountains, where he closed in an army of 40,000 rebels and let them starve to death.

Is Hamilcar not a charismatic leader of a special order? The judges and prophets of the *Old Testament,* for instance, were consumed by their mission; and they pursued it without swerving from the narrow path prescribed by the Lord. Uncompromising and single-minded, they felt no need to change tactics to achieve their ends, but based their harsh demands on the conviction of their righteousness. In this regard Hamilcar's charismatic leadership is rather different, for he does not claim to be the mouthpiece of the gods. He is a statesman and politician. As such, he is flexible and ready to adapt his methods to the requirements of a given situation. His attitude toward the mercenaries is characteristic. At first he treats them with leniency by releasing prisoners on their word of honor not to fight against Carthage any more, and he instructs the authorities of the city to spare the lives of captured Barbarians. When the mercenaries respond with senseless atrocities against Carthaginian captives, and he realizes that "clemency toward the defeated had been pointless [. . .], he resolves to be ruthless" (202). After heralds have announced that between Carthaginians and Barbarians there will be "no faith, no mercy, no gods," the conflict indeed becomes the "truceless war" of which Polybius writes. Hamilcar, for one, no longer finds it necessary to keep the word he has given this enemy.

While Hamilcar's character is marred by several blemishes, he also has a real weakness which can be defined as his "planetary faith." This has to do with his belief that he has grasped "the unchanging spirit behind appearances. Something of the vital planetary forces penetrated him, while for death and all events of chance ["hasards"][13] he felt a more informed and intimate contempt" (107).[14] The Punic leader relies on his own instinct and superior intelligence to turn politics into a calculable domain, and he finds confirmation in the all-determining, "eternally regular" movements of the planets. Yet, he deceives himself thereby into assuming that the future course of human affairs is predictable. As a politician and statesman Hamilcar is a proponent of the rational theory of history which Flaubert criticizes by confronting the seemingly sovereign Carthaginian who had nothing but contempt for the workings of chance, death, and the baalim with the unforeseen death of his daughter and its unpredictable political consequences.[15] The meaning behind the author's representation of Hamilcar's political projects becomes transparent. Since the suffete, in spite of his outstanding abilities, fails to make allowance for human frailty and the irrational element in all human enterprises which join to become history, his ultimate goal of gaining world supremacy for Carthage under a Barca dynasty is doomed from the beginning. As has been said, the historical Hamilcar's own accidental death in Hispania, the hidden country (another uncanny entity), supports the authorial conception of historical fatalism, which holds that all individual endeavors make no marked difference in the general course of things.[16] The Greek concept of "moira" reasserts itself triumphantly.

Flaubert's Hamilcar Barca is an early literary incarnation of the "Realpolitiker" of the nineteenth century (e.g. Cavour, Bismarck), yet one with the gifts of divine grace characterizing the charismatic leader. Although the qualities of the "Realpolitiker" and the charismatic leader seem to be mutually exclusive, in Hamilcar they coexist since he consciously uses his charismatic gifts to further his calculated political projects. One might even say that Hamilcar is quite cynical about the effects his gifts of divine grace have on his audiences and followers. In unison with his readiness to change his methods whenever expedient, the cynical use of his special talents and powers likens him to those French charismatic leaders of the nineteenth century who also pursued royal and dynastic ambitions: Napoleon Bonaparte and Napoleon III. In such affinities lie the modernity and real significance of Flaubert's innovative historical Oriental novel.

Hamilcar's charismatic ascendance to power is made possible by his victories over two socio-political groups. In the first place, there are the mercenaries, all of non-Carthaginian origin and tied to the Punic state by contracts. Since the republic had delayed fulfillment of these contracts, the deceived soldiers felt justified in taking up arms against their employer. Except for the slaves and the poor, the foreign mercenaries constitute the lowest social class in the Punic world so that their victory would have signalled a social revolution the repercussions of which throughout the organized states of the Mediterranean would have been incalculable.[17] For this reason, the established powers in the immediate vicinity of Carthage, Rome and Syracuse, decided to support the Carthaginian cause in the Mercenary War. In the case of Rome this meant that Carthage returned former Roman slaves (including Spendius) taken prisoner; and that in turn Rome declined requests for protection made by the rebellious Punic mercenaries in Sardinia as well as the secessionist Tyrian city of Utica. The tyrant Hiero of Syracuse was even more obliging. Since he knew that he needed a balance of power between Carthage and Rome in order to keep his realm independent, he sent a great number of oxen and a large amount of wheat to the succor of the North African republic. The text explains the socio-political situation: "a deeper reason brought help to Carthage. People knew very well that, if the mercenaries won, from the soldier to the scullion there would be a general insurrection, which no government, no household would be able to resist" (245–246). Hence the unexpected support from the established hostile powers Rome and Syracuse. With his defeat of the mercenaries Hamilcar suppresses a social upheaval that was menacing the entire social order of the ancient world.

The other social group at whose expense Barca rises to power is the maritime republic's oligarchy or bourgeoisie represented by the Council of Elders and the Grand Council. As the analysis of his meeting with the Council of Elders revealed, the Rich of Carthage had become ineffective as a ruling class because of petty selfishness, reluctance to make substantial financial sacrifices for the republic, and mutual distrust. Such liabilities rendered them incapable of mastering a major national crisis like the Mercenary War. A national state of emergency is of course a precondition for Hamilcar's rise to absolute power, which he can achieve only by being successful. The reduction of the bourgeoisie to mere rubber-stamp assemblies constitutes a significant change of the socio-political order within the Carthaginian state. Essentially, it means a destabilization of Punic political life. For Hamilcar bases his rule on the fickle favor of the masses,[18] and he will not hesitate to use plebiscites in support of his causes, a proven instrument of charismatic leaders to stifle opposition from established interest groups. It is a legitimate question whether an empire of the Barcas built on such shaky foundations could indeed last "forever."

Within the novel *Salammbô,* Hamilcar is the incarnation of what in the 1880s Nietzsche was to call "the will to power": "All 'purposes,' 'goals,' and 'meanings' are only expressions and metaphors of the *one* will that is inherent in all happenings: the will to power. To have purposes, goals, intentions, to *will* altogether signifies the will to become stronger, the will to grow, and the will to obtain the means."[19] Hamilcar not only embodies this type of leader from antiquity, but also points to comparable figures of the nineteenth century.

Notes and References

1 Although Hamilcar had a daughter who was to be married to Narr'havas (Polybius), I nevertheless write "non-historical" heroine because posterity does not know anything about her, not even her name.

2 George Sand, Letter to Flaubert, January 1863.

3 Max Weber, "Die drei reinen Typen der legitiminen Herrschaft", *Gesammelte Aufsätze zur Wissenschaftslehre,* third ed. (Tübingen: J.C. Mohr, 1968) 481–482.

4-5 Abraham Malamat, "Charismatische Führung im Buch der Richter," in *Max Webers Studien über das antike Judentum,* ed. Wolfgang Schluchter (Frankfurt a.M.: Suhrkamp, 1981) 110–133 and 114.

6 Aside from the "suffete" ("schofet") only key words of Phoenician/Hebrew origin that occur in the text have been listed.

7 Ernest Renan, "Histoire générale et système comparé des langues sémitique," *Oeuvres complètes* (Paris: Calmann-Levy, 1958) VIII, 313.

8 According to Martin Bernal, Romans and nineteenth-century Europeans considered this Carthaginian custom the "ultimate abomination." See *Black Athena,* 358.

9 It is quite telling that Hamilcar had performed comparable theatrics when the priests of Moloch came to his house in order to fetch his "only" son.

10 The setting down of the statuette is all the more provocative since the Elders know very well that a struggle for power will ensue in which the maritime suffete will use every available trick to gain the upper hand.

11 In *Flaubert Writing,* Michal Ginsburg maintains that "Hamilcar resists knowledge": "[. . .] he withholds information (about the goddess, from Salammbô; about his son, from Carthage); he resists knowledge (in his vow not to ask Salammbô whether the allegations are true); and he avoids the physical equivalent of knowledge—direct contact with others (by absenting himself from Carthage, by avoiding direct contact with the Mercenaries). Hamilcar's strategy from beginning to end is a willed manipulation of ignorance" (130). Not all of these assertions are plausible. When Hamilcar returns from Hispania, the war has already begun, and even he would not be able to end it by confronting the embittered rebels, for tempers have risen too high. Instead he responds to the situation by deeds, i.e., by freeing captive rebels on their word of honor. Whatever information about Tanit he withheld from Salammbô is meant to preserve her innocence regarding the wayward practices of the goddess's cults. To be a virgin was a precious quality in antiquity, and her father Hamilcar sought to preserve her innocence. On the other hand, the fact that he refuses to lend an ear to the allegations about his

daughter's relationship with Mâtho is an example of his prudence, for he thereby preserves *his* innocence and can give his will to power free and unencumbered reign. Aside from all this, a great figure of Oriental antiquity like Hamilcar cannot be assessed by paradigms derived from the behavioral patterns of average protagonists of the modern novel.

12 Diodorus Siculus, *Bibliothek der Geschichte,* transl. Joh. F. Kaltwasser (Frankfurt a. M.: J. C. Hermann, 1786) VI, 58 (my translation).

13 This is one of several instances where I had to change the English translation of A.J. Krailsheimer because of inaccuracies. Here, for example, the French word "hasards" is translated as "dangers," although an English expression like "events of chance" is undoubtedly much closer to Flaubert's thought and argument.

14 Needless to say, for a Carthaginian whose pantheon was dominated by planetary and stellar representations of the gods, Hamilcar's "planetary faith" is appropriate. It is quite noteworthy that in the late eighteenth and nineteenth centuries writers showed once more interest in such matters. A parallel to Flaubert's Hamilcar and his faith in the planets is, for instance, found in Friedrich Schiller's play *Wallenstein* (1798/99), whose titular hero, another outstanding military leader, tries to schedule his actions according to astrological directives.

15 The political consequences of Salammbô's unexpected death are historical, not fictional. We know from history that Masinissa's siding with the Romans was a major cause of Hannibal's loss of the battle of Zama (202 B.C.). If Hamilcar had succeeded in cementing an alliance with the Numidians, Scipio might never have earned the title "Africanus."

16 Here, I am referring to Flaubert's fatalist, "mechanistic" conception of history as discussed in Chapter I.

17 The ancient world had indeed seen a precedent of the mercenaries' war with Carthage: that of the Mamertines. Former mercenaries of Agathocles, they took Messina in 289 B.C. When Hiero of Syracuse threatened their positions, some of these soldiers of fortune called Rome, others the Carthaginian Republic, for assistance. This dispute was one of the causes of the first Roman-Punic war. The fact that Flaubert lets his rebellious soldiers sing the anthem of the Mamertines ("sons of Mars") at the beginning of the second chapter of *Salammbô* is ominous.

18 This is only a conjecture, derived from the historically documented features of charismatic rule. In the Barcas' case, the favor of the masses did not quite suffice in their fight with Rome. For, as historical evidence seems to show, and despite contrary claims by Charles Lamb, for example, the Carthaginian Republic did not provide adequate support for Hannibal in its second war with Rome.

19 Friedrich Nietzsche, *Werke in drei Bänden,* ed. K. Schlechta, eighth ed. (München: Hanser, 1977) III, 679.

Chapter IV

An Allegory of Bonapartism

> "Nichts ist zarter als die Vergangenheit; Rühre sie an wie ein
> glühend Eisen; Denn sie wird Dir sogleich beweisen, Du lebest
> auch in heißer Zeit."
>
> Goethe, "Zahme Xenien," III

The preceding discussion of *Salammbô* suggests that Flaubert had not written his Oriental novel for the purpose of resurrecting a lost civilization. A conscientious Realist, he did not know enough about this metropolis of antiquity to make it the principal focus of his narrative. Rather, he saw his depiction of the city as a "fata morgana" in the very sense of the term, as a vision containing real components. Comparable reservations apply to the titular heroine, an intriguing Oriental princess who necessarily remains a mysterious figure to the European observer and reader. From such premises, it would be difficult to assume that the author intended to write his historical novel for the primary sake of the ancient metropolis or the titular heroine. Instead, *Salammbô* presents a political allegory of nineteenth-century France.

Until less than thirty years ago the reception of *Salammbô* had, for the most part, been an uninterrupted series of critical misreadings. At the very least, they were one-sided and unconcerned with political themes. At the source of this tradition stand two eminent figures in French letters: Gautier and Sainte-Beuve. The foremost spokesman of l'Art pour l'Art and author of *La Momie* celebrated Flaubert's novel as an escapist indulgence in aesthetic and erotic dreams, whereas the outstanding French critic of the nineteenth century perceived it as an essentially ahistorical historical novel (provided there were such a hybrid). Sainte-Beuve's principal objection was that the subject matter of *Salammbô,* an obscure war between Carthage and its mercenaries, had no bearing on the present.[1]

Most important for Sainte-Beuve's misprision is the fact that despite his critical flexibility and shrewdness, he held on to the norms of classical literature and thus measured *Salammbô* strictly against the conventions of Scott's novel. Flaubert's narrative belongs, however, to the new literature that emerged in France in the aftermath of the abortive revolution in 1848, for which the established critic evidently had little appreciation. His stature and authority appear to have borne his strong reservations forward through time. Even in the twentieth century they have survived (often with the admixture of Gautier's aestheticism) in the erudite and thoughtful criticism of Thibaudet, Lukács, Victor Brombert, Maurice Nadeau, Maurice Bardèche, and Sartre.

Lukács's main argument that Flaubert attempted "to reawaken a vanished world of no concern to us,"[2] echoes Sainte-Beuve's pronouncement. Another legacy of the norms of classicism under which Sainte-Beuve labored is the notion that there are innately beautiful or worthy literary subjects and, consequently, also undeserving ones. As Flaubert repeatedly demonstrated in his correspondence, the new aesthetics he represented no longer found this premise acceptable. In a letter to Louise Colet of June 25–26, 1853, he asserts that "poetry is purely subjective, that in literature there are no beautiful artistic themes, that hence Yvetot is as good as Constantinople, and that one can write on one thing as well as another. *The artist must elevate everything* [. . .]." This statement proclaims the equality of all literary subjects (e.g. the Mercenary War is neither more nor less suitable than Carthage's confrontation with Rome), and it asserts that the merit of a literary work derives from the authorial treatment of the subject matter. In this letter to Colet the verb "élever" has a double meaning. It connotes what classical aesthetics understood as the ennobling function of art. But the continuation of the letter shows that in addition Flaubert assigned to literature another, altogether different purpose by insisting that the author penetrate to "the entrails of things" and make visible that which "lay hidden underground and which one did not see." In short, literature has the task of disclosing things and situations, presenting new insights, making the reader aware of conditions he had not observed before.

The preceding chapter has argued that a considerable part of *Salammbô* is devoted to describing conditions favoring the appearance of the charismatic leader, and what his attributes and deeds are to be. It analyzed the circumstances under which Hamilcar had assumed command of the Punic forces and showed how he gradually expanded his power by taking over the direction of all crucial Carthaginian affairs at the expense of the

Council of Elders and the Assembly of the Rich, whose authority he undermined or disregarded. The uneasiness and distrust of the Punic oligarchy, which never turned its weary eyes from Hamilcar's alarming activities, culminated in the accusation that he wanted to make himself king. This charge was confirmed by Hamilcar's vision of a future empire of the Barcas in Spain. Although his monarchist and dynastic ambitions have since been verified by historical research, some of the evidence was not yet available to Flaubert.[3] He relied, instead, on his intuition and, as Collingwood would have said, on historical construction. Thus, Hamilcar's monarchist project does constitute a significant narrative element in *Salammbô*. In the face of this fact it is impossible to regard Flaubert's novel as essentially apolitical, i.e. an escape into a colorful and aesthetically attractive era of history. Moreover, one can contend without hesitation that the Carthaginian novel relates to Flaubert's own political, social, and economic present in a rather concrete way: The conditions in Carthage and Hamilcar's rise to power both reflect and comment on the political situations in France during and after the revolutions of 1789 and 1848. From amidst internal dissent and turmoil (in the case of the first revolution, there was in addition the threat of aggression from abroad), Napoleon Bonaparte and Louis Napoleon emerged as charismatic leaders.

It is not at all surprising that French and German criticism, which was imbued with social and political thought over the last thirty or forty years, has been in the forefront of pointing out the parallels between Flaubert's Carthage and nineteenth-century France. Critical works of such provenance are often disregarded in the bibliographies of Anglo-Saxon studies of Flaubert's oeuvre. Yet even if they are listed, they have not caused any noteworthy reorientation in English or American approaches to *Salammbô*. Anne Green, for one, has labored assiduously to unearth evidence of parallels between Carthaginian and nineteenth-century French political and economic attitudes. What she failed to discuss, however, was the major thrust of Flaubert's novel: the emergence of the charismatic leader from the midst of a decaying bourgeoisie clinging to power at all cost.

The studies to which I refer are by Christa Bevernis, Bosse/Stoll, and Jeanne Bem.[4] Bevernis's article, based on the Marxist conception of history, recognizes in the representation of the Carthaginian oligarchy "the most successful and artistically strongest part of the book," the "actual core of the novel" which "reveals the nature of the ruling class."[5] Aside from frequent references throughout the text, Flaubert offers a penetrating portrayal of the Punic merchant patricians in Chapter VII during its confrontation with Hamilcar, which has been discussed in the previous chapter. It has been shown that the Carthaginian oligarchy was divided into representatives of an "ancien régime" grouped around the incompetent and moribund Hanno, and a smaller segment of nouveaux riches supporting Hamilcar and looking for a place in the sun. Both groups had become wealthy not only through trade, industry, and agriculture, but also through piracy, slavery, usury, and the ruthless exploitation of subject peoples, and of women and children. Although Bevernis regards the two factions of the oligarchy as "nothing but two versions of the same social phenomenon," this generalization also misses the intent of the novel.

Rather, Flaubert describes an evolutionary political process by which a debilitated ruling class no longer able to rise above the pursuit of private interests is supplanted by a younger, more far-sighted, and enterprising group. Indeed, the text leaves no doubt about the fact that Hamilcar is the military savior of Carthage (just as after the victorious conclusion of the Mercenary War he and his son-in-law Hasdrubal rebuilt the economic foundations of the Punic realm with the silver from Hispanic mines).[6] Therefore it is inappropriate to lump all Carthaginian merchant bourgeois together, although most of them display the same drive to enrich themselves or to augment their possessions. In any case, the group around Hamilcar combines greed with the knowledge that wealth is most conveniently accumulated in the shadow of a strong army. This view of the ruling class(es) of Carthage is convincing because it is based on experience, i.e. the author's first-hand knowledge of the bourgeoisie of his own time. A comparison of the Carthaginian bourgeoisie of the third century B.C. and the French bourgeoisie of the nineteenth century was feasible because Flaubert subscribed, as has been shown in my first chapter, to Vico's cyclical view of history according to which the phenomena of a certain stage in one civilization are comparable to those of another at a corresponding phase of development. To put the matter more concretely, it is undeniable that the author of *Salammbô* believed that the ruling classes of Hamilcar's Carthage were similar to that of the financiers and entrepreneurs in France after 1830. In her extensively researched study of *Salammbô* Anne Green claims that it would be "misleading to draw [. . .] direct analogies between characters from the novel and individual figures in France."[7] General similarities nevertheless do exist, but these are, along the conventions of Realism, based on generic traits which Flaubert observed and transferred to some of his characters. More important, however, is the fact that he grasped the very nature of revolutionary situations as preconditions for the rise of charismatic leaders. Such a position seems reasonable, for *Salammbô* was indeed not conceived as a "roman à clef." However this should not imply that the novel does not treat the great political movements and events of its own time. Monika Bosse and André Stoll read the novel not as "a recapitulation of so-called historical facts," but as a "socio-psychologically and aesthetically differentiated transposition" of developments in revolutionary France. For Bosse and Stoll the common denominator of late Carthaginian and modern French political history is Bonapartism, which signifies the cynical abuse of the revolutionary forces and their transformation into "sacrificial matter" for the purpose of buttressing the power of the enlightened despot. While Bosse and Stoll emphasize the analogies between Hamilcar and Napoleon I and relegate the rise of Napoleon III to an afterglow of his uncle's mythical light, the case is far from clear.[8] Surely, Flaubert must have had his reasons for depicting Carthage as the citadel of the Rich and stressing the role commerce and industry played in the daily life of the republic. For the Carthaginian oligarchy even war was commerce transacted by other means; and when the interest of war and commerce collided as in the first long conflict with Rome over Sicily, the plutocratic leaders of the republic tended to terminate hostilities in order to save their trade and their profits.

In *Salammbô* there are three contenders for power: the mercenaries, the Rich, and Hamilcar Barca. An amorphous group of soldiers of fortune from all shores of the Mediterranean, the mercenaries and their North African allies under the leadership of the irrational Mâtho and the wily, but cowardly Spendius who occasionally falls back into his former slave habits, as well as their lieutenants Autharite and Zarxas, attract the reader's interest less for their own sake, but function primarily as instruments of disclosure. In the treatment they are accorded by the Carthaginian authorities, "the nature of the ruling class is revealed."[9] The lack of interest in the rebels' cause may be partially due to the fact that Flaubert did not empathize with the socially underprivileged, except when they existed in a "state of primitive naturalness." Thus, he indulged in excessive descriptions of fierce battle scenes where the raw courage and bestial instincts of the uncivilized could jubilate in their gory triumphs (e.g. Zarxas who, after a Garamante had cut Gisco's throat, throws the severed head into the Punic lines).

On the other hand, Flaubert was evidently hardly capable of entertaining any less alarming thought than that of proletarians on the verge of seizing power. The symbolic figure of the young prostitute in *L'Éducation sentimentale* who, on a heap of royal clothes, assumes the pose of the symbol of liberty during the revolution of 1848 is more revealing than many loquacious sentences. What he dreaded most, he wrote in one of his letters, was "the dream of democracy to raise [through education] the proletarian to the bourgeois' level of stupidity."[10] He would have been willing to grant the masses liberty, but not the right to vote. If the masses were to gain power, he feared, this would mean the advent of democracy and, in due course, socialism which would crush the individual, lead to the abolishment of great art, and usher in the inevitable and indisputable reign of mediocrity. Flaubert voiced such views in many epistolary tirades to Louise Colet: "According to the socialists the ideal state is a kind of huge monster which swallows up every individual action, the entire personality, every thought; it will direct everything, take care of everything. [. . .] What is Equality after all if not the negation of all liberty, all superiority, and nature itself? Equality is slavery."[11] On the premise of such convictions or prejudices Flaubert's treatment of the mercenaries is ambiguous; it constitutes a strange mixture of human sympathy for their miserable situation, admiration for their strength and desperate perseverance, and ultimate negation of their goal to overthrow an organized state. As *L'Éducation sentimentale* and *Bouvard et Pécuchet* show, he regarded the fight of the French workers of 1848 with similar emotions. Since the mercenaries of *Salammbô* are "foreigners" and "Barbarians" (i.e. "others"), it might seem contrived to compare them to French workers. Yet one can argue that to the French bourgeoisie and the nobility that had survived politically into the 1830s, their own proletariat appeared as "foreign" and "barbaric" as did the exotic mercenaries to the Rich of Carthage.

If Flaubert set little store by the working classes, he had even less regard for the bourgeoisie. Actually, if there is one certainty about Flaubert, it is his hatred of the class into which he had been born. The adjectives he heaps upon it with undiminishing malice include hypocritical, stupid, foolish, greedy, and corrupt, just as he speaks repeatedly of the "bêtise bourgeoise." Undoubtedly, the Carthaginian oligarchy represented by the Council of Elders and the Assembly of the Rich was conceived as the political, social, and economic counterpart of the French bourgeoisie, the main difference consisting in the obviously greater resoluteness of the ancient guardians of vested interests. By using the device of presenting a contemporary problem in an Oriental setting of the past, i.e., by distancing and estranging it, Flaubert offered his readers the chance to perceive the real issue in their midst: a narrow-minded and selfish ruling class that was always ready to sell out the welfare of the whole for the sake of its own interest. Appropriately enough, Hamilcar's somber prophecy, "You will fall, Carthage!," had its French equivalent prior to the publication of *Salammbô*. Indeed, many French intellectuals shared the apprehension that under bourgeois leadership France was tottering toward its ruin. By the 1860s it had become commonplace opinion that the destruction of France was close at hand and would most likely be accomplished by "barbarians" (workers) from within. It was fashionable to evoke the demise of Carthage as an ominous parallel of the impending fall of the French capital.[12]

With combatants like the mercenaries and the merchant oligarchy contending for political power in Carthage, and with the historical precedent of the Mamertines, countless cases of oligarchic misrule, and the political forces of his own country in mind, it seems only logical that Flaubert was reluctant to treat either group with excessive political sympathy, or to accord either final victory. Instead, it appears, another solution was required in this desperate struggle, one that held out the promise of genius in politics and gave some recognition to the voice and energy of the "people." Hamilcar Barca and his charismatic leadership embodied this solution; its French equivalent was Bonapartism.

Much has been said and written about Flaubert's political views and, allowing for exceptions, there is a consensus that essentially he was either apolitical, or so fickle in his opinions that no firm position could be discerned. He did not belong to a political party, nor did he ever hold political office. Hence his politics are deduced from three sources: his conversations, his letters, and his fiction. His contemporaries attest to his lack of interest in political discussion and relate that whenever he voiced opinions, they were highly contradictory. The impressions of the Princess Mathilde, whose salon in the rue de Courcelles Flaubert frequented, are quite typical: "Absolute and versatile, wanting to die for his country, yet getting along well with everyone, victors and vanquished, he had no political convictions whatever. One moment he demanded all kinds of repression, and another he did not accept any."[13] Maxime Du Camp, his friend, writes in *Souvenirs littéraires* that he appeared as little affected by the revolution of 1848 as by the coup d'état of 1851. A similar case can be made on the basis of Flaubert's letters where 1848 and the ensuing events find scant mention, and when they are mentioned one cannot ascribe firm political opinion to their author. On the basis of such evidence the sagacious Anatole France, who called Flaubert's politics "an abyss of uncertainties and errors," noted in bewilderment: "[. . .] his ideas will drive every man of good sense crazy. They are absurd and so contradictory that anyone who attempted to reconcile only three of them will soon clasp his temples with both hands in order to prevent his head from bursting."[14]

The lack of direction in his pronouncements and the absence of substantial commentary on the most significant political events during his young adulthood may be all the more surprising since the author of *L'Éducation sentimentale* and *Bouvard et Pécuchet* has won recognition as one of the foremost transcribers of the revolution of 1848 into fiction. Several explanations may be offered regarding the discrepancy between Flaubert the private person and Flaubert the novelist. Venturing occasionally into good society, the hermit of Croisset may have enjoyed playing the role of "l'enfant terrible," or "le poète maudit," or the devil's advocate who provoked his listeners in order to draw out their responses as raw material for his fiction. His letters, however, are an altogether different matter. As we know, he wrote them late at night in a state of nervous exaltation, after he had completed his literary labors. Hence the violence of their assertions and the crassness of their formulations.[15] They express his intuitions of a given moment, and they are addressed to a particular person, facts that most likely had an impact on what he said and how he said it. An explanation by Thomas Mann of Theodor Fontane's relationship to politics should throw light on the matter: "His political awareness was complicated by his temperament as an artist, it was, in every elevated sense, not reliable. [. . .] A great painter may become official, a great writer never. For everything that constitutes the rank, the charm, and value of his personality, the subtle intellectual distinctions, the problem-posing, the wilful undiscipline, must make him seem in the eyes of the ruling classes both disloyal and suspect."[16] Although Mann was highly self-conscious about the writer's unreliability regarding specific political situations and choices, this did not prevent him from authoring *Betrachtungen eines Unpolitischen,* an apology of the politics of cultural conservatism, nor did it prevent Flaubert from offering in *Salammbô* a penetrating analysis of the rise of charismatic leadership. Ultimately, however, the writer's gift of empathy or negative capability may be the cause for his/her contradictory political views. Nevertheless, in his fiction political figures and events are presented in a balanced and, as Flaubert thought, objective way. As a critic he assumed the same position, for concerning Louise Colet's fulsome poem *Servante* he reproached her for allowing personal animosities and dislikes to set the tone of her work and determine her characterizations to the detriment of her poetic achievement.[17]

As a novelist, then, Flaubert tried not only to be objective, but also "impassible" toward what he described. His ambition as a writer consisted in ferreting out the truth about things, for which task he was resolved to employ all resources available to the modern novelist. Of course he relied on this approach in his portrayal of Hamilcar, the man who won the Mercenary War which had been caused by the avarice of the Rich. He is the political hero of the novel, yet a mixed character with extraordinary gifts and grave flaws. In his retort to Sainte-Beuve's criticism Flaubert points out that he had "not been commissioned to sing [Hamilcar's] praises," but that he had drawn him as a character who, aside from his merits, forges his merchandise, orders the incompetent and disloyal masters of his slaves to be whipped bloody, substitutes the child of a slave for his own son as a sacrificial offering to Moloch, and has the leaders of the mercenaries crucified. He is a complex figure, a fact Flaubert stresses by observing that "people who let themselves be addressed as Son of God or Eye of God (e.g. the inscriptions of Hamaker) are not that simple [. . .]."[18] As has been shown, Flaubert depicts Hamilcar as the embodiment of the charismatic leader whose gifts of divine grace are manifest in his names, his military leadership, his administrative skills, his resourcefulness, his oratory power, and his claim to prophecy. These gifts and qualities combine to make him the savior of the Punic nation. If one reads *Salammbô* with an open mind, the similarities and correspondences of its politics to those of France since 1789 become evident. The critical effort of Bosse and Stoll who see the novel as an allegory of the era of Napoleon I or the phenomenon of Bonapartism is a valuable contribution to our understanding of the work. It is also true, however, that they do not make sufficient political distinctions in their interpretation of the historical narrative as an allegory of Flaubert's own political present.[19]

Bosse and Stoll perceive the Carthaginian suffete as another incarnation of "Bonapartism" without properly defining the concept. The same pertains to the adjective "charismatic," which they use once in a general way to characterize the rules of the two Napoleons. Max Weber's significant work on charismatic leadership receives no mention, nor are its insights applied to the study of *Salammbô*. The origin of the title "suffete" is disregarded. This is most likely due to the authors' assessment of Hamilcar, whom they portray as a monster, for his reign appears to build on such immense horror that it destroys its own legitimacy. Since the sympathies of Bosse and Stoll lie with the rebellious soldiers who are perceived as defrauded revolutionaries, and with Salammbô, the "paternally oppressed woman" who is sacrificed to the interests of a male-dominated world, Hamilcar and Bonapartism are not treated impartially.

For is it altogether appropriate to regard Hamilcar in terms of Bonapartism without qualifying the concept, particularly when recent scholarly investigations make such qualifications necessary? Bonapartism is a particular form of charismatic leadership, and a modern form at that. It signifies the rule of an individual who has attained this position through a coup d'état, justified by the perilous state of the country. In 1799 Napoleon claimed to have acted because of the danger posed by the "exclusifs"; in 1851 Louis Napoleon pointed to the threat of the "Reds" as his justification for seizing power. Like Hamilcar, both Napoleons presented themselves as saviors of their country. They rose out of revolutionary fermentation and tamed the unruly forces of society. Both Bonapartes pretended to stand above all political parties and resorted to plebiscites in order to demonstrate that their rule expressed the will of the entire nation.

At this point it is important to point out a distinction between "Bonapartism" and "Bonapartisme" made by a group of experts at a recent Franco-German symposium. While the German scholars tended to see Bonapartism[20] as a modern version of Caesarism and were prepared to apply it to similar political phenomena outside France, their French colleagues insisted that "Bonapartisme" owes its peculiar character to its commitment to the nation and the revolution of 1789. "The Blue-White-Red," Karl Ferdinand Werner summarizes, "had definitely replaced the colors of the dynasty; royalty by divine right no longer had a place in France; and the politically organized people, which expressed their will in elections and plebiscites, was no more the subject, but the sovereign whom even the emperor or the president had to serve. The country and its wealth did not belong to the ruler, but to the nation [. . .]. In universal suffrage, in the ideals of 'liberté, égalité, fraternité' and in the concept of the 'citoyen' the achievements of the great revolution lived on, even if the strong central executive power and administration Napoleon imposed on the revolution as its most permanent features were suited to prevent new revolutions."[21] Although this definition of Bonapartisme sounds rather idealistic (particularly the claim that even the emperor served the people rather than vice versa), Bonapartisme was attractive to large segments of French society which, on the basis of the gains of 1789, expected to live in a national community united in and stratified by the central government.

In contrast to Bonapartist forms of rule outside France, Bonapartisme displayed a republican character and claimed democratic legitimization, even if the parliamentary component was not given much weight. The denigration of parliament undoubtedly meant that the government had to contend with fewer checks and balances. In spite of outrageous transgressions, Imperial France was a state under the rule of law. The basis of government and its most formidable counterweight consisted in the people and public opinion. There are three other important elements of Bonapartist rule: control of the press which is used to celebrate the achievements of the sovereign and to mythify his name, effective administration, and success in foreign policy where military victories figure prominently.

The military exploits of Napoleon I have become proverbial; Napoleon III sought to emulate his renowned uncle (though not as the general in command) by participating in the Crimean War, by intervening in the Italian states' confrontation with Austria, and by sending an expeditionary force under Bazaine to Mexico where a puppet emperor was installed. The Mexican adventure, which turned out to be a costly failure, was conceived as the first step toward establishing a mystical French protectorate over all Latin peoples. It also proved to be the beginning of the end for Louis Napoleon, for having become unsure of himself, he allowed his subordinates to draw France into war with Prussia (and its Southern German allies) against his own better judgment. His defeat at Sedan, his capture, ensuing deposition, and exile corresponded to the great Napoleon's fortunes at and after Waterloo. It is significant that both dynasties ended with their founders' removal from office, signalling the termination of imperial government. Bonapartisme obviously requires success abroad in order to maintain itself. Hamilcar's career in Flaubert's novel and that of his son Hannibal in history confirm this view.

Although the people and public opinion could be influenced and controlled by the press, such manipulation had its limits of effectiveness. The press proved especially useful in identifying the name of the Bonapartist leader with noteworthy deeds and accomplishments, and thus was instrumental in justifying his coup d'état and securing his rule. It was also employed to gloss over internal conflicts and scandals. Ultimately, however, the fate of Bonapartist rule depended on the standing of France among the leading nations of Europe. Regarding Bonapartisme in this light, Jean Tulard observes: "The legend celebrates at one and the same time the fate of an exceptional individual and a national adventure. Therein lies the explanation of its success."[22] Of recurring significance in the discussion of Bonapartisme is the cult of the leader's name. The case of Napoleon Bonaparte serves as a model of the devices a charismatic leader might employ in order to make himself a legend in his own lifetime, to create a personal myth, and to inscribe himself in the annals of history. Louis Napoleon, on the other hand, who could not point to any great personal deed when he staged his coup d'etat, relied solely on the mythical quality of his inherited name in his proclamation of December 2, 1851 to the

French people: "My name guarantees strong and stable government, and good administration."[23]

The place allocated to the propertied classes during the rule of the two Bonapartes is considerably more difficult to describe. In general terms one can say that in both cases they had to share power and opportunities with groups of political neophytes. Because of its claim of impartial detachment from all parties, Bonapartisme invited the political and economic participation of socially stratified elements. While the first Napoleon relied on the best from the middle-class, the nobility (in 1801 he even allowed the émigrés to return to France), as well as genuine talent of socially non-descript origin, the social background of those supporting the reign of Napoleon III is at once more complicated and dubious. The latter was, by and large, supported by an uneasy coalition of the bourgeoisie and the peasantry, which had been legitimized by Napoleon I in their aspirations of securing possessions or political influence. The peasantry, reeling in debt due to mortgages and taxation, did not play a significant role in the government of Louis Napoleon except as a provider of "blind" votes he could always count on. The "bourgeoisie" constituted a considerably more thorny problem.

Although the bourgeoisie had been one of the motivating forces of the revolution of 1848 by demanding a share of power for its yet unrepresented segments, and though its representation was enlarged considerably, this class proved unable to consolidate its gains after 1848 because of internal divisions. Aside from defrauding the proletariat of its spoils from the overthrow of the July-Monarchy, the bourgeoisie with its factions of moderate and radical republicans, Legitimists, and Orleanists, all of which were united for some time under the banner of the Party of Order, felt unable to resist consistently the pressure exerted by the left, i.e., by the discontented and ambitious elements of the peasantry and the urban workers. Hence the bourgeoisie, distrustful of its radical opponents and its own fragmented interests, opted to support Louis Napoleon in 1848 and in subsequent elections, partially because he promised law and order, and conditions conducive to the unimpeded pursuit of happiness, partially because the popularity of his name among the majority of rustics allowed him to mobilize a broad social spectrum of the electorate. Karl Marx has characterized the strange interaction between the president and later emperor and the bourgeoisie with sardonic acumen:

> As the autonomous power of the executive, Bonaparte felt it was his calling to secure "bourgeois order." Yet the middle-class is the backbone of this bourgeois order. Thus, he sees himself as the representative of the middle-class and issues

appropriate decrees. On the other hand, he is what he is only because he has broken the power of the middle-class and continues to do so every day. Hence he sees himself opposed to the political and literary power of the middle-class. Yet by protecting its economic power, he generates once more its political power. The cause must therefore be kept alive, whereas the effect must be erased whenever it shows itself. However, this cannot be done without confounding cause and effect since both lose their marks of distinction in their reciprocal affects. Therefore he issues new decrees devised to blur the borderlines. At the same time Bonaparte sees himself as the representative of the peasants and the people at large against the bourgeoisie, who wishes to improve the lives of the lower classes. He issues new decrees designed to deprive the "true socialists" in advance of their future government wisdom. But Bonaparte sees himself above all as Head of the Company of December 10, as the representative of the rabble, to which he himself belongs, his entourage, his government, his army. Their main concern is to take care of themselves [. . .]. [24]

The most striking feature of the relationship between Napoleon III and the bourgeoisie was a trade-off. His government created an economic climate in which the entire class was able to enrich itself, together, of course, with the emperor and his clique of adventurers in the government and at court. The price for these economic gains was a reduction of bourgeois political influence. For as Emperor who stood above all parties, he could not afford to be ostensibly identified with a particular social class. In order to appear equitable, he had to take away one thing after he had bestowed another. Marx even claims that Louis Napoleon stole all of France in order to give it back to the French, whereby he deducted a certain percentage for himself and his own. He had, as his critic notes, transformed the imperial eagle into a thieving crow.

Much of this is present in the Carthaginian "realities" of *Salammbô*. Hamilcar, for instance, evinces personal greed the major aspects of which are comparable to those of Bonapartist avarice displayed by Napoleon I and his nephew. According to the standards of the Punic oligarchy of landowners, manufacturers, and merchants he is, like the Bonapartes, a parvenu bent on increasing his possessions in order to beat his rivals for power on their own turf. Michelet observes that of the spoils of war which fell to his Carthaginian armies, Hamilcar delivered one third to the state, handed over another third to his soldiers, but kept the remaining third for himself: thirty-three percent. This explains some of his wealth, but the larger part is probably due to his highly diversified commercial enterprises, and to fraud. As Jeanne Bem has pointed out, Hamilcar even defrauds the goddess Tanit (a parallel to his defrauding Moloch of his son) who is to receive ten percent of all revenues. By declaring only seventy-five percent of his commercial income, he deprives Tanit of the taxes from the remaining fourth.[25] The forging of goods from his factories, though a measure of the private Punic citizen Barca, must nevertheless be seen as a bad omen for a future empire dominated by the practices and interests of his family. For does this kind of fraud, arising from the discrepancy between appearance and substance, not point directly to the discrepancy between the outward glitter of the Second Empire and its inner rot? In *L'Éducation sentimentale* Flaubert contrasts the conspicuous extravagance of the public balls and dinner parties of high society with the immorality of their participants. Long before Flaubert published *Salammbô* or *L'Éducation sentimentale* Karl Marx had labeled the government of Napoleon III as an assembly of "kept men,"[26] thus preparing the way for seeing the Second Empire as an era where everything was for sale and prostitution reigned ubiquitously.

Hamilcar's position between the Punic Rich and the masses, which he plays off against one another, constitutes another major parallel to the political stance of Napoleon III. The novel shows how, once given command because there is no alternative, Hamilcar gradually disempowers the Council of Elders and the Assembly of the Rich by two means: military and organizational urgency, as well as the wrath of the masses with which he threatens his social peers. However, while taking away their political power, Barca also does not touch the private wealth of the Rich, except when military expenditures require contributions. He is prudent enough not to drive them to despair. After the end of the Mercenary War his strong rule and the conquest of Spain allowed Carthage to make a stupendous economic recovery, which enabled the Punic bourgeoisie of merchants and financiers to enrich themselves on an unprecedented scale. Also, like Louis Napoleon, Hamilcar did not promise to bring economic benefits just to one class, but he held out the prospect of wealth for all Carthaginians to motivate them.[27] Thus he, too, presented himself as a truly national leader with the well being of all at heart. The fact that his actions are occasionally motivated by cynicism make him—in contrast to Alexander for instance—a more modern figure whom readers of the nineteenth and twentieth centuries can more readily understand. The charge of "modernization" Lukács levelled against *Salammbô* is based on such grounds, yet it is, as shall be shown later, inappropriate since it disregards historical facts and crucial aspects of historical fiction.

Other parallels between Flaubert's Carthaginian novel and France under the reign of the Bonapartes consist in the use of religion as a political instrument and the entire range of military questions. As has been shown, Hamilcar is not a religious man in the sense of Punic orthodoxy. At one point the text states that the gods are but symbols and names for him (107), at another he feels "stronger than the baals and full of scorn for them" (235). Although he does not believe in the gods, he accepts the people's acclamations of "Eye of Khamon!" His red mantle connects him with the priests of Moloch. As a lay priestess of Tanit, his daughter Salammbô is the most exalted woman of the city in religious matters. Through his own associations with Khamon Baal and Moloch, and Salammbô's with Tanit, the house of Barca appears to enjoy privileged relations with the three foremost Punic gods. Quite obviously Hamilcar uses religion as a means to buttress and increase his political power by playing on the credulity of the people and by acting as champion of Carthaginian beliefs.

Napoleon III behaved in a comparable way. While his support did not come from the "people," except for the conservative farmers and the petits bourgeois—the radical workers whom he first disenfranchised and then bloodily suppressed (1850–51) were his bitter enemies—he exploited the religious sentiment of the nation, although he himself was a free thinker. In 1848, as President of the Second Republic, he dispatched French troops to break up the Roman Republic and to restore the pope. A year later he allowed the clergy to regain a large measure of control over the educational system in France by signing the Falloux law. In other words, the free thinker Napoleon III followed and used the mood of the time, which was characterized by a religious revival among the middle classes and the farmers. Fearing the rise of socialism and the outbreak of social revolution, they considered the church a bulwark of the status quo concerning property rights. His marriage to the Spanish countess Eugénie Montijo capped his religious policy, for her clerical inclinations and charitable activities made her the favorite of France's devout Catholics, and even of a good number of workers. On the other hand, Napoleon III's encouragement of Italian nationalism alienated him from the clerical party of France. He was no Hamilcar, but only a weak modern reflection of the antique leader.

Bosse and Stoll have interpreted the immense horror of the military operations in *Salammbô* (without mentioning the inhumane, frequently outright sadistic, treatment of Punic prisoners by the Mercenaries) as a phenomenon characterizing the establishment of Barca's rule. According to their reading, the victims include the woman Salammbô, Mâtho and his army, the troops of the republic, the sons of the old oligarchy, and the (Carthaginian) slaves.[28] This view of events in Flaubert's novel appears to be arbitrary, if not unduly polemical. Indeed, it is conditioned by the critics' own political convictions, although no political stance justifies the distortion of facts. Bosse and Stoll have, however, done just that in order to account for their indictment of Hamilcar. In their interpretation of *Salammbô* he is the villain. But is that really so? While it is true that he annihilates the rebellious mercenaries, he does so only after they rejected all offers of reconciliation. It also is erroneous to classify the Carthaginian dead as victims of Hamilcar's political ambitions.

Contrary to the assumption of Bosse and Stoll, Hamilcar does not sacrifice his daughter; rather, she is victimized by the mystical causality determining the religious and moral life of Carthage. In political terms she dies because in the secularized world of the new politics represented by her father, there is no longer a place for comet-like figures she embodies (i.e., she follows a course of action incomprehensible from a rational perspective). In this sense, and only in this sense, does Hamilcar's political advent necessitate Salammbô's demise.[29] As to the troops of the republic, the sons of the Rich, and the slaves,[30] none of them can be considered victims of Barca's rise to power, for with whom should he have defended Carthage against the deadly threat posed by the insurrection? In the face of the extreme military situation threatening the existence of the Punic state, it is inappropriate to downplay the merits of Hamilcar's leadership in saving his people and to blame him for Carthaginian casualties. Michal Ginsburg's thesis that the mercenaries are a multi-national entity, in whose ranks no particular segment dominates, and who would therefore be willing to take in the Carthaginians as one additional group (whereas the latter insist on their racial exclusiveness), is just as questionable.[31] For the Mercenary War was a struggle between an ancient state and "barbarians," and although an infusion of "alien blood" might have benefitted Carthage (Michelet), the mercenaries' demand for Carthaginian women could never have received a favorable response from the republic. Ginsburg argues from a postmodernist position, but there is the textual reality of proportions. The Carthaginians numbered around 500,000 as compared with the rebels' force ranging from 40,000 or 80,000. How could the Barbarians absorb or integrate the former?

To be sure, Carthage approached the problem of the rebellious mercenaries in the worst possible way. Regarding the annihilation of the rebels an analogy can be drawn to an event of 1848, the June insurrection of the Parisian proletariat, where the workers of the city tried to safeguard their stake in the revolution. In the course of this truceless conflict between the proletariat and the united bourgeoisie, which Marx termed "the most colossal event in the history of European civil wars,"[32] three thousand insurgents were brutally cut down by the regular army of the new republic under the command of General Cavaignac and Colonel Bernard, while another fifteen thousand men were deported without trial. The brutality of the suppression, supported by the bourgeoisie, the middle-class, the clergy, most of the peasants, and many intellectuals, undoubtedly moved Flaubert, for in *Salammbô* he graphically describes the analogous fate of the "barbarians." Thus, the reigns of Napoleon III, who was elected President of the French Republic on December 16 of the same year, and of Hamilcar were built on comparable acts of brutality.

As a charismatic leader, Hamilcar embodies elements of both Bonapartisme and Bonapartism. A Carthaginian of the third century B.C. he could of course not build on the achievements of the French Revolution (in particular "les droits de l'homme") but, on the other hand, his deeds correspond so closely to those of the Bonapartes that analogies cannot be denied. Moreover, parallels to the reign of Napoleon III appear to predominate. Obviously Flaubert used the historical Carthaginian setting, where such gruesome events took place, in order to decry the political confrontations and ruthless means of settling them in his own present. In his France he took issue with class warfare; in Carthage the case was more complex. There tens of thousands of uprooted and impoverished foreign soldiers of disparate national backgrounds fought with a reputedly rich nation of transplanted Canaanites led by wealthy merchants, industrialists, and landowners. Hence the Mercenary War was not only a class struggle of the poor against the rich, but it was also a fight of "Barbarians" with a state. The conflict displayed noteworthy racial overtones, a feature of Carthaginian history Flaubert found fully developed in Michelet's treatment of the subject.

In his preoccupation with questions of race, Michelet was by no means an eccentric thinker and scholar. Quite the contrary, the nineteenth century was awash in racial theories which frequently went hand in hand with the new nationalism engendered by the wars of the French Revolution, the Napoleonic armies, and Romanticism. In France, historians and critics such as Guizot, Thierry, Renan, and Taine followed Michelet's lead by attributing the characteristics of nations to their constituent races. Between 1853 and 1855 Joseph-Arthur, Comte de Gobineau published his influential *Essai sur l'inégalité des races humaines* which thematized the racial problem and declared it predominant over all other issues in history. Yet these historians did not voice uniform views on the question of whether racial purity was more desirable than racial braiding. Michelet, for instance, thought that an occasional infusion of barbarian blood would reinvigorate older civilized nations, whereas Gobineau argued that the imminent decline of France was due to racial intermingling, as a consequence of which social status was no longer based on racial descent, but on wealth.

It is hardly surprising that Flaubert's attitude toward racial questions was ambiguous. What can be said with certainty, however, is that he considered "race" an interesting issue, though he was not a racist. His diary and letters from his Oriental journey do not contain any disparaging remarks about other races. In *Salammbô* he presents the Carthaginians as an exclusive race that tenaciously adhered to the ancient Canaanite gods and missed the opportunity of expanding and solidifying Carthage into a truly North African empire. Yet in his description of the Punic Elders he points out that the physiognomies of some betrayed an admixture of African nomad ancestry, but he refrains from making any value judgments. He also read in Michelet's *Histoire romaine* that Hamilcar's bravery and outstanding qualities of military leadership derived from his North African heritage (his family came from Kyrene), while Hanno, greedy, ruthless, and incompetent at war, embodied the true Carthaginian. All this indicates that Flaubert may have favored a mingling of the races in *Salammbô*,[33] particularly in view of Michelet's implication, confirmed by Gobineau, that the Carthaginians, contemptible as they were, could only be improved by foreign admixture. On the other hand Flaubert deplored in his correspondence that "there was no [French] race any more!" or that in France "the aristocratic blood was exhausted,"[34] lamentations which ought, however, to be read with some caution.

What interested him much more as a writer and a thinker of the nineteenth century were two other aspects of the new racial consciousness. One of them clearly had to do with the fact that when filtered down to the crowd, racism could—like nationalism, democracy, and socialism—become an instrument of mass hysteria and unprecedented destructiveness. In two letters to George Sand shortly before the outbreak of the Franco-Prussian War Flaubert asks whether "we have returned once more to racial wars" and the horrible slaughter they entail, for which there is no reason but the lust of fighting for the sake of fighting." A fortnight later he writes more explicitly:

> Perhaps the racial wars will commence again. Before this century will have run its course, we shall see how several million people will kill each other in a single clash of arms. The entire Orient against the whole of Europe, the old world versus the new. Why not? The great collective works like the Suez Canal are perhaps—

in another form—projections and preparations for such immense conflicts we are yet unable to imagine![35]

These, then, were Flaubert's apprehensions about the future which, as a retrospective prophet, he depicted on a large canvas in *Salammbô* in terms of the social and racial conflict of the Mercenary War. The large number of combatants (at its peak the 40,000 rebellious soldiers were augmented by another 40,000 African insurgents and adventurers), the merciless nature of the conflict, and the shameless abuse and torture of prisoners (by rebels and Carthaginians alike) combined to make this struggle the kind of truceless war that was enacted once more in his own time and in the twentieth century. Obviously, the author of *Salammbô* shared the apprehension of many thinkers and artists of the nineteenth century that the involvement of the masses in politics would cause a lowering of standards and turn wars into instruments of savagery and mass destruction. This dread of politically and militarily mobilized masses was, for instance, also widespread among British intellectuals and members of the upper classes who believed that extension of the franchise beyond that of the Reforms of 1832 would bring about chaos and doom.

Another aspect of racial and class struggles that interested Flaubert was the question how a civilized group or class behaved when confronted by a relatively primitive aggressor. Would it be able to maintain civilized demeanor, or would it allow itself to be dragged down to the enemy's level? Evidence suggests that Flaubert considered "culture" but a thin veneer that readily peeled off when put under pressure. Counting its Canaanite-Phoenician origins, the civilization of Carthage was more than two thousand years old at the time of the Mercenary War. Nevertheless, it resorted all too quickly in kind to atrocities committed by the Barbarians. After some fierce fighting, especially the siege of Carthage and the battle for the city walls, no distinction exists any longer between Carthaginians and the Barbarians with respect to giving free reign to the lower instincts of vengeance, blood-thirstiness, and cruelty. Hamilcar, the Rich, the artisans, and the "people" are equally guilty of atrocities. The French experience of a comparable outburst of inhumanity during the June insurrection of 1848, which the military suppressed with rare brutality, became inscribed in Flaubert's consciousness. In this respect, too, ancient Carthage provided a suitable model for the present and the future.

The acts of organized violence Flaubert describes in his Punic novel as a precondition of charismatic rule and as a reflection of that of Napoleon III are all the more remarkable as an authorial accomplishment since he was not opposed to the emperor or Bonapartisme. Rather, the contrary is true, for as Jean-Paul Sartre has demonstrated along the lines of Flaubert's thought, "the personal regime, which is demonic in essence and anti-bourgeois in principle, cannot exist without constructing a strict hierarchic order from the top downward; hence it is the only [regime] that suits the artists or, at the very least, does not harm them. Therefore they must not question the Second Empire, but the props it had to pick [. . .]."[36] Flaubert not only forgave the emperor the insult of 1857 (the trial concerning *Madame Bovary),* but after being received in Saint-Gratien, Compiègne, and the Tuileries, and after he had indeed become the representative writer of the Second Empire, he identified with it. "Absolute art, pessimism, and the Second Empire, they all hang together."[37]

While Flaubert supported the Second Empire and the institution of personal rule, his attitude toward Napoleon III remained ambivalent. Occasionally he belittled him as "Badinguet," yet on the whole he approved of his reign for several reasons, both good and bad. As to the latter, the Realist writer and dissector of Emma Bovary was deeply gratified in perceiving the new president as a demoralizer who, on account of the poverty of his ideas and his lack of respect for everything, appeared to be the very leader the nation deserved: "[. . .] I am not of this century, for among my compatriots I feel as if I were in Nubia, and I am beginning seriously to admire the Prince-President who squashes this noble France under the heel of his boot. I would even kiss his behind in order to thank him personally, if there were not such a crowd that has already taken up this position."[38] Flaubert even took sardonic pleasure in the thought that with Louis Napoleon an incarnation of "le Garçon," a foolish, humdrum, and conventional bourgeois, had seized power in France. But this was only one side of the coin. Flattered by the attentions of the imperial family (including the soirées at the residence of Princess Mathilde), he evidently was not quite able to keep his distance from the court and came to appreciate the advantage of personal rule, particularly since he favored such government on ideological grounds. Undoubtedly it also pleased Flaubert that Napoleon III sought to aestheticize the state by supplanting the prosaic routine of public life during Louis Philippe's bourgeois July-Monarchy with the glitter and pomp of imperial ceremonials. Sartre even believed he had discovered correspondences between Louis Napoleon's coup d'état and that of Flaubert in the realm of literature: both were the results of serious application and concentration.

It should have become clear that Hamilcar was not conceived as an ancient embodiment of either Napoleon. He is considerably larger in stature than the second emperor of the French, and he differs in too many personal aspects from the first. Hamilcar is described in the process of carving out for himself the position of an ancient tyrant, according to Flaubert "the most splendid manifestation of man that ever was." Modern tyrants he held in lesser esteem; they struck him as "stupid, weak, and timid."[39] As a figure of antiquity, Barca is more original and daring than his modern European equivalents; everything he achieves he brings forth out of himself, whereas both Bonapartes can be seen as incarnations of the tempers of their times. They seized the opportunities their epochs offered by means of charismatic abilities, became focal points of specific political, social, economic, and moral conditions, and of the disposition of the nation as a whole. What Flaubert tried to portray in *Salammbô*, then, was not an ancient mask of particular French statesmen in his own age, but a political process disclosing the rise of the charismatic leader, of Bonapartism, and of the necessary preconditions, realities, and consequences of personal rule.

There are, to be sure, other parallels that can be drawn between the Punic Empire and modern France such as the similarity of their administrations in North Africa, the much-decried decadence of their civilizations, as well as possible analogies in the grandiose architectural reconstructions of Carthage and Paris. These correspondences have been treated by Anne Green. Nevertheless, a few annotations are necessary regarding Punic and French colonialism in present-day Tunisia and Algeria. Flaubert repeatedly emphasizes that Carthage exploited the native populations of its North African dominion, including the Numidians. Particularly in times of need it squeezed and pressed them as one does grapes at wine-making. As we have seen, the Punic state inflicted horrible punishments on those who failed to meet its requirements. The Numidian king Narr'havas explains his initial siding with the rebellious mercenaries with these very "facts." And there is the impressive metaphor/simile of the "Phoenician galley anchored on Libyan sand," which is rocked by the slightest storm because the suppressed natives join every invader. Undoubtedly Flaubert was very effective in presenting the Carthaginians as grasping masters whose subjects desired nothing as much as free themselves from their yoke. This would confirm Bernal's assertion that on such grounds and its well-publicized abominations the total destruction of Carthage was justified in the eyes of nineteenth-century Europeans and in Flaubert's.

Yet was it? As I have demonstrated, the sexual perversions of the Punics (e.g. holy prostitution, mass copulations, and orgies) may have attracted Flaubert to Carthage in the first place, for he and Du Camp engaged in comparable practices in the Orient, from Cairo to Beirut. Also, the sexual mores of the Parisian Bohème in Flaubert's time, especially the circle of the sculptor James Pradier, whose studio Flaubert frequented in the late 1840s and 1850s, were not that different from those of the Orient; if anything, they were more perplexing.[40] Concerning Punic colonialism, Flaubert unquestionably knew two publications that compared Carthaginian and French methods of administration in dependent territories: Saint-Marc Girardin's article, "De la Domination des Carthaginois et des Romains en Afrique comparée avec la domination française" (1841) and Simonde de Sismondi's *Les Colonies des anciens comparées à celle des modernes* (1837).[41] Both studies conclude that Carthaginian colonialism was more benign toward the native populations than that of modern France. For example, when French prisoners of war were murdered by Algerian freedom fighters, the French army responded with "razzias" in which natives were systematically slaughtered in order to intimidate the population as a whole and prepare it to submit more readily to French rule. The colonial French administration also expropriated the natives in order to settle French colonists. Of course Algerian Arabs and Berbers were not allowed to vote.

In his rendering of Carthaginian colonial measures, Flaubert obviously exaggerated their severity. One must assume that he who loved the Orient and did not voice any objections to the cudgelings in Alexandria, overstated the faults of the ancient Afro-Oriental empire in order to alarm his fellow Frenchmen about the perilous direction of their own government in Algeria. What should the fictional Carthaginians have done in lieu of their oppressiveness, emulated by the French? While it would be fashionable in today's sense of political correctness to demand that they should have built a multicultural society, such societies did not exist in antiquity nor in nineteenth-century Europe. In antiquity those genuinely "other" were "barbarians" or "gentiles" from Greek, Phoenician, and Jewish perspectives. In the nineteenth century such views continued to be upheld. Could Carthage have created a vast North African realm by granting citizenship to its subject peoples, as Rome did later?[42] Rome survived for several centuries after enacting such legislation, but it, too, perished in the end.

Notes and References

1. This criticism of Sainte-Beuve, which he advanced in his well known review in *Le Constitutionnel* (December 8, 15, and 22, 1862), lies at the heart of all subsequent rejections of *Salammbô* as an Oriental historical novel.

2. Georg Lukács, *The Historical Novel*, transl. H. and S. Mitchell (Boston: Beacon Press, 1963) 185.

3. Indeed, some archaeological discoveries were made long after Flaubert had published *Salammbô*. This also pertains to a number of important coins which were either found or identified later.

4-5. Christa Bevernis, "Vergangenheitsdarstellung und Gegenwartsbezug in Gustave Flauberts Roman *Salammbô*," *Beiträge zur romanischen Philologie*, XI (1972) 22-38 and 29. See also Monika Bosse and André Stoll, "Die Agonie des archaischen Orients—eine verschlüsselte Vision des Revolutionszeitalters," in Gustave Flaubert, *Salammbô*, transl. G. Brustgi (Frankfurt a.M.: Insel, 1979) 401-448; and Jeanne Bem, "Modernité de 'Salammbô,'" *Littérature*, 40 (1980).

6. As to Hasdrubal, Gilbert and Colette Charles-Picard write in Chapter V of their study *Daily Life in Carthage at the Time of Hannibal*, transl. A.E. Foster (New York: Macmillan, 1961), that Hasdrubal determined Punic policy because he controlled the main revenues of the state and commanded the only large military force.

7. Anne Green, *Flaubert and the Historical Novel—Salammbô Reassessed* (Cambridge, London, etc.: Cambridge University Press, 1982) 88.

8. Monika Bosse and André Stoll, "Die Agonie des archaischen Orients—eine verschlüsselte Vision des Revolutionszeitalters," 435.

9. Bevernis, "Vergangenheitsdarstellung und Gegenwartsbezug . . .," 29.

10. Flaubert, Letter to George Sand, October 4 or 5, 1871.

11. Flaubert, Letter to Louise Colet, May 15/16, 1852.

12. Anne Green, *Flaubert and the Historical Novel—Salammbô Reassessed*, 60.

13. Princess Mathilde, quoted in Flaubert, *Lettres inédites à la Princesse Mathilde*, ed. L. Conard (Paris: 1927) XXII.

14. Anatole France, *La Vie littéraire*, III (Paris: Calmann Levy, n.d.) 298-299.

15. See Eugen Haas, *Flaubert und die Politik*, Diss. (Heidelberg: 1931) 4-7.

16. Thomas Mann, *Essays of Three Decades*, transl. H.T. Lowe-Porter (New York: Knopf, 1948) 303.

17 See Flaubert, Letter to Louise Colet, January 10–11, 1854.

18 Flaubert, Letter to Sainte-Beuve, December 23–24, 1862.

19 In his essay "Flaubert et le réel," *Mercure de France*, Feb. 15, 1934, Jean-Jacques Mayoux asserts in a footnote that Hamilcar *is* Napoleon I.

20 Karl Hammer and P.C. Hartmann, ed. *Le Bonapartisme * Der Bonapartismus* (Zürich und München: Artemis, 1977).

21 Karl Ferdinand Werner, "Vorbemerkung," *ibid.*, XV–XVI.

22 Jean Tulard, "Aux Origines du Bonapartisme: Le culte de Napoléon," *ibid.*, 8.

23 Guided by the Code Napoléon as a guarantee of civil rights, the administration of Napoleon III regenerated the economic progress of the early 1840s through new banking institutions, international trade agreements, the tripling of railroad track, and public works improving the cities and harbors of France. Paris itself was transformed by the cutting of broad, tree-shaded avenues through ancient quarters, laying out large public parks, and the construction of monumental public buildings.

24 Karl Marx, *Der achtzehnte Brumaire des Louis Bonaparte* (1852), (Berlin: Dietz, 1946) 111–112 and 113. See also Karl Marx, *Die Klassenkämpfe in Frankreich 1848 bis 1850* (1850), (Berlin: Dietz, 1951).

25 Jeanne Bem, "Modernité de 'Salammbô,'" *Littérature,* 40 (1980) 24.

26 Karl Marx, *Der achtzehnte Brumaire des Louis Bonaparte,* 114. The theme of prostitution, male and female, is also ubiquitous in *L'Éducation sentimentale,* where it manifests itself with particular explicitness in the figures of the banker Dambreuse, his wife, and Rosanette.

27 This is a striking parallel to the reign of Napoleon III. Hamilcar not only poses as the spokesman of the people, but he also promised them their share in the golden future of Carthage. Indeed, once he launched his Hispanic venture after the conclusion of the Mercenary War, Carthage made a most speedy and remarkable recovery. Hispanic silver, labor, and troops provided the foundations of the Second Punic War with Rome. The North African metropolis enjoyed another, though short- lived, flourishing from which the people at large also benefited.

28 Bosse and Stoll, *op. cit.*, 433.

29 At the conclusion of *Wilhelm Meisters Lehrjahre* a comparable measure is enacted, when Mignon, another comet-like figure, is excluded from the rational Society of the Tower.

30 The claim of the authors above that Hamilcar denies the proletariat a future by sacrificing his slave's child in lieu of his own son, cannot be maintained. Cruel as the deed is, the interpretation is all too pointed. The son of a slave does not constitute the proletariat, nor does the sacrifice of this one child signal the destruction of an entire class.

An Allegory of Bonapartism

31 Michal P. Ginsburg, *Flaubert Writing* (Stanford, CA: Stanford University Press, 1986) 117–119.

32 Karl Marx, *Der achtzehnte Brumaire des Louis Bonaparte,* 17.

33 Anne Green sees in the breaking down of the walls separating the various sections of Carthage a symbol of the mixing of the races. See Green, *Flaubert and the Historical Novel—Salammbô Reassessed,* 68.

34 Flaubert, Letter to Louise Colet, March 25, 1853.

35 Flaubert, Letters to George Sand, July 20 and August 3, 1870.

36–37 Jean Paul Sartre, *L'Idiot de la famille: Gustave Flaubert de 1821 à 1857* (Paris: Gallimard, 1972) III, 463 and 469.

38 Flaubert, Letter to Louise Colet, May 29, 1852.

39 Flaubert, Letter to Louise Colet, August 6 or 7, 1846.

40 In mid-century fashionable Parisian society it was for example a disgrace to be seen with one's wife in the theater (only a mistress would do). As to sexuality, women were divided in two groups: those who were taboo and raised on a pedestal (mother, sister, bride) and available ones such as working girls (e.g the proverbial "grisette"), married women, and prostitutes. During the July monarchy of Louis-Philippe there was a proliferation of brothels in Paris, where customers could select from an extensive menu of sexual favors, including encounters with children and pregnant women. Child prostitution was not abolished in France untl 1908. See Francine du Plessix Gray, *Rage and Fire: A Life of Louise Colet* (New York, etc.: Simon and Schuster, 1994) 128–129.

41 Saint-Marc Girardin, "De la Domination des Carthaginois et des Romains en Afrique comparée avec la domination française," Revue des Deux Mondes, May 1, 1841, 413–414; and J.C.L. Simonde de Sismondi, *Les Colonies des anciens comparées à celles des modernes* (Geneva, 1837).

42 The Romans granted citizenship to their allies (socii) in 89 B.C.; the inclusion of all "free provincials" followed with considerable delay in the the *Constitutio Antoniniana* (A. D. 212).

Chapter V

Making the Old Orient Present

"In *Salammbô*," Lukács contends, "the tendencies of decline in the historical novel appear in concentrated form: the decorative monumentalization, the devitalizing, dehumanizing, and simultaneous privatization of history. History becomes a large, imposing stage for purely private, intimate and subjective happenings."[1] If one adds to these alleged flaws the charges of modernization (feelings, ideas, thoughts) and ubiquitous brutality, one has, together with disparaging remarks about Flaubert's "archeologism," all of Lukács's conceptual reservations about the Afro-Oriental narrative. Lukács does not view *Salammbô* as an isolated literary phenomenon, but as a representative work of the "new" historical fiction that also includes Sainte-Beuve's *Port-Royal* and the narratives of Conrad Ferdinand Meyer, as well as the aesthetically much lesser narratives by Felix Dahn and Georg Ebers. Within the larger scheme of the history of the genre, all of them are purported to reflect the "crisis of bourgeois realism."

According to Lukács and Barthes, this crisis was the direct result of the failure of the democratic-proletarian forces to gain power in 1848. The bourgeoisie reconfirmed once more its hold on the means of production, while ideologically it ceased to be the leading class in Western European nations. Instead, it subscribed to a flabby liberalism and promoted a simplified conception of progress. For the bourgeoisie defined progress as an orderly evolutionary process rather than one propelled by revolutions. Appropriately, Lukács holds that in the German-speaking countries the profoundly historical philosopher Hegel, who had formulated the dialectical method of development, fell from favor after 1848 and was supplanted by the anti-historical thinker Schopenhauer, and by Nietzsche. Most important, however, was the fact that in the aftermath of the abortive revolution and the suppression of the June insurrection in Paris the French people, and most others in Europe, were divided into "two nations" on political, economic, social, and ideological grounds. Marx, on the other hand, perceived the events of 1848–51 in France as a farcical detour, for how could the derailment of one revolution, aborted by the little schemer Louis Napoleon with "liquor and sausage" (his means of bribing the military), ultimately halt the inevitable historical process?

For Lukács, the reverberations of this event permeated all aspects of intellectual life, including history and art. Symptomatic of the new spirit was the esteem accorded to the historicism of Leopold von Ranke whose tenet that all epochs of history are equal before God provoked Lukács's ire. Ranke "denies the idea of a contradictory process of human advance" and claims that "history has no direction, no summits and no depressions."[2] Although Lukács acknowledges that Ranke's conception of history was formed prior to 1848, he dismisses the fact by arguing that it only became a dominant trend after the failed revolution (just as the ascendence of Schopenhauer). However, if one takes into account that historicism emerged in the works of Vico, Herder, Goethe, and the Romantic historians, the picture looks quite different, for ever since its inception historicism was a constituent element of "modern" historiography. Despite Lukács's claims to the contrary, it has also continued to be the principal approach of the discipline into the twentieth century. After its decline in the 1920s it was quite recently revived in the approaches of the New Historicists and multiculturalism.

Another kind of historiography to which Lukács objected was that based on racial distinctions. Although this strain had its origins in the Enlightenment's attempt to apply the findings of the natural sciences to the study of society and the past, it rather quickly collided with two of its principal ideas: those of tolerance and human brotherhood. For, as the New Historicists have shown, certain scientifically inspired "findings" of the Enlightenment eventually led to the justification of racism and colonialism. While in *Histoire de la conquête de l'Angleterre par les Normands* (1825) Augustin Thierry explains the emergence of modern European nations as the result of class struggles that were in part grounded in race (Saxons versus Normans in England, or Gauls versus Franks in France), and thereby presents a conception of history incorporating social progress as essential, this is no longer true of racial conceptions inspired by Charles Darwin. In Hippolyte Taine, with whom Flaubert was personally acquainted, race constitutes a basically ahistorical element among the three determinants of Naturalism—"race, milieu, moment"—which he proclaims as the foremost conditioners of human existence.

Taine also pays homage to Balzac's monumentalism, which becomes a characteristic feature of music, literature, and the fine arts in the second half of the nineteenth century (e.g. the oeuvres of Richard Wagner, Émile Zola, and Auguste Rodin).

Lukács detected echoes and premonitions of this creative volition in *Salammbô*. Most astounding is the fact that, as a socio-cultural critic, he failed to perceive the political relevance of the events depicted by Flaubert. Surely, his disinterest in matters lying outside his ideological orbit may account for his misreading of *Salammbô,* as he tended to discard historical phenomena which either did not contribute to social progress or oppose it decisively. Punic civilization, from which no direct connections to modern Europe were immediately obvious, could not seem to be of import to a critic concerned with "realities." His insistence on the exclusive significance of progress as defined by Marx's application of the dialectical method required that the forces and events portrayed in historical fiction themselves belong to the line of development designated as the only valid one. In its Afro-Oriental setting *Salammbô* does indeed present one of the most important problems of nineteenth-century French politics: charismatic leadership in the wake of social revolutions and the institutionalization of Bonapartism.

In lieu of Lukács's monolithic reading of history which, due to foregone conclusions, necessarily limits literary tradition to a slim canon, Walter Benjamin's theses on history and literary history in particular offer a more rewarding approach.[3] Accordingly, historical events and periods or, to be more precise, images of historical events and periods, become accessible only at certain times. Benjamin speaks of a kernel of time ("Zeitkern") in a given present encompassing both "what is known and in the knower"[4] that recognizes itself in a particular phase of the past. This, then, constitutes the spark that engenders historical encounter, as for instance that of Flaubert and Hamilcar Barca's Carthage. Far from being a subjective whim of the novelist, Flaubert's Punic setting was determined by the sociopolitical history of modern France, and by his own interests as a historically conditioned individual. Revolutionary politics and eroticism were the dominant themes of the author's most productive period, and in *Salammbô* he treated them with the consummate skill of the modern novelist and the dispassionate empathy one frequently encounters in superior historians, especially of the historicist school.

The charge of "modernization" is even more easily refuted. Since the past can only come alive and be representationally enlivened when the present beholder rethinks it (Dilthey/Croce), the perception of historical events must necessarily contain values of the present and its perspectives. Of course Lukács would argue that in the Western tradition nothing is foreign to us for the very reason that it is our tradition. But is it not conceivable that a given "foreign" historical period might arouse our interest, even if it were alien to us at first sight? It is possible to recognize that "exotic" historical events can very well serve the purpose of illuminating problems of a Western author's own society and of placing them into cognitive focus.

Lastly, is the "monumentality" of *Salammbô* really as inappropriate and false as Lukács holds? The impression of the grandiose arises from the raw materials of the novel provided by history (Polybius/Michelet), particularly from the large armies of the antagonists, the fierceness of the battle scenes, and the brutality accompanying most forms of human interaction in the course of the truceless war between Carthage and its former mercenaries. The rampant incidents of inhumanity in the novel contribute in Lukács's view directly to the readers' sense that they are witnessing events of monumental proportions. However, there is no question that the Mercenary War of three years was one of the major military conflicts in antiquity, with respect to the political and social stakes, and the scale on which it was carried out (e.g. 80,000 men besieging the walls of Carthage). Indeed, this is a large number of soldiers and warriors. When the Roman armies and their adversaries (Phillip of Macedon and Antiochus the Great of Syria) struggled for domination of the Eastern Mediterranean after the defeat of Hannibal, they did not muster more than 30,000 men each. Thus, the conflict Flaubert recreated was monumental in itself; moreover it had to be of a large scale if it were to reflect adequately the forces involved in the rise of Bonapartism.

A comparable case can be made regarding Lukács's objection to Flaubert's "archeologism," supposedly a sure indication of the fact that the Carthaginian material was beyond resurrection. But had Flaubert, well aware of the linguistic problems posed by a setting removed in place and time, not said that his presentation of Carthaginian life required a sort of "permanent transcription," and had he not emphasized in his replique to Sainte-Beuve that Phoenician terms were used quite sparingly in the narrative? In support of the novelist's contention one can add that his transposition was, by and large, geographical-exotic rather than ethnic-linguistic. By this method he achieved a degree of estrangement comparable to what a profusion of Punic names and designations would have effected. Thus, it is only fair to say that the ingrained misunderstanding of *Salammbô* must be ascribed to the failure of its critical detractors to read the work on its own terms, that is, as a new kind of historical novel with an Oriental setting. Flaubert's original contributions to the genre of historical fiction consist in the nature of the contemporary political problems he presents in an exotic milieu, in the types of protagonists he portrays, in the way he organizes his narrative, in his "écriture," and forms of discourse.

The analogies between the historical events of *Salammbô* and modern French, if not European, politics have been discussed at length. Such analogies constitute in themselves an innovation within the history of the genre, for until Flaubert historical novelists—except for Vigny—had described likeable average characters (representatives of the "people") in whose private lives the great happenings of their times reverberated. At the heart of most older historical novels the reader perceived the uplifting moral of a personal fable and, quite frequently, and with allowance being made for the ultimate imperfection of everything, a justification of the ways of the world. Since the genesis and first flowering of the genre coincided with Romanticism, the specimens of this period tend to confirm the existing socio-political order, primarily because of the conservative dispositions of the authors. In the United Kingdom and the German-speaking countries Romanticism regarded itself as an inexhaustible well of the national spirit which was marshalled in defense of national independence and national peculiarities during the French Revolutionary Wars and the Napoleonic era. Such decisive intellectual and moral engagement built on the belief in a preordained world order and saw the nation as an organism whose orderly development must not be tampered with from the outside. (Later developments showed that this notion, too, was an illusion).

In contrast to certainties of this kind, Flaubert's spiritual situation was markedly different, if not quite desperate. He scarcely believed in anything and wavered with dependable inconsistency in his social and political views. And he disliked or hated almost everything pertaining to public life because he felt manifestations of the will of the many were necessarily incorrigibly stupid. Yet Flaubert respected facts and had some faith in the positivist sciences. He spent his entire life in the service of art, although he often doubted its ultimate value. In this respect he shared the scruples of other bourgeois artists like Goethe and Thomas Mann who sometimes viewed their literary accomplishments with profound irony. In writing *Salammbô* Flaubert tried to apply the insights and methodologies of the natural and social sciences to the novel. This meant not only scrupulous research and the establishment of plausible data, but also comparative historical, cultural, and religious studies. For despite his seemingly disparaging remark that his Carthaginian novel was nothing but a "soap-bubble," Flaubert nevertheless tried to paint his panorama of Punic life, love, and politics with the greatest possible accuracy. Although he was but an amateur historian, he not only asked himself whether his portrayal of the lost civilization was coherent in itself, but also whether it could be true. It was for good reason that in his reply to Sainte-Beuve he compared his endeavor with the attempt "to fix a fata morgana." Striking as the simile is, it has frequently been cited by critics of the novel, but has also evidently failed to pique their interpretative curiosity. What does this bon mot imply, after all?

A fata morgana is an optical illusion produced by a layer of hot air across which are seen reflections of distant objects. An ephemeral image, the phenomenon of the fata morgana or mirage became known in Europe during the eighteenth century through travelogues depicting exhausted wanderers in arid lands suddenly confronted with visions of oases, ponds, and verdant splendors. The analogy of such a situation to Flaubert's own becomes transparent at once. After his immersion in the prosaic world of *Madame Bovary,* which could be likened to an odyssey in a spiritual wasteland, the conception of Carthage—original, colorful, and ferocious—must indeed have struck him like a mirage. But could such a fleeting vision be "fixed" and if so, how was that to be accomplished? By what means was it possible to conjure up the Punic metropolis once more from the sea of oblivion, endow it with seeming reality, and imbue it with life?

When he started the novel, Flaubert believed he was sufficiently familiar with the Punic capital to write a massive first chapter in the descriptive manner of Balzac. It was to introduce the reader to the location and topography of Carthage, views of the city, its people, their customs, religion, government, commerce, and industries. This chapter has been lost, but Max Aprile has ingeniously and patiently reconstructed it from Flaubert's draft papers and provided it with an explanatory essay.[5] The decision of the novelist to delete this chapter was a prudent one. To take up the comparison with Balzac once more, it is obvious that Flaubert's knowledge of Carthage was greatly inferior to his predecessor's familiarity with Saumur or Paris. Because of the indeterminacy of historical Carthage, many of its aspects and characteristics remained open questions and would have been presented discursively, uninterrupted by action. Another disadvantage of this mode of presentation lay in its point of view since it was conveyed by a third person "omniscient" narrator.

Instead of confronting his readers and critics with such an extensive description, Flaubert opted for breaking up the chapter in order to integrate information about the maritime republic in bits and pieces in the narrative as a whole. This practice offered the advantage that the point of view could be multiplied, thus diminishing the principal narrator's responsibility for the correctness of the facts. Free indirect discourse, public speeches, and dialogues are the major forms of substitution for the omniscient narrator's voice. The three descriptions of the city in Chapters I, IV, and VII of the definitive edition confirm this point. By means of indirect discourse they convey images of the city through the perceptions of Mâtho and Spendius, the barbarian army, and Hamilcar. Yet Flaubert was not content with creating a deceptively solid physical setting down to the last plausible detail of weapons, household furniture, perfumes, and trinkets (G.W.F. Hegel on the epic) with the help of painstaking research, scholarship and imaginative construction, but he also relied on the psychology of his figures, on striking images, as well his treartment of time in order to meet the challenge.

The "écriture" of *Salammbô*

It has been the practice of literary historians and critics to describe, analyze, and evaluate Flaubert's style.[6] However, over forty years ago Roland Barthes and the Deconstructionists coined the technical term "écriture" as opposed to style, in order to distinguish consciously chosen elements from "natural" ones in an author's writing. Under the name of style, Barthes claims, "a self-sufficient language is evolved which has its roots only in the depths of the author's personal and secret mythology, that subnature of expression where the first coition of words and things takes place, where once and for all the great verbal themes of his existence come to be installed. Whatever its sophistication, style has always something crude about it: it is a form with no clear destination, the product of a thrust, not an intention, and, as it were, a vertical and lonely dimension of thought." Hence, "imagery, delivery, vocabulary spring from the body and past of the writer and gradually become the very reflexes of his art."[7] 'Écriture," on the other hand, is the result of a writer's confrontation with society where he makes conscious decisions about the purpose of his work, his rhetoric, tone, and morals. These factors combine to make écriture an act of literary engagement emanating from the writer's freedom to respond in a chosen way to challenges posed by his time. According to Barthes, a modern writer[8] can select one of several possible écritures, yet the ultimate determinant is and remains his conscience.

If one accepts Barthes's thesis that images are subsumed under the concept of style, distinctions must be made, for there are different kinds of images. Barthes's coordination of image and style surely is most appropriate for metaphor, the form of imagery that reveals more than anything else the quality of a style since it is the purest expression of a writer's imaginative originality. Matters are altogether different with similes and symbols, which in contrast to metaphors are consciously sought or constructed, and therefore are the results of intellectual application. In Flaubert's texts similes occur with much higher frequency than metaphors, a fact for which there are sound reasons. Flaubert was not a poet, and a metaphorical style was not one of his innate gifts. He lived, moreover, in an age in which confidence in the natural and social sciences steadily gathered strength. It is well known that Flaubert set himself the goal of becoming a scientific writer, and that he was determined to live up to the obligations of such a profession. Lastly, during his aesthetically and politically formative years he lived in a society dominated by the bourgeoisie which he hated with a passion and remarkable persistence. Thus, he did not identify with the social world of his time and, innate gifts aside, was unable to write in a predominantly metaphorical style which equates disparate things on the strength of the author's sense of being and his poetic imagination. Also, as a scientific writer, he could not equate different phenomena. Instead, Flaubert's descriptions and imagistic comparisons seek to approximate a thing as closely as possible, an intent that requires the simile.

This method of gradual approximation to the true nature of an object, can be observed in *Salammbô*. One such instance is the afore-cited harbor scene at the opening of Chapter VII when the Moon Herald first notices "something like a bird skimming the surface of the sea with its long wings," only to correct his impression shortly thereafter by recognizing the phenomenon as "a ship with three banks of oars." Another such example occurs at the end of Chapter III: "Suddenly he [Schahabbarim] saw on the horizon, behind Tunis, what looked like wisps of fog, trailing along the ground; then there was a great curtain of grey dust extending vertically, and in the eddies of this numerous throng appeared the heads of dromedaries, lances, shields. It was the Barbarians' army advancing on Carthage" (57). In this case the perception is set right three times. Wisps of fog turn for the beholder into a curtain of grey dust out of which components of an army appear, and finally the apparition is recognized as the mercenary host. What Flaubert is enacting here is not the drama of language—in other words, not his authorial despair over the inability of language to describe reality in a reliable manner—but he is depicting the stages of the cognitive process. At its end, the object emerges as what it really is, and it is named. The initial and the last perceptions are not interchangeable; rather, the final perception blots out the first two and subsumes the third. Fog moving toward the city would not endanger it, whereas the Barbarians' army threatens its very existence. The precise description of the approaching enemy host across the isthmus is based on Flaubert's observations of oncoming caravans in the deserts of Egypt, which he minutely recorded.[9] The trend in the scholarship of our time to view such passages as examples of metonymy is based on the erroneous assumption that utterly different things can be equated.[10] Instead, the cited passage is an example of synecdoche. Yet if metaphor and metonymy are not Flaubert's favored figures of speech in *Salammbô*, neither is synecdoche. Granted that the depiction of the barbarian army's march on the Punic capital is an outstanding illustration of synecdoche (where a part or parts stand for the whole), in the same way the image is outstanding, it is also rare and isolated in the text. For Flaubert's uncertainties about the very characteristics of Carthage did not allow him to make synecdoche his dominant trope. Rather, all images are undermined by the pervasive trope of irony.

Salammbô presented the additional problem that except for the outline of the military action, a handful of names and brief characterizations, as well as some explanations of the causes of the Mercenary War, the author could not be sure of much regarding Carthage. The method of analogy, on which he relied and eloquently defended against the archaeologist Froehner,[11] points to his presentational goal of approximation (i.e. allegory) in lieu of equation (metaphor or symbol). To turn to the images involving serpents, snakes, vipers, and dragons: Undoubtedly, they were not part of the novelist's early experiences, and thus not personal-natural givens. As creatures indigenous to the homeland of the Canaanites and North Africa, the serpent images of *Salammbô* are freely chosen, though suggested by the setting of the novel and the bible. Hence my reservations voiced above with respect to Roland Barthes's assertion that images are components of style rather than écriture. In Flaubert the contrary seems to be true.

What are the obligations of the scientifically oriented writer, as Flaubert sees them, and what is their impact on his historical Oriental novel? He was no moralizer in the sense of his English contemporaries Dickens or George Eliot, nor a Realist writer of fairy-tales like the German-Swiss Gottfried Keller, and he did not believe it was his task to portray a better world. Instead, Flaubert wished to describe things and events as they "really" were, or how they most likely have been; he wished to show, to disclose, and to reveal how things were in themselves to the complete exclusion of his own likes and dislikes, as he insisted again and again in his numerous letters to Louise Colet. Since he disapproved of most things he observed in his own time (e.g. the social structure and its constraints, the quality of life, and the individual's prospects of realizing one's aspirations), and since he thought that those in power were quite successful in concealing their abuse of power, his acts of representational disclosure often turn into deeds of unmasking. In *Salammbô* the social, political, and personal preconditions of charismatic rule are brilliantly described, as well as the horror and the suffering meted out in the process of establishing such rule.

Flaubert's determination to reveal the truth by unmasking reprehensible social and political conditions and practices in nineteenth-century France by means of a historical novel about Carthage deserves all the more appreciation as the author was lionized by the highest representatives of the Second Empire. However, his scrupulous honesty and his painstaking endeavors to get to the heart of things and to make the truth visible with the help of his consummate skills, was a decision of conscience, an act in the spirit of the yet unborn Existentialist philosophy. It was, above all, a crucial resolve regarding his écriture in the essential sense of Barthes's definition of the term. It would certainly have been appropriate for Barthes (and Sartre) to emphasize this aspect of Flaubert's uncompromising art, rather than the undisputed, and indisputable, fact that like other representative writers after 1848 he achieved what he achieved primarily because of hard work. In any case, Barthes failed to perceive the politically subversive criticism of *Salammbô,* and so did Lukács and Sartre.[12] In all three, Flaubert appears once again as an antibourgeois bourgeois novelist who bites the hand that has been feeding him (e.g. his bourgeois class), but who nevertheless refrains from challenging directly the entire socio-political order in which he flourished. The preceding analysis of *Salammbô* has shown that in this historical novel, seemingly utterly detached from French life in the nineteenth century, Flaubert was eminently successful in unmasking its socio-economic and political inadequacies by means of an Oriental foil.

Of course the modes in which Flaubert cast his historical narrative are also part of his écriture. For Hayden White, emplotment, formal argument, and trope in a given writer ultimately derive from his ideology. As has been shown, Flaubert did not have an explicitly formulated ideology, although he was, by and large, a conservative, if not a reactionary, with occasional outbursts of anarchist sentiment. The emplotment of his Carthaginian novel is satirical, a classification which applies to both strains of the narrative. To be sure, the story of Salammbô displays features of tragedy, but these elements are ultimately subordinated to the rules of power politics which must, of necessity, be coordinated with the norms of satire. "The advent of the satirical mode signals a conviction that the world has grown old."[13] With the end of Carthage less than one hundred years away, a historical fact, and France, as Flaubert thought, tottering towards its undoing, a satirical emplotment of his novel was justified.

Flaubert's formal, or discursive, argument is mechanistic. Surely, as a creative writer he must have been tempted to emulate the formist stance (of which Michelet was an outstanding practitioner). This historical school is distinguished for depicting history in all its variety, color, and vividness. Nevertheless, the author of *Salammbô* obviously opted for a mechanistic conception of history with its cyclical laws Vico had proclaimed. The very fact that even the great Hamilcar's almost superhuman efforts (not to speak of the incomparable deeds of his son Hannibal) led to nothing less than the destruction of Carthage, appears to confirm the theory that history is fatalistic. By 146 B.C., the history of Carthage had run its course.

In the absence of a firm ideological premise, the trope of irony becomes instrumental in Flaubert's work. All-pervasive in *Madame Bovary, L'Éducation sentimentale, Bouvard et Pécuchet,* as well as in *Trois Contes,* it also constitutes the principal force in the casting of his Oriental historical novel. In contrast to the tropes of metaphor, metonymy, and synecdoche, figures of speech that may be considered naïve since in them the object and its signification presumably coalesce, the trope of irony stands as a "sentimental," i.e. self-conscious counterpart. This distinction, which is indebted to Friedrich Schiller's essay "Über naive und sentimentalische Dichtung" (1795)[14] and draws on the latter's definition of satire deduced from Kantian aesthetics, most likely forms the basis of White's finding that irony "is in one sense metaphorical, for it is deployed in the self-conscious awareness of the possible misuse of figurative language. Irony presupposes the occupation of a 'realistic' perspective on reality"; yet it also "points to the potential foolishness of all linguistic characterizations of reality as much as to the absurdity of the beliefs it parodies."[15]

Although there are different kinds of irony, this trope is, in cultural terms, a late mode of expression. While Romantic irony, for example, actualizes the discrepancy between the artist's aspirations toward the infinite and the poverty of his fragmentary achievements [Friedrich Schlegel's highly self-conscious novel *Lucinde* (1799) is a salient illustration], the ideal nevertheless persisted like a Platonic idea, or a non-contingent mathematical figure, precisely because it never existed. In contrast, this is no longer the case in the age of Realist irony. For, as Realist writers discovered, the rational conquest of reality only led to the insight that it was ultimately meaningless.[16] At the time when he undertook the project of *Salammbô*, Flaubert still believed that the two muses of the modern age were history and science. Yet even the Afro-Oriental world of ancient Carthage, to which he had hoped to escape after laboring in the deprecated world of *Madame Bovary*, proved inadequate to his revived Romantic expectations. Except for their more colorful milieu and trappings, Carthaginian society and politics turned out to be allegories of modernity. As a result, the trope of irony permeates his historical novel.

"[. . .] as the basis of a world view," Hayden White writes, "irony tends to dissolve all belief in the possibility of positive political action. In its apprehension of the folly or absurdity of the human condition, it tends to engender belief in the 'madness' of civilization and to inspire a Mandarin-like disdain for those seeking to grasp the nature of social reality in either science or art."[17] This observation applies only partially to *Salammbô*. Although the novel can be read as an unmasking of the madness of civilization, its author was also convinced of having properly depicted Carthage's upper classes, especially since he had recognized in them striking correspondences to the French bourgeoisie of his own time. Above all, he had masterfully traced the nineteenth-century French political phenomenon of the charismatic leader. As the author shows, the rise of the Punic tyrant required, just as in modern France, the connivance of the bourgeoisie.

In Flaubert's uses of irony, the trope becomes a scalpel that dissects the powerful social classes of Punic merchants and landowners in order to lay bare their compulsive motivations of avarice, greed, selfishness, and jealousy. Irony also dispels the notion that "culture" is capable of protecting man from his own lower impulses. As Flaubert's saga of the Mercenary War demonstrates, a nation's culture and personal culture do not amount to much more than a thin veneer. The scalpel of irony cuts away the embellishing cover when the former masters of North Africa are confronted by a barbarian host and must fight for their own survival. In this extreme situation of "either/or" they readily adopt the uncivilized practices of their barbarian enemies. In addition, the irony of *Salammbô* also teaches the lesson, in this particular instance in complete accord with Flaubert's mechanistic "formal argument," that the efforts of individuals, however great they may be, are nonetheless to no avail when pitted against the inevitable march of history.

Unquestionably, Flaubert's reliance on irony as his trope for *Salammbô* was a conscious decision. But why did he utilize this trope which he chose for his narratives with contemporary settings since he had wished to depict another world in his historical novel, "loin du monde moderne dont j'ai plein le dos"? Obviously he wished to drive home an alarming point by revealing undeniable correspondences between his own time and the Carthaginian past: The other is but a variation of the same. His choice of irony as the all-pervasive trope in *Salammbô* is conscious, indeed, for it constitutes a crucial force in his écriture.

Discourse, Dialogic Failure, and Intratextuality

Aside from creating a Punic setting acceptable to the reader accustomed to the conventions of the Realist novel, a formidable problem Flaubert confronted was that of language. In 1858 he gave succinct expression to an important aspect of the challenge: "No one since the beginning of literature has ever undertaken such an insane project. It's bristling with difficulties. To make people speak a language in which they didn't think!"[18] The question how to let the ancient Carthaginians, an Oriental people with an alien culture dominated by strange gods, utter their concerns in modern French, was but part of the problem. The stilted dialogues of the medieval figures of *Ivanhoe* illustrate the hazards of recreating the speech of a cultural whole wholly past. Yet was Scott's task not considerably easier since he evoked an older form of his own language of which substantial documents existed? The father of the modern historical novel was quite familiar with medieval British culture, and he practised a derivation of medieval European Christianity. The reverse of the problem which Flaubert confronted with his project must have troubled him all the more: Could he describe how the Carthaginians thought and felt since he did not know their language?

While the author of *Salammbô* is beset by doubts and uncertainties, the narrator of the novel "knows"[19] the Punic capital, its people, and its hinterland. In the case of Flaubert's novels, the author and narrator are particularly close since the latter is not dramatized and remains "impassible" in regard to the characters he presents and the events he relates. Thus, there is little difference between the author Flaubert and his narrator except for their attitudes towards narrative discourse. The author struggles with every word and sentence, whereas the equally heterodiegetic narrator delivers his discourse with seeming ease. The two may be distinguished in another way. The author creates the fictional illusion of a real world and its indigenous life, and the narrator conveys it as a matter of fact.

As is customary in the vast majority of novels, the narrative alternates between scenic representation, which not infrequently takes the forms of the tableau, and summary. In scenic representation people, objects, and events are shown, in the summary the narrator tells about them. Flaubert's summaries are often enlivened by memorable images and epic similes, at times they are rather laconic. It stands to reason that scenic representations show such things and events the author was most knowledgeable about. In Gérard Genette's understanding of narrative discourse, the narrator has four functions: Besides his main task of conveying the "story", he has a "directing function," addresses the (ideal) narratee, and plays an "emotive" role.[20]

While in *Salammbô* the narrator's personal presence is hard to detect, he nevertheless guides the reader by providing signals concerning the narrative text. Examples of such signalling are the repeated references to Hamilcar's absence in Chapters I–VI, which awaken and steadily increase the reader's curiosity about this figure which looms large in the consciousness of those present and whose name is constantly on their lips. As to Hamilcar himself, the narrator's directing and emotive functions coalesce at the very end of Chapter VI where in an instance of psychonarration regarding the public's faith in his leadership, the arrival of the anxiously expected savior is heralded. To be sure, this paragraph of three lines would perfectly suffice to prepare the opening of Chapter VII which is couched in mythologizing language, but the narrator adds one final short paragraph relating Salammbô's nightmares arising from her sight of the zaïmph: "[. . .] she woke up screaming with terror. Every day she sent food into the temples, her servant Tanaach was worn out with obeying her orders, and Schahabarim never left her" (104).

The few sentences emphasize Salammbô's firm belief in the reality of the goddess Tanit whom she seeks to placate through offerings. The fact that this information about her devoutness immediately precedes the description of Hamilcar's return invites a direct comparison between the religiosity of father and daughter, for the reader learns a few pages later that the maritime suffete banishes "from his thoughts every form, every symbol and name of the Gods, the better to grasp the unchanging spirit behind appearances" (107). In other words, the narrator makes it plain that Salammbô and her sire live in different worlds. On the personal level this difference has led to an estrangement. It is not the father who comforts and reassures the terrorized young woman in her need, but the priest Schahabarim. This rift between the father's and daughter's approaches to things is not expressly stated by the narrator, but an issue of "intratextuality."[21] It is dramatized in their first encounter which occurs in the very place where Salammbô pacified the riotous mercenaries only to become the cause of the deadly rivalry between Narr'havas and Mâtho: Hamilcar's gardens. As to narratorial signals concerning the titular heroine, her ecstatic nature manifested in the first chapter explains her ardent patriotism and her ability to embrace Mâtho (Chapters X and XI) as an incarnation of Moloch. Even more explicit are the multiple death-omens that foreshadow her stunning demise in the last chapter.

Undoutedly Flaubert wrote for the ideal reader, just as the narrator addresses the ideal narratee. Stendhal dedicated *Le Rouge et le Noir* to "the happy few," and he expressed the apprehension that his novel might not be understood for another two generations. Meanwhile we have realized that there is no single correct reading of a given narrative. Instead, every literary narrative should be read from a double perspective, one attempting to empathize with the authorial intention, the other relating to the reader's own context of temporality.[22] With this solution Mikhail Bakhtin sought to do justice to the author and his time while acknowledging that a historical work can acquire meaning only when it is related to the reader's own horizon of expectation, preferably in the form of a challenge. In any case, this solution does take the sting out of the heated controversy surrounding authorial intentionality. However, by recognizing aspects of one's own present in the narrated image of the past, the reader enters into a dialogue with this particular image of the past, and in this very sense every historical narrative (provided it is not purely antiquarian in Nietzsche's sense) must be called dialogical in nature.

Even a quick reading of *Salammbô* shows that this work contains even less dialogue than Flaubert's other novels. One reason for this difference has already been pointed out: the author's lack of knowledge of neo-Phoenician and his uncertainty how the Carthaginians thought and felt. To make matters worse, Flaubert had to make them speak in a credible manner in modern French. Since one of the foremost concerns of the author was the avoidance of absurdities, he was prudent to limit dialogue to a necessary minimum. However, there was a second reason for the paucity of dialogue in the Punic novel which essentially constituted a problem for the writer Flaubert. Salammbô's encounter with her father in Chapter VII demonstrates that the two fail to understand each other verbally. Their abortive attempt to communicate is symptomatic for the entire narrative. Its protagonists do not talk to each other, they rather speak past one another. As conversation partners they are not aware of the other's situation, motivation, and intention. They live in different worlds, have strong, if not exclusive, personal desires, and little empathy. They act like monomaniacs, obsessed by one idea to the pursuit of which they have wholly devoted themselves. This is the primary cause underlying their inability to "hear" the other and the intonations of his or her voice. (In his exchange with his daughter, by the way, Hamilcar does not even want to hear). Hugo Friedrich has offered additional explanations for this non-existence of communication. Accordingly, most protagonists of Flaubert's novels actually have nothing to say, either to one another, or in the form of monologues. Their "fate is not the confrontation between a projecting self and a contrary condition, but it consists in a soul overtaken by situations, although the soul had never wished for such situations, nor had it ever willed anything. Charles Bovary, Mâtho, Frédéric Moreau, Saint Julien are individuals who change without expression [. . .] from one condition to another. They are driftwood on the indifferently flowing stream of fate."[23]

Friedrich's listing of figures who are unaware of their fate or remain remarkably inarticulate about it, could easily be expanded by the inclusion of comparably disposed characters such as Jacques and Marie Arnoux, Dussardier, and Louise. Conspicuously absent from this enumeration are, however, Emma Bovary, Salammbô, Hamilcar, Schahabarim, Spendius, as well as Bouvard and Pécuchet. Emma and the two former clerks (the latter resemble parodistic embodiments of Faustian man) are excluded, for despite their different personalities and desires, all three are modern seekers and display a good deal of nervous energy. On the other hand, except for Mâtho, the characters of the Punic novel cannot be discussed in the same way since they are figures from antiquity. As such, they do not appear to have much of an inner life, or to put it differently, Flaubert appears to have conformed to the conventions of the classical epic by not displaying their inner lives. Instead, these characters realize themselves through actions and deeds. Nevertheless, in a few instances that which inwardly moves them is shown by means of free indirect discourse, the indirect mode, and psycho-narration. These isolated glimpses at the contents of their consciousness reveal their essential interests and make *Salammbô* a novel in which heterology constitutes an important element.

The main characters think and speak in the languages reflecting their provenance, profession, and personal desires or ambitions. Hence each voice is not pure in the heterologic sense, but a mixture of languages. For example, in Salammbô's utterances the language of the prehistorical, chthonic Canaanite religion fuses with the language of a Punic princess and that of an ecstatically disposed virgin with vague erotic urges. Hamilcar, on the other hand, thinks, feels, and speaks the language of power. The liberated slave Spendius expresses himself in terms of servility and resentment reflecting his former social status, and in the language of his desire, that of freedom. Shortly after the mercenaries have liberated him, he offers his services to Mâtho and acknowledges him as his new master: "You freed me from prison. I am yours! You are my master! Give me your orders" (29).

It is noteworthy that in *Salammbô* the most important and extensive figural utterances are made in the form of public addresses. This pertains, above all, to the titular heroine, the freedman Spendius, and the Carthaginian leaders Hanno and Hamilcar. In *The Poetics of Prose* Todorov distinguishes between "speech as action," which is accompanied by risk (and frequently linked to rebellion), and "speech as narrative," an art that is primarily enacted by some sort of bard within the narrative to provide an audience with pleasure. Salammbô's narration of Phoenician myths in Chapter I, a chant she accompanies on the lyre, obviously is of the latter type, for it is meant to entertain the riotous soldiers and, thereby, please and appease them. Although she presents the adventures of Melkarth in an old Canaanite dialect which the Barbarians do not understand, she nevertheless achieves her end through her sheer presence and manner of presentation. Thus, Salammbô's success confirms Todorov's assertion that an "auditor never remarks on the content of the song but only on the bard's art and his voice."[24] Even Hanno's dishonest address to the mercenaries awaiting their pay is more of a narrative than "speech-as-action," for it is a litany of the woes of Carthage and the Rich who, he suggests, bear the brunt of dire post-war times.

In the *Odyssey,* Todorov has pointed out, the characters lie to one another more often than not, and so does Hanno to the disgruntled soldiers in order to persuade them that the little money he has brought with him is all the Republic can spare at the moment. The ineffectiveness of his speech has been assured from the very beginning since the mercenaries do not understand Punic. In contrast to Salammbô, his physical presence and his delivery neither intrigue nor captivate the soldiers. One of the foremost plutocrats of Carthage, it is characteristic of Hanno that his language emphasizes words and concepts denoting expenses, losses, accounts, merchandise. Beyond all this, however, the suffete's speech also contains direct threats, above all that of making Carthaginian slaves of the "free" mercenaries. Hanno's lies and misrepresentations engender even bolder lies when Spendius proceeds to "translate" them into the major languages of the mercenaries assembled:

> "First he [Hanno] said that all the Gods of other peoples were only dream things compared to the Gods of Carthage! He called you cowards, thieves, liars, dogs and sons of bitches! The Republic, but for you (he said) would not be compelled to pay the Romans tribute; and through your excesses you have exhausted its stock of perfumes, spices, slaves, and silphium, for you are in league with the nomads on the Cyrenaican frontier! But the guilty will be punished! He read out the list of their punishments; they will be sent to work at paving the streets, fitting out ships, embellishing the Syssitia, and the others will be sent to scratch the earth in the Cantabrian mines!" (47)

Spendius pours salt into the troop's emotional wounds. Because of his clever repetition of a few proper names Hanno had used, his listeners are convinced that he is giving them a truthful account of the suffete's speech. The purpose of his forgery is to incite the soldiers into rebellion against their employer Carthage, for this is his only chance of retaining his newly gained freedom. While Hanno's lies are prompted by Carthaginian avarice and miserliness which he personally embodies, those of Spendius arise from his fear of being enslaved once again.

The other outstanding speech is that of Hamilcar in the Council of Elders; it constitutes a foil to Hanno's inept utterances. Delivered partially in the prophetic future tense, this powerful oration visualizes the fall and destruction of Carthage. The future of this passage contains two perspectives in that it is prospective from Hamilcar's point of view, but retrospective from the positions of the narrator and reader. In Flaubert's historical novel the great oral presentations and speeches encompass the principal levels of time: Salammbô evokes the mythical and the historical past (the latter in the war with Rome), Hanno and Spendius the present, whereas it is Hamilcar alone who envisions the future.

Additional forms of speech in *Salammbô* are free indirect discourse, the indirect mode, and psycho-narration.[25] Here is an excerpt from the extensive passage displaying Hamilcar's subterranean treasures of precious stones and metals, another part of which has been cited previously:

> The light from the stones and the flame of the lamp were reflected in the great golden shields. Hamilcar stood smiling, arms crossed—and he did not so much

delight in the sight as in awareness of his wealth. It was inaccessible, inexhaustible, infinite. His ancestors, sleeping beneath his steps transmitted to his heart something of their eternity. He felt very near the underground spirits. It was like a Cabirus's joy; and the great rays of light striking his face seemed to him like the end of an invisible network which spanned abysses to attach him to the center of the world. (129)

Scrutiny of this paragraph discloses that it constitutes more than straightforward description, for it contains changes in perspective and voice. To be sure, the first sentence continues in the same manner in which the precious stones were named and characterized in the preceding paragraph. The opening of the next sentence which relates Hamilcar's pose is also conveyed from the narrator's point of view, whereas the utterance after the dash seems at least open to question. Is it the Punic leader who realizes that he enjoys more the awareness of his wealth than its sight, or is it the narrator's perception? Who considers these riches "inaccessible, inexhaustible, infinite"? Undoubtedly this must be the voice of Hamilcar presented by the device of free indirect discourse. For it can only be he who holds this triadic esteem of his own resources, whereas the narrator knows better. The following two sentences refer to the Barca ancestors and the reassuring presence of their spirits. However, the last sentence braids the narrator's and Hamilcar's perspectives. "It was like a Cabirus's joy" must be the narrator's observation, as it is not probable that the suffete would have likened himself in this situation to a Cabirus, a special type of god. The long clause after the semicolon describes once again Hamilcar's own reflection. It is his intuition that the blazing rays springing off the golden shields form a network connecting him to the center of the earth.

In *Salammbô,* just as in Flaubert's other narratives, the transitions from the narrator's voice to the figural ones are fluid; at times it is difficult, and occasionally impossible, to distinguish one from the other. Free indirect discourse allows the narrator to describe figural consciousness. In the case of Flaubert's narratives this is done in the narrator's language. Thus the perspective is that of the character or figure, yet the style is typically Flaubertian. Vaheed Ramazani has described this practice in *The Free Indirect Mode:* "In this problematic instance of free indirect discourse, as in its more canonical manifestation, the rhythmic, syntactic, and idiomatic sameness of narratorial and figural voices constitutes an 'innocently unaware' nondifferentiation of different perspectives."[26] It should also be pointed out that according to Ramazani Flaubert's dictum, "Madame Bovary, c'est moi," ironically includes the "style" of the narrative which renders "undifferentiable the verbal and nonverbal, the conscious and unconscious, the narratorial and the figural."[27] In the case of his historical novel, the voice of the narrator also is that of Salammbô, Hamilcar, Schahabarim, and Spendius whose consciousness he enters. These are the only figures in the narrative who are portrayed from the inside.

The fact that the figures of his novel think and feel in Flaubert's very own language means that they are not entirely independent. Rather, they are caught up in his écriture, living beings in the Flaubertian "trottoir roulant." This predominance of the narratorial voice over the figural voices, or its presence in their unvoiced utterances, makes genuine dialogue between the author/narrator and his characters impossible in the sense of what Bakhtin ascribes to Dostoevsky and his human creations.[28] To put it differently, the characters of *Salammbô* are not sufficiently autonomous to enter into a real dialogue with the author/narrator. Instead, they appear to be other possibilities of his own self. This practice stands in sharp contrast to Dostoevesky's, for his extraordinary negative capability enabled him to conceive of figures seemingly different from himself. In the course of his narratives he also refrained from encroaching on the personal space he had granted them at the outset. In this respect the novelist Dostoevsky is comparable to the God of the Judeo-Christian tradition who granted Adam and Eve freedom of the will and made them responsible for their words and deeds. In conjunction with his narrator, on the other hand, the author Flaubert subjects the very figures he imbues with life to the requirements of his écriture and to one of its most salient features: the trope of irony. This is the reason why *Salammbô*, which initially was conceived as a counter-statement to *Madame Bovary* by presenting events in the antique Orient, ultimately offers, despite its more grandiose and colorful "realities," similar insights about the human condition.

There exists, then, a "dialogic problem" in Flaubert's narratives. The characters speak to one another, but they do not communicate, and the author/narrator cannot enter into a real dialogue with his figures because his very écriture does not allow them sufficient autonomy. However, like all successful novels *Salammbô* contains other dialogic elements that contribute to the formation of the human and ideological matrix of the narrative. The speeches of the protagonists are an excellent example of this particular form of dialogism or intratextuality. In his definition of the dialogic essence of the utterance, Bakhtin offers a succinct formulation:

> No member of the verbal community can ever find words in the language that are neutral, exempt from the aspirations and evaluations of the other, uninhabited by

the other's voice. On the contrary, he receives the word by the other's voice and it remains filled with that voice. He intervenes in his own context from another context, already penetrated by the other's intentions. His own intention finds a world already lived in.[29]

This affirmation makes sense and is acceptable in all its ramifications. As the most extensive utterances beside the narrator's conveyance of the story and his discourse, the public speeches of the figures are of particular interest. A look at their content and delivery discloses a curious fact. In contrast to the failure of person-to-person dialogue, they prove to be highly effective. Salammbô's narrative performance pacifies the marauding soldiers, Spendius's "translation" of Hanno's speech prompts them into open defiance, and Hamilcar's prophetic oration fills the Council of Elders with fear and trembling and prepares his rise to extraordinary power. Why, then, is there such a difference in effectiveness between straight dialogue and public speaking? To paraphrase Bakhtin, an utterance is a three-role-drama enacted "between author, listener, and those whose words resonate in the words of the author."[30] As to figural discourse in the novel, one must add a fourth component: the reader who is usually better informed to perceive dialogism in the form of intratextuality. Except for Hanno and Gisco, the figures of *Salammbô* who engage in public speaking are successful because they know their audience and its disposition, they are skilled mass-psychologists who can play on and manipulate the feelings of their listeners. The same speakers are utterly helpless when facing another individual because they either fail to or do not take the trouble to understand the "other."[31] Thus, all major characters are preoccupied with the pursuit of their own interests to such a degree that they prove incapable of empathizing or communicating with their respective partners-in-dialogue. In almost every dialogic situation the speaker sees in the object of his discourse an instrument to further his own projects. This applies to the verbal exchange between Hamilcar and his daughter, Schahabarim and Salammbô, as well as Spendius and Mâtho. Even the first two verbal encounters between the heroine and Mâtho cause grave misunderstandings as her conciliatory invitation "drink" to the Libyan soldier is interpreted by Autarite as an offer of herself. The chapter entitled "Tanit" ends in an even sharper dialogic dissonance, for Mâtho's wooing of Salammbô with the zaïmph ends in a tragic-comic reversal: the heroine suddenly curses the thief of the sacred veil and shouts for her attendants.

Of course both, the personal dialogues and the public addresses, resonate with previous utterances. Since the speeches to large audiences are considerably longer than the abortive dialogues, they necessarily are charged with more verbal and thematic echoes. Paradoxically, what appears to be monologic is essentially dialogic in Flaubert, and vice versa. Last but not least, it should be pointed out that Flaubert's dialogue with his "ideal readers" did not begin until the 1970s.

Aspects of Imagery: Serpents, Snakes, Vipers, and Dragons

Another crucial element that contributes to making *Salammbô* an extraordinary novel about the Old Orient is its écriture which strikes one to be almost as dense as that of a prose poem. This density reveals itself most notably in the matrix of its imagery. One of the most memorable images equates Carthage with a Phoenician galley anchored on Libyan sand. The image and its meaning were discussed at length in Chapter II. Of comparable importance is the symbol of the zaïmph whose rainbow colors appear and reappear through much of the text. The veil of the goddess has been thoroughly treated in two articles.[32] The écriture of *Salammbô* is further enriched by the many splendid similes drawing on the sea, the natural element to which Phoenicians and Carthaginian had traditionally tied their destinies.

There also is the prominent reptile imagery which is paradigmatic of Flaubert's conscious deployment of images. They refer to the Phoenicians' provenance from the Sinai Peninsula, a desert wasteland of Biblical renown. Were the poetic possibilities of subsistence desert dwellers who turned themselves into rich and powerful seafarers not infinite? And is it not equally remarkable that the Phoenicians/Punics never forgot their humble beginnings but enshrined them in their theology? The significance of the chapter entitled "The Serpent" for Salammbô's development has been probed, i.e. the heroine's ritual of sexual initiation with the python, a "male" creature associated with the bisexual goddess Tanit.[33] The serpent is also the genius of the House of Barca, and it plays an important role in the mythical past of the Canaanites and Punics, as well as in their cosmology. Had not the conger eels, similar to snakes in appearance, hatched the mystic egg in which the goddess Tanit lay hidden? (24) Another example is found at the opening of the narrative, where Salammbô tries to placate the riotous soldiers in her father's gardens by entertaining them with patriotic and mythical chants. One of them relates the struggle of the god Melkarth with Masisabal, a monster half serpent half dragon, for the purpose of avenging the serpent queen. Having conquered Masisabal, Melkarth cut off the head of the fiend and affixed it to the prow of his ship, where the sun embalmed it and made it harder than gold.

Thus, the unruly soldiers receive a lesson in Punic mythology and hear that the fearful decorations of Carthaginian galleys are the bloody work of a god. Hamilcar himself displays the sign of the national fetish in his face, "a long scar on his forehead; it twitched like a snake between his eyebrows" (118). In the battle of Macar, moreover, the trunks of the Carthaginian elephants, daubed with red lead, stand up straight in the air, "like red serpents" (147).

The reality, the image, and the symbol of the serpent represent essential components of Carthaginian life. Closely related to the serpent is the dragon (in German, the kinship is linguistically still recognizable[34]), to which the text refers several times. In "Un Chapitre inédit de *Salammbô*," Flaubert compares the city of Carthage itself to a "dragon sprawling from the white rocks in the North across the hilly peninsula to the harbors in the South, with the fortification walls outlining its shape."[35] In the novel proper, there are the women with the hindquarters of dragons whom Melkarth encountered during his pursuit of the serpent-dragon Masisabal, and there is Hamilcar's battle horse, "covered with yellow spots like a dragon, and throwing up spray all round him" (124). The image of the dragon, as unreal as it became when myth was severed from history, nevertheless continued to stimulate even the modern imagination in a powerful way. There is, for example Richard Wagner's dragon Fafner in *Der Ring des Nibelungen*. Fafner is apparently not an altogether unfriendly dragon and even voices his grievances in song. Yet, essentially, he is evil, for as a giant he slew his brother Fasolt out of greed, and he is doomed because he possesses and jealously guards the cursed ring and the treasure of the Rhine. Wagner's *Das Rheingold, Siegfried* and Flaubert's *Salammbô* are contemporary works, for although the premiere performances of the music dramas took place in 1869 and 1874 respectively, the libretti had been completed by 1856. While the authors put myth to utterly different uses, both resorted to the image of the dragon. Thus, they must have perceived attitudes in mid-nineteenth century society, namely greed and coveting power, which this symbol expressed most adequately. In the 1870s, Wagnerians—and there was a growing number of French admirers following Baudelaire's article of 1861 "Richard Wagner et *Tannhäuser* à Paris"[26]—could have read Flaubert's likening of the city's shape to a sprawling dragon as an analogy to Fafner and his treasure, for Carthage also holds riches and tries to protect them from the mercenaries. In addition, by comparing Hamilcar's horse to a dragon, Flaubert adds, if nothing else, another "petit fait vrai" to the character of the Punic leader, for does he not ruthlessly seek wealth and absolute rule? To be sure, a horse and its rider are not quite the same, yet the two might as well be seen as one creature since nineteenth-century French readers, steeped as they were in classical mythology, would be reminded of centaurs.

Salammbô offers additional versions of the serpent and its images. In Mâtho's tent the titular heroine's golden chastity chain snapped when the soldier seized her heels, and as the two ends flew off, "they struck the canvas like two vipers recoiling" (187). Whether these reptiles were consciously invoked as "Carthaginian vipers," or whether Flaubert habitually associated snakes with the prelude to the sexual act remains an open question since a comparable image is used to convey Emma Bovary's frenzy in undressing for Leon: "She pulled so savagely at her corset string that it hissed around her hips like a gliding adder/viper" ("comme une couleuvre qui glisse").[37] In the penultimate chapter of *Salammbô* the heroine is haunted by the memory of her ravisher and conceives the idea "that this man's death would free her thoughts, as the cure for viper bites is to crush vipers on the wound" (269). Here, Mâtho is equated with the viper, and again this is an image charged with sexual connotations. In the concluding scene when Mâtho collapses in front of her and the balustrade occupied by the Carthaginian dignitaries, this antidote is figuratively enacted. Significantly enough, in the midst of the high-ranking Punics lies the tribal python from the temple of Eschmoûn (Aesculapius) "between flasks of rose oil, biting his tail to describe a great black circle" (278). Aside from the figurative equation of Mâtho with a viper in Salammbô's thought, the entire novel contains only two snake similes visualizing someone or something non-Carthaginian. They pertain to Spendius who compares himself to a viper (29), and to Mâtho running the gauntlet, whereby he "made such an effort to break his bonds that his arms crossed on his bare back swelled up like the coils of a snake" (279). The latter image can be recovered for the scheme of the novel when one considers the perceivers of the spectacle. They are Carthaginians who have a fixation on serpents.

Images of the serpent and its relatives occur throughout the text, and they are mainly associated with the Carthaginians after the reptile has been established as a national symbol and the genius of the Barcas. It connects the Punic people and the House of Hamilcar with the origin of the cosmos, the gods, their mythical past, and thereby opens up all dimensions of past time behind the historical events the novel describes. Through the device of these images that cut vertically through the layers of time, the action of the narrative gains import by being embedded in a temporal continuum. As a symbol of Carthage and its culture, the serpent is also a fitting image with respect to place. It is as much at home in the primordial slime of all beginning and Tanit's life-giving moisture as in the deserts burned down to sand crystals in the Sinai by the power of the sun or destructive Moloch. Hence the image of the serpent encompasses in space and time the migration of the Phoenicians from the desert of the Sinai to the moist lowlands of the Levant, and from there to the arid peninsula of North Africa. Altogether, the serpent plays a conspicuous role in Oriental mythology. In contrast to the Judeo-Christian tradition which views it with a mixture of fear, hatred, and contempt because it prompted the fall of man, God's subsequent curse on the seducer, and His decree that there be perpetual enmity between the serpent and woman, the Phoenicians regarded the serpent affirmatively. While it is a Biblical punishment that the serpent must crawl on its belly, the Canaanites considered its ability to move about without feet a mark of distinction. In this respect, too, the world of the Punic imagination appears as "other." According to Carthaginian mythology the circle of the python biting its own tail suggests the planetary system, Eschmoûn's intelligence, just as its skin with golden spots on a black background is reminiscent of the splendors of the firmament.

Yet even in the context of *Salammbô* the image of the serpent is not without ambiguities. The titular heroine and her father are clearly coordinated with it. In Hamilcar's case, however, the image of the dragon intervenes. Outside of Chinese mythology where the dragon possesses positive traits, the dragon represents lust for power, violence, greed, and thus evokes the protagonist's less attractive qualities. Also, one must keep in mind that Flaubert wrote for nineteenth-century French readers who approached his novel with preconceived opinions. Thus, no matter in what positive light the text might present the serpent, it was improbable that readers steeped in the Judeo-Christian tradition would discard what they had been taught about the creature since early childhood. Next to the zoological definition of serpent as reptile, the *Petit Larousse,* for instance, provides the figurative meaning of "personne perfide et méchant," while "langue de serpent" means "personne très médisante." There also is the proverbial expression, possibly common to all European languages, "rechauffer un serpent dans son sein," explained as "accorder ses bienfaits à un ingrat qui se retourne contre son bienfaiteur." With the serpent having been the national fetish of the Phoenicians, we have returned full circle to the notions of "perfida Carthago" or "forked-tongued Tyrians" perpetrated by Roman apologists in literature and historiography. This was also the view of the mercenaries whom Carthage denied just compensation. In distinction from the Carthaginians, the rebellious soldiers are frequently compared to lions and wolves. As a matter of fact, the military-historical actions of the novel could be discussed in terms of animal imagery, which sets serpents, snakes, vipers, and dragons (the Carthaginians) against lions and wolves (the mercenaries), or intelligence, knowledge, and cunning against brute strength and instinctive courage.

All this demonstrates that the image of the serpent and related species is complex in *Salammbô,* and that on account of its literary history, its field of linguistic gravity and suggestiveness, it opens up dimensions of time and meaning which lift the work high above mere reportage or the representation of forgotten historical events admixed with scenes of exoticism and unbridled erotic self-gratification. Rather, the image of the primordial serpent with its chthonic and heavenly references, and its function of integrating the Canaanites' mythical past into the Carthaginian present as symbolic reality, endows life in the Punic capital with a poetic lustre Flaubert and many of his contemporaries missed so dearly in their own modern present.

Time and Repetition

In the system of Hegel's *Aesthetics* Romantic poetry comprises all literature since the advent of Christianity, and it is distinct from classical Greek poetry and the immanently meaningful cosmos of the latter by its depreciation of the world outside the self.[38] The only reality it can recognize is that of interiority or subjectivity. Thus, *Parzival,* Wolfram von Eschenbach's medieval romance par excellence, depicts the adventures of a hero who is essentially homeless in the natural and social world of his time, and who, in his quest for the Holy Grail, seeks reunion with God. As a result of the breakdown of belief in the eighteenth century, precisely the age when the modern novel emerged as a literary form, man also became transcendentally homeless. It was only then, i.e. as a consequence of the individual's severance from the conception of an all-encompassing redeeming eternity, that time could become a decisive factor in narrative.

In his Hegelian *Theory of the Novel* Lukács characterizes Flaubert's narratives set in the author's own time, above all *L'Éducation sentimentale,* as works representing the nineteenth-century phenomenon of romantic disillusionment. Merciless accounts of to what end Romantic expectations must lead in prosaically ordered contemporaneity, these novels nevertheless juxtapose the fragmented minds of their protagonists and the fragmentariness of outer reality with one continuum: time. For time,

Making the Old Orient Present 139

ungraspable and invisible, "gradually robs subjectivity of all its passions and imperceptibly forces alien contents into it." More than that, time the relentless procurer of disillusionment, gradually saps the constructive energies of the characters, and wears them down and out. In the end they are, as for instance Frédéric Moreau and Deslauriers of *L'Éducation sentimentale,* reduced to utter passivity. Instead of continuing to pursue unattainable objectives, or trying to act in one way or other on the world, they reminisce about their common experiences, which were most uplifting when their longings remained ungratified. "And so, by a strange and melancholy paradox, the moment of failure is the moment of value; the comprehending and experiencing of life's refusals is the same source from which the fullness of life seems to flow. What is depicted is the total absence of a fulfillment of meaning, yet the work attains the rich and rounded fullness of a true totality of life. Herein lies the essentially epic quality of memory."[39] As Emil Staiger has shown in *Grundbegriffe der Poetik,* the mode of epic writing about past events constitutes an act of making them present, of creating a "Gegenüber."[40] Time past and time present become one. Making past events present also constitutes, as we know from Wilhelm Dilthey, Benedetto Croce and R. G. Collingwood, one of the foremost tasks of historiography, which is realized by the historian's empathetically rethinking the thoughts of the participants in a historical event. The professional historian, Geoffrey Elton writes, must immerse himself in the period of his choice until he hears its people speak; he must "read them, study their creations and think about them until [he] knows what they are going to say next."[41] During this process the historian's crucial faculty for recapturing and enlivening the past is "imaginative construction" (Collingwood).

In *Salammbô,* a narrative about the "timeless" Orient, the memory of the characters plays only a comparatively modest role. As figures of antiquity, they either do not have much of an inner life, or the novelist has, by and large, followed epic conventions by disclosing only occasional glimpses of it. There are, to be sure, noteworthy exceptions. One such incident takes place in the Building of the Admiralty on an island within Carthage's military harbor, immediately after Hamilcar's popularly acclaimed return from Hispania. The ensuing moment of the protagonist's turning inward commands the reader's attention (the second half of his reflections has been quoted before in a different context):

> This was not how he had hoped to return! All he had done, all he had seen unfolded in his memory; the attacks, the fires, the legions, the storms, Drepanum, Syracuse, Lilybaeum, Mount Etna, the plateau of Eryx, five years of battle—up to

the melancholy day when arms had been laid down and Sicily had been lost. Then he saw again the lemon-groves, goatherds on the grey mountains; and his heart leapt at the idea of another Carthage established there. His plans, his memories, buzzed in his head, still dazed by the ship's pitching; he was overwhelmed with anguish, and in sudden weariness he felt the need to approach the Gods (106–107).

Hamilcar's thoughts recollect and revive his heroic, but futile, struggle with the Romans over Sicily, including the major scenes of the conflict. A bitter lesson, especially since he was not responsible for the ultimate Carthaginian naval defeat at the Aegates Islands. All these memories come to him in the dismal present of his Carthage whose very existence is threatened by his former mercenaries. Yet in the aftermath of the Carthaginian defeat Hamilcar resolved to stem the expansive power of Rome. In order to meet the new challenge, Carthage had to rebuild its formerly invincible fleet and conquer larger, economically even more rewarding dependencies such as fabled Hispania. At this point, the past and the future coalesce in Hamilcar's mind, despite the fact that it is still confronted with the desperate present of a revolutionary uprising. In any case, the past and the future appear, because of their juxtaposition, not only to be succeeding each other directly, but they also absorb the yet undecided "realities" of the present. As far as the maritime suffete is concerned, no divisions of time exist: the past, the present, and the future form a "durée" in which the individual (i.e. Hamilcar) has the unprecedented opportunity of realizing himself.

According to Bergson, time is a function of consciousness and memory. Its "essence is to flow without ceasing,"[42] and it is basically indivisible. This concept of time is radically opposed to Isaac Newton's "absolute time" which flows equally whether anything is happening or not. In other words, the latter is the time of mathematicians, i.e. clock or calendar time. Since Bergson describes his understanding of time as subjective (in contrast to the objective criteria of space), it remains bound to an individual, whereas for the purpose of a historical account an accommodation, if not the coexistence, of subjective and calendar time is required. In order to enable the reader to maintain clarity about the time narrated events take, occasional references to chronological time are appropriate. Flaubert tends to avoid such benchmarks although Polybius's *Histories* would have allowed for divisions. For this reason the narrator of the novel emerges as the one all-encompassing consciousness keeping time.

Hamilcar's own sense of time is neither mathematical nor Bergsonian, but dramatic. Events of the past unfailingly condition his future enterprises. The fact that his present, in contrast to the Latin concept of "being," does not matter much to Hamilcar, although it requires his utmost exertions, might be attributed to the different notions of time he and his Roman adversaries held. Hence, in Hamilcar's reflections, time past and time future become one composite, in which the future must redeem the past and the present. Since he has failed in the past and is struggling with the present, his greatness as a builder of empire can only lie in the future. For in contrast to the objective passing of time, nothing matters to the Carthaginian leader but his personal deeds and achievements. He knows who he is, and what he can do, and given adequate support by the two Carthaginian assemblies, he will be able to direct the course of state in an awe-inspiring manner. Barca attains his complete stature when narrated time has run its course. The reader, who has been witness to his outstanding leadership, cannot question the soundness of his calculated risks and daring plans.

In *The Theory of the Novel* Lukács writes with respect to *Salammbô* and C.F. Meyer's historical narratives that "the central character in works of this kind is in essence a contemplative rather than an active one," so that the novelist's task consists in transforming reflection, lyricism, and psychology into "genuinely epic modes of expression," i.e. into action. While these observations may be appropriate for the titular heroine, they do not pertain to her father, the other hero of the novel. For Hamilcar is by no means a reflective character, but a man of quick resolve and vibrant action. As my reading of the novel has shown, Hamilcar is not only the other hero of the narrative, but he is also a truly exceptional protagonist of the modern novel because of his energy, his resourcefulness in solving military, social, and political problems, and his ability to make quick and circumspect decisions. He is a complete hero of antiquity, with all of the latter's strengths and flaws. In his case it is utterly impossible to speak of a predominance of contemplative features, or of an essentially "hesitant behavior" the novelist must transcribe into action. Rather, Hamilcar realizes himself and the possibilities of his people through deeds in the block of years constituting his lifetime that reaches beyond the narrated time of the novel. The fact that his achievements were undone by historical events long after his death does not diminish them, although this kind of historical undercutting likens the basic tenor of the Carthaginian novel to the ironic authorial predilection pervading Flaubert's fiction set in nineteenth-century France.

The "durée" of the historical action and events, conveying the slow flow of time, is occasionally ruptured by two other kinds and dimensions of temporality: "immobile" time and lyrical time. The former results, by and large, from the extensive descriptions of figures, settings, and other exteriors. Whenever the narratorial discourse gives way to such depictions, "action disappears," Mario Vargas Llosa contends, "people, things, places remain motionless and, as though transported out of the nightmare of chronology, live an eternal moment. The fictitious reality shown in this plane is [. . .] a plastic presence, a body that exists solely to be contemplated. [. . .] everything is matter and space as in a painting."[43] This claim that the elaborate descriptions in *Salammbô* again and again petrify the characters and suspend the action is substantiated by the text, but it requires modification. For instance, the elaborate portrayal of human figures usually takes place in the context of panoramic tableaux covering from one to ten pages of narrative space. Although these tableaux contain sections displaying background paraphernalia such as landscapes, buildings, and groups of people, they are highly complex constructs full of life, tension, and motion. Often they issue from the perspective of a particular character in the narrative. Primary examples are the first and last chapters of the narrative, the former circumscribed by the bounderies of Hamilcar's gardens, the latter by the limits of the space between the prison and the square of Khamon. These tableaux are not merely decorative, but with respect to the "story" they function as instruments of disclosure. Thus "The Feast" informs the reader about the causes of the mercenaries' rebellion, lays the foundation of the love interest, and shows the beginning rivalry between Mâtho and Narr'havas, whereas the closing chapter resolves the conflict of the novel in an ironical manner. Structurally, the tableaux mirror the narrative as a whole in that they are composits of description, scenic representation, discourse, dialogue, and, occasionally, indirect discourse and the free indirect mode. They resemble short films, and whenever the narrator or a character of the novel focuses on a particular figure, object, or event in order to describe it, all action disappears and immobile time reigns for a mythical moment.

Salammbô whom Lukács accuses in *The Historical Novel* of having no necessary connection to the crown-and-state action of the work, nor to the lives of the common people, performs—aside from enlivening Punic mythology and retrieving the zaïmph—through memory another crucial integrating function at the end of the narrative. She is facing Mâtho once more whom Punic vengeance, ire, and sadism have reduced to a spectre no longer human:

> [. . .] and soon all the outside world was blotted out and she saw only Mâtho. Her soul was filled with silence, one of those abysses in which the whole world

> disappears beneath the pressure of a single thought, memory, look. This man walking towards her attracted her to him. [. . .] these dreadful eyes looked at her, and she suddenly became conscious of all he had suffered for her. Although he was dying she saw him again in the tent, on his knees, with his arms around her waist, stammering gentle words; she yearned to feel those arms, hear those words again; she did not want him to die! (281)

Indeed, pertaining to a historical novel set in antiquity, these reflections undoubtedly constitute a rare moment. Where else in such a setting is the entire world blotted out for the sake of recollecting intimacies with a Thou? Salammbô's memories are sentimental; they evoke her encounters with the leader of the vanquished insurgents from the feast of the mercenaries to their fateful and redeeming embrace in his tent. They make the past present once more. The reader recollects the military exploits Mâtho performed in order to win her, as well as the preceding and following actions. In contrast to the reclusive heroine, who must necessarily remain uninformed about many occurrences, the reader is much more knowledgeable. Ultimately, of course, he/she is the judge of events, even beyond the intents voiced by the narrator and ascribed to the author.

Salammbô's concept of time is subjective-lyrical. She punctures the epic "durée" by remembering events of the past and illustrates Hegel's principal theme of the modern novel: the confrontation of the poetry of the heart with the overwhelming forces of reality. In such a scheme, time plays a crucial role. It is the only concept that matters to subjectivity embodied by the heroine in contrast to the slow flow of time characterizing "epic" literature. Yet in her confrontation with Mâtho, time is suspended altogether. Salammbô is oblivious to the individuals near her and the excited crowd below. Her destiny fulfills itself in narrated time. While Salammbô tries to overcome the present by recalling the past, Hamilcar directs his thoughts to the future in order to correct history. As a result, father and daughter fail to meet once again in the present.

There is yet another aspect of time to which Flaubert resorts and which acquires thematic significance in *Salammbô*. The word revolution itself, the subject matter of the historical strain of the novel, connotes in itself repetition. For aside from a forcible overthrow of an established government and political system, or a radical change in the social structure, revolution also designates a "course as if in a circuit, as back to a starting point in time" and "a turning round or rotating, as on an axis" or "point."[44] The first two definitions name the actions and interests of the mercenaries while the last two refer to revolutionary motions in space and time. If one takes the fourth specification and uses the dial of a traditional clock as an example, one has the two arms of the clock on a point and performing repeated revolutions. While the two arms repeat their revolutions with the same regularity, one at twelve times the speed of the other, they return again and again to their starting point and thereby indicate the passage of time. In cosmic terms the movements of the arms of the clock have their analogies in the rotation of the earth on its own axis and its eliptical revolution around the sun, man's premises for measuring human time.

The concept of time and the term repetition are indissolubly connected.[45] Thus, the uprising of the foreign mercenaries against the government and political system of Carthage is in itself not original, but an attempt to emulate the Mamertines, former mercenaries of King Agathocles of Syracuse, who captured the city of Messina, Sicily. The Mamertines (sons of Mars), who called on Carthage and Rome for support in their struggle with Agathocles's successor, were the immediate cause for the first war between the Punic Republic and Rome. The mercenaries depicted in *Salammbô* fought this war and are still awaiting their pay at the opening of the narrative. Since they admire the Mamertines, they sing their song, part of which Flaubert cites (35). Concurrent with this imitative revolution at the bottom of society, Flaubert describes a revolution at the top, that is, within the political system of the Punic state, which Hamilcar precipitates with calculated moves.

As I have shown, the "inviolable" maritime suffete plans to make himself absolute ruler or "king" (Diodorus Siculus) with the help of his charismatic gifts. The realization of this ambition would signify a return to the monarchy which had been the sole government of Carthage since its mythical founding by Dido in the eighth century B.C. to 480 B.C. More intriguing yet is the fact that the suffete's revolutionary designs are an imitation or repetition of changes in the forms of tribal government that occured in Canaan-Israel about one thousand years earlier. Subsequent Punic history shows that Hamilcar established a Barca empire in Spain with himself, his son-in-law Hasdrubal, and his son Hannibal as rulers who controlled the (new) wealth and military forces of Carthage. It must be emphasized that Hamilcar's charismatic road to power was not made up by Flaubert, the author of "fiction," but developed in analogy to Biblical accounts of early Semitic society and on the basis of the Carthaginian leader's historical deeds. Regarding evidence, the aforementioned Punic coins minted in Spain showing portraits of Hamilcar and Hasdrubal support Flaubert's conjecture.

Within *Salammbô* repetition also appears as a structural characteristic, as Flaubert remarked in a letter to Jules de Goncourt of September 27, 1861:

> The more I advance, the better I can evaluate the whole, which appears to me too long and full of repetitions. The same effects recur all too often. One will tire of the wild soldiery. Yet the outline is designed in such a way that deletions would cause too many obscurities [. . .].

Flaubert refers here to the repetitious battle scenes of horrifying gore in which Hamilcar always triumphs, whereas encounters lost in his absence are merely reported or summarized. Undoubtedly Flaubert depicted the protagonist's military campaigns to display his strategic and tactical genius. Of course it was the author who designed the outline of the novel, and as a civilian of the nineteenth century he well knew that strategic and tactical variations in battle plans would not excite the majority of his readers. Was the achievement of greater clarity the only reason for these repetitions? For repetition is one of the foremost features of his Realist narratives, manifesting itself as metonyme or substitution from *Madame Bovary* to *Bouvard et Pécuchet*. One might very well say that Flaubert considered monotony and repetition essential features of nineteenth-century life limited by bourgeois constraints, against which a figure such as Emma Bovary rebel while others like Frédéric Moreau, "the weakest of men,"[46] accept them without too much agonizing, and the simple-hearted Félicité embraces them fervently. All three fall victim to the "modern temper" although they assess the closures of their lives differently. Poor Félicité dies in a state of apotheosis confusing her stuffed parrot Loulou, the last substitution for those she has loved and lost, with the holy ghost. The tandem of Bouvard and Pécuchet presents an extreme case. Trying out the intellectual disciplines and practical pursuits of their century, they fail for one reason or other, possibly because they do not learn anything from their experiences. They just substitute one enterprise for the preceding one and repeat their errors until they have exhausted their constructive energies.

The fact that repetition also made its way into his historical novel set in antiquity can only mean the following: What Flaubert had initially embraced as the Oriental other, turned out to be something similar, although on a grander, more poetic scale and closer to the origins. The disparity in personal stature is the principle difference between Hamilcar and the two Bonapartes, for on the basis of the modern division of labor neither of the

Napoleons could attain the completeness of the tyrant from antiquity, although their methods of attaining power and silencing their opposition resemble each other more than modern consciousness would care to admit. As to *Salammbô* as an allegory of nineteenth-century France, the rise of Napoleon III is a repetition of the achievements of his uncle and of Hamilcar Barca. The three revolutions ended with the restoration of absolute rule; they are comparable to a huge wave broken near the shore whose successive waves become ever smaller. If Marx thought that Louis Napoleon's coup d'état was a farce because it promised a repetition of his uncle's reign, it becomes even more ludicrous as the repetition of a repetition.

Hamilcar's ascendence was reluctantly supported by the Punic bourgeoisie and enthusiastically embraced by the people's party, representatives of a class that had little say before his advent. He also raised the poor, who had no rights at all, to the status of citizens, provided they served well in his army. Similarly, Napoleon I built on the professional middle class and the bourgeoisie, the classes that had carried the French Revolution, and he opened up opportunities for the gifted, regardless of their social provenance. In a sense, then, these two usurpers' rules entailed social changes, whereas Louis Napoleon, according to Marx, relied on the "Lumpenproletariat," non-working shifters and drifters, so that his government represented no class, but only himself. Since he resorted to support his regime with forces from outside the established class antinomies, Marx believed that his rule constituted a suspension of time. Yet was this really the case, or did it signal a rupture in the historical process, despite the Paris Commune of 1871 and the seventy-year existence of the Soviet empire?

Lastly, with respect to the theme of repetition it is noteworthy that Flaubert favored the cyclical view of history. Vico's conception is as much based on the comparative analyses of different national histories, as it points to the organic theories of Romanticism. Just as with an organism a national culture has its origin, youth, flourishing, and decline. In short, it follows a life cycle. Is it therefore not inviting to compare the same developmental stage of cultures belonging to different historical ages, if not millenniums, since later ones repeat the rise or decline of former ones? For Flaubert the study of Carthage in the third century B.C. was intriguing because it was a culture at a stage of decline which he believed was being repeated in the France of his own time.

With his complete victory over the rebellious mercenaries, Hamilcar seems to have returned Carthage to normalcy, i.e. the ante-bellum order.

Besides, the Punic nation is positioning itself to make the great leap forward into a golden future, one promising an unprecedented expansion of Carthaginian power, and riches for everyone. However, this is only how things appear. The splendid future of Carthage and its projected dependencies is inseparably linked to the House of Barca and the abilities of its members. Yet Hamilcar has already undermined the constitution of the state and made himself de facto tyrant of the maritime republic, with troops at hand to enforce his wishes. It is a fatal blow to the plans of the Barcas that Salammbô suddenly expires and the alliance with the ruling house of Numidia cannot be reinforced through marriage. Hannibal paid for this lost opportunity with the crushing defeat at Zama in 202 B.C., where Massinissa and his Numidian cavalry fought for Publius Cornelius Scipio and sealed his fate. This decisive Carthaginian defeat occured in spite of Sophonisbe, a tragic historical Punic woman (and subsequent operatic heroine), reminiscent of Salammbô, who for political reasons was married off to the aging Syphax, "king" of the Numidians. Ultimately, it was Numidian encroachments on Punic territory by a younger and more powerful usurper (Massinissa) that provoked the third war of Carthage with Rome, Numidia's new protector, and led to the historical destruction of the Punic capital and state.

Of course historical events relating to Hamilcar's death in Spain, Hannibal, or the third Punic War are not part of *Salammbô,* and therefore the literary critic might disregard them, on formal grounds. But can one, seriously? This poses an important problem for the historical novel dealing with a segment in the chain of recorded historical events and historical personages. The results are well known. Such knowledge on the reader's part detracts from narrative tension. For a modern work, this is not much of a disadvantage since the "how" of a work is more important than the "what." The modern narrator must captivate the reader's interest by means of his discourse, his language and tropes, the motivations he ascribes to his figures, and by the inevitable discrepancy between the goals they set for themselves and the extent to which they are able to realize them.

The fates of Hamilcar and his daughter illustrate the ancient conception that every personal gain demands an equivalent price so that a balance is maintained in the ancient Greek concept of "moira." It is precisely here that the author's irony finds its lever. It is only fitting for *Salammbô* as a historical novel that the irony undercutting its action is *historical.* For history records that the endeavors of the Barcas to maintain and aggrandize the position of Carthage by braving vastly superior Roman forces (in the Second Punic War Rome's numerical superiority in manpower was about 10:1) were all in vain. In the end the ancient metropolis and its empire were totally annihilated, and the memory of Carthage was left to Roman propagandists. Cato the Elder's dictum, "Ceterum censeo Carthaginem esse delendam," has reverberated through twenty-two centuries; the destruction of the Punic capital was the most thorough holocaust perpetrated by one nation upon another.

Would all this have taken place if the Barcas had not overstrung the bow? Instead of seeking the confrontation till death with Rome for hegemony in the Mediterranean, Carthage might have lived on as a prosperous, though politically unimportant, city state. In that case it might have shared the fate of Byblos, Sidon, and Tyre which gradually faded from history as Phoenician cities. Yet this is but speculation. The ironic fact is that the North African capital perished as a consequence of the Barcas' almost superhuman endeavors. There is a good deal of fatalism in this, which was conceptionalized by Vico and revived by other nineteenth-century historians Flaubert had studied. Of course the novelist had been drawn to historians of such persuasion because their views were congenial to his own: one of extreme scepticism. His novels with contemporary settings all express the same scepticism, if not pessimism, about the individual's fate in the world.

Notes and References

1-2   Georg Lukács, *The Historical Novel*, transl. H. and S. Mitchell (Boston: Beacon Press, 1963) 199 and 176.

3   I can only make this assertion since Walter Benjamin's approach is more differentiated and makes allowances for the peculiarities of historical periods in relation to a given present.

4   Walter Benjamin, "Über den Begriff der Geschichte," in Walter Benjamin, *Gesammelte Schriften*, ed. R. Tiedemann and H. Schweppenhäuser, Werkausgabe (Frankfurt a. M.: Suhrkamp, 1980) II, 704.

5   Max Aprile, "Un Chapitre inédit de *Salammbô*," in Gustave Flaubert, *Oeuvres complètes* (Paris: Club de l'Honnête Homme, 1971-75) XII, 263-303.

6   See for instance Hans-Martin Gauger, *Der Autor und sein Stil* (Stuttgart: Deutsche Verlags-Anstalt, 1988) 57-80.

7   Roland Barthes, *Writing Degree Zero*, transl. A. Levers and C. Smith (New York: Hill and Wang/Farrar, Straus and Giroux, 1987) 10-11.

8   In Barthes, the "modern writers" emerged in the aftermath of the abortive revolution of 1848 when French society was split into (at least) three mutually hostile classes. See *Writing Degree Zero*, 60-61.

9   Flaubert, *Flaubert in Egypt*, transl. and ed. Francis Steegmuller (New York: Penguin, 1996) 181-182.

10   For the metonymic approach, see Veronica Forrest-Thomson, "The Ritual of Reading *Salammbô*," *MLR*, 67 (1972) 787-789 and 798. Related to this approach is Michal Ginsburg's discussion of "substitutions," *Flaubert Writing*, 124-131. Perhaps more in tune with the subject is Jean Rousset's article, "Positions, distances, perspectives dans Salammbô" in *Poétique* 6 (1971) 145-154, which describes first impressions in the novel as "misunderstandings."

11   Flaubert to Guillaume Froehner, January 21, 1863.

12   See also Jean Bruhat, "Napoleon et sa légende: le mythe et la réalite," *Europe*, Avril-Mai, 47 (1969) 52-61.

13   Hayden White, *Metahistory: The Historical Imagination in Nineteenth-Century Europe*, 10.

14   Friedrich Schiller, "Über naive und sentimentalische Dichtung," *Sämtliche Werke*, V (München: Hanser, 1975) 694-780.

15   Hayden White, *Metahistory: The Historical Imagination in Nineteenth-Century Europe*, 37.

16 Erich Heller, "The Realistic Fallacy," in *The Artist's Journey into the Interior* (New York and London: Harcourt, Brace, Jovanovich, 1965) 96.

17 Hayden White, *Metahistory: The Historical Imagination in Nineteenth-Century Europe,* 38.

18 Flaubert, Letter to Ernest Feydeau, mid-October 1858.

19-20 See Gérard Genette, *Narrative Discourse,* transl. J.E. Lewis, Fourth Printing (Ithaca: Cornell UP, 1990) 24.

21 I use the term "intratextuality" for referrals within the same text; for referrals to other texts the term "intertexuality" applies.

22 Mikhail M. Bakhtin, *The Dialogic Imagination,* transl. C. Emerson and M. Holquist (Austin: University of Texas Press) 313-315. See also Tzvetan Todorov, *Mikhail Bakhtin: The Dialogic Principle,* transl. W. Godzich, Third Printing (Minneapolis: University of Minnesota Press, 1988) 99-100.

23 Hugo Friedrich, *Drei Klassiker des französischen Romans,* 6th ed. (Frankfurt a.M.: Vittorio Klostermann, 1970) 142 (my translation).

24 Tzvetan Todorov, *The Poetics of Prose,* transl. R. Howard, Fourth Printing (Ithaca: Cornell UP, 1987) 57.

25 See Dorrit Cohn, *Transparent Minds: Narrative Studies in Fiction and Film* (Ithaca: Cornell UP, 1978).

26-27 Vaheed Ramazani, *The Free Indirect Mode: Flaubert and the Poetics of Irony* (Charlottesville: The University of Virginia Press, 1988) 70 and 73.

28 Bakhtin, *The Dialogic Imagination,* 349.

29 Bakhtin, quoted in Todorov, *Mikhail Bakhtin,* 48.

30 Todorov, *Mikhail Bakhtin,* 53.

31 It is worth noting that the epistemological importance Bakhtin attributes to the "other" in a publication of 1922 is close to the role of the "other" in Jean-Paul Sartre's philosophical work *L'Etre et le Néant.*

32 See the bibliography for the articles by Sima Godfrey and Jacques Neefs.

33 Michal Ginsburg, for instance, argues that Moloch and Tanit, the two principal Carthaginian deities, are not stable or fixed entities, "but dissolve into each other," and that, therefore, "the characters identified with them cannot have unambigous identities or behave in coherent or consistent ways." *Flaubert Writing,* 116. The male character of the python, at least as far as its grammatical gender is concerned, seems to support Ginsburg's hypothesis. On the other hand, the Moloch of Flaubert's novel does not display feminine traits. Thus, one could argue that the Punic Tanit is simply the more comprehensive or inclusive goddess, a quality in complete accordance with her feminity.

34 I am referring to word compunds such as "Lind-wurm" and "Tatzel-wurm."

35   Max Aprile, "Un Chapitre inédit de *Salammbô*," 274.

36   Charles Baudelaire, "Richard Wagner et *Tannhäuser* à Paris," *Curiosités esthétiques, L'Art romantique*, ed. Henri Lemaitre (Paris: Garnier, 1962), 689–728.

37   See also Gustave Flaubert, *Madame Bovary*, transl. Francis Steegmuller, The Modern Library (New York: Random House, 1957) Part III, VI, 32.

38   G.W.F. Hegel, "Die Romantische Kunstform," *Werke in zwanzig Bänden* (Frankfurt a.M.: Suhrkamp, 1970) XIV, 127–242.

39   Georg Lukács, *The Theory of the Novel*, 126.

40   Emil Staiger, *Grundbegriffe der Poetik*, 6th ed. (Zürich: Atlantis, 1963) 84.

41   Geoffrey Elton, *The Practice of History* (New York: Crowell, c. 1967) 17.

42   Henri Bergson, *Mélanges*, ed. A. Robinet (Paris: Presses Universitaires de France, 1972) 353.

43   Mario Vargas Llosa, *The Perpetual Orgy: Flaubert and Madame Bovary*, transl. H. Lane (New York: Farrar, Straus and Giroux, 1986).

44   *The Random House Dictionary*, unabridged edition, ed. Jess Stein (New York: Random House, 1966).

45   Àpropos the theme of repetition I am not referring to Gilles Deleuze's *Repetition and Difference* because this work is based on Nietzsche's concept of "the eternal recurrence of the same." At the time he wrote *Salammbô*, Flaubert was still innocent of its implications.

46   Flaubert, *A Sentimental Education*, 298.

Epilogue

What has been shown, argued, and explained in the preceding pages should furnish convincing reasons why *Salammbô* is an extraordinary Oriental historical novel. No single aspect, but all of its major components contribute to the casting of the new genre. Its political theme, the depiction of revolutionary warfare and the rise of a charismatic leader from amidst chaos, fear, and despair, presents in an Oriental garb an allegory of Bonapartism, the epoch-making political force of nineteenth-century France. Flaubert viewed this phenomenon with curiously mixed feelings. While the reigns of the two charismatic Napoleons, however different they were in themselves and in their appeals, achievements, and failures, granted him a Pyrrhic triumph over his countrymen's low spiritual and moral state, his aesthetic self had profited from such rule (J. P. Sartre). Also, he was deeply troubled about the future of France. The reigns of the three members of the House of Barca, glorious as they were, had led to the destruction of Carthage. Flaubert feared that Napoleon III might precipitate a comparable catastrophe.

Flaubert's narrative reflects with unprecedented acumen his own political present in the image of a "re"-constructed Afro-Oriental civilization. In the earlier, or "classical," historical novel, there existed no such compelling correspondences to an author's present. Scott had above all conceived of his "romances" as instruments of telling how things had been sixty or seventy years ago, that is, as memorials to a past way of life and as means to a better understanding of how the present had become the way it was. But he did not write his narratives as critical political and social mirrors of his own actuality. The Romantic authors inspired by his work (von Arnim, de Vigny, Hauff, Mérimée, Hugo, etc.) followed his lead in their attempt of evoking the past for its own sake. As far as its political thematics are concerned, the publication of *Salammbô* thus constitutes a watershed in the evolution of the historical novel: The past does not explain how the present has become what it is, but it functions as its critique.

The greater part of Flaubert's accomplishment would probably have remained unrealizable, had he not encountered the Orient with rare empathy and immersed himself in historical study. Aside from his acquaintance with Greek and Roman historians, his knowledge of Vico and Voltaire, Montesquieu and Herder, Hegel, Chateaubriand, Michelet, Thierry, and Barante, where he encountered the competing claims of historicism, critical history, and philosophies of history, made him acutely aware of the problems he faced as a historical novelist in the second half of the nineteenth century. It is his great merit to have anticipated later innovations of seminal historians and critics such as Dilthey, Croce, Collingwood, and Walter Benjamin. Based on documentary evidence, historical events are thought through once more, internalized, i.e. reexperienced, in order to be enlivened. Hand in hand with his historical scrupulousness went his dedicated study of Oriental matters where his empathetic personal experiences allowed him to rise above the prejudices of de Volney, Chateaubriand, Lamartine, Michelet, and Renan. In this respect, Flaubert could be confident about his labors concerning Carthage, despite the reservations of contemporary experts such as Guillaume Froehner. But he also knew, as his various epistolary asides attest, that what he had resurrected was only an image of ancient Carthage. This very Carthage of Salammbô and Hamilcar functions as a revealing reflection of socio-political developments in France beginning with the great Revolution of 1789.

According to Nietzsche's division of historiography, *Salammbô* is not an "antiquarian" narrative. The irrefutable affinities of Punic society and politics, as conveyed by the narrator's discourse, to those of France during the first two thirds of the nineteenth century exclude this option. Although the novel undoubtedly displays "monumental" features, the thrust of *Salammbô* makes it clearly a "critical" specimen. This assessment comes close to Collingwood's defintion of history, although the latter claims the concept of "critical" history (in his case, "scientific" historiography) exclusively for historians. However, the late philosopher Louis Mink has demonstrated that concerning "truth," narratives of historical novelists and historians are much closer to one another than has been generally assumed. This view finds support in the writings of Walter Benjamin (an extreme advocate of "critical history"), Claude Lévi-Strauss, and Hayden White.

By writing an Oriental historical novel set in antiquity, Flaubert accommodated his dreams and the socio-political demands of his own time.

This hybrid genre, juxtaposing past and present while prospecting the future, allowed him to achieve two ordinarily exclusive goals and unite them aesthetically. In Salammbô and Hamilcar he could portray two strong characters with great desires and spectacular lives. At the same time Flaubert was in a position to reflect the modern, or at least his and his favorite historians' view that the outcome of the individual's collision with the superior forces of reality was always the same. If one looks for meaning, Flaubert's Oriental novel offers several possibilities. There is, first of all, Salammbô's and Mâtho's fulfillment in love which they experience as impersonations of the gods Tanit and Moloch. They find a kind of love-death while lost in the eyes of each other, oblivious to everything else. Their end has the mood of tragedy, and that can be seen as something positive in itself (Nietzsche). With Hamilcar's career Flaubert was able to portray a complete military and public success unparalleled in modern novels. At the closure of the narrative, the historical Hamilcar's star is still rising, its curve arching beyond the author's fictional cosmos. His fate is a key to determining meaning in this particular narrative.

Meaning always is, in one way or other, related to space and time. The English linguistic order of "space and time"—in contrast to the German convention of "Zeit und Raum" (time and space), with which French usage, though less unequivocally, seems to agree—may not be able to hold its ground against empirical evidence. For what kind of evidence do we have, provided we are concerned with events in the "real" world, that is, indeed, not "historical"? While there have been a few historical movements for which space was more important than time (such as the massive retreat from the everyday world enacted by Christian monks and hermits around the Eastern Mediterranean in the third and fourth centuries A.D.,[1] to which Flaubert's own *La Tentation de Saint Antoine* is a monument), these occurrences have been exceptions. Neither Salammbô nor Hamilcar withdraw from life but, sensuous Oriental pagans as they are, they seek to realize their dreams and ambitions in their here and now. Moreover, since they act upon their world, their fictional careers must be evaluated against the omnipresent and inexorable judge of time. This is only appropriate because the genre of the historical novel is indissolubly wed to the concept of temporality. Both protagonists live audaciously and realize most of their extraordinary potential in the life-spans allotted to them. Yet is not the relative brevity of their full lives that which makes them precious, as Thomas Mann has one of his characters observe: "Transitoriness did not destroy value, far from it; it was exactly what lent all existence its worth, dignity, and charm. Only the episodic, only what possessed a beginning and an end, was interesting and worthy of sympathy because transitoriness had given it a soul. But that was true of everything—the whole of cosmic Being had been given a soul by transitoriness, and the only thing that was eternal, soulless, and therefore unworthy of sympathy, was that Nothingness out of which it had been called forth to labour and to rejoice."[2]

This insight about being and life relates directly to the microcosm of *Salammbô* which Flaubert created almost "ex nihilo." The narrative, its figures, and their Afro-Oriental world come to life in the consciousness of the reader. On account of the paucity of sources, all of Flaubert's characters are, strictly speaking, creations of his imagination. Some of them are "round" figures (according to E.M. Forster's classification of fictional characters) and capable of surprising us. With Hamilcar, Salammbô, Schahabarim, and Spendius the author formed human beings who hardly have their equals in historical fiction. Hamilcar is more memorable than whoever emerged from Scott's Scottish mists, and because of her Oriental otherness Salammbô need not shy away from comparison with Jeanie Deans, the Cameronian lass, surely one of Scott's most original heroines *(The Heart of Midlothian),* or from Rose Bradwardine and Flora MacIvor of *Waverley,* not even from Rachel and Beatrix of *Henry Esmond,* although Thackeray's ladies are considerably more complex. Whereas Jeanie stands fully illuminated and is utterly comprehensible in her quest to save her sister, the honor of her family, as well as her own conscience, Salammbô remains mysterious and can be perceived only through a veil, the rainbow-colored zaïmph. And what about Spendius, the ingenious Greek who is at the same time a coward? There is also Schahabarim, the doubting priest, who finally leaves the goddess he serves for the stronger god. Flaubert's characters are so very intriguing because their personal, metaphysical, and representational qualities are often not in agreement with one another,[3] and because the author leaves a considerable part of their selves to the imagination of his audience. In addition to Flaubert's psychological perceptiveness and political acumen, the very strength and innovative quality of *Salammbô* lie, like the author's novels on contemporary subjects, in the employment of effective narrative devices: the iterative-durative approach combined with focussing on the unique, the style, "écriture," imagery, the "trottoir roulant" of the narrator's discourse, and the handling of time. One of Flaubert's foremost stylistic merits consists in that precise, crisp, and laconic mode of narration. Contrary to Roland Barthes's assumption, this kind of style was not innate to the author, for the "natural" Flaubert, however paradoxical this may sound, tended toward a verbose and hyperbolic Baroque-Romantic manner.

While two crucial instruments in the novelist's arsenal, his style and his imagery, do not conform to Barthes's definition, this critic was evidently right in his assessment of the purposes of creative writers after 1848. Accordingly, post-1848 novelists were no longer innocent of the crucial socio-political problems of their era. In *Salammbô* Flaubert went to great length to present them to his readers. But neither they, nor the critics of his day, or literary historians understood him. This is rather regrettable since all Flaubert wanted to impart to his contemporaries and succeeding generations is allegorically spelled out in his only Oriental historical novel. This case is even more extreme than that of Stendhal who feared that it would take two more generations to understand him.

It is likely that *Salammbô* would not have been misunderstood if its readers and critics had been less Eurocentric and accustomed to reading narratives as allegories. Regarding the Afro-Oriental setting and Punic politics, French readers of the second half of the nineteenth century, citizens of one of the two most progressive and powerful European nations, were quite unprepared to see the principal events of their recent history reflected in the civil war and power struggle of an ancient Oriental people such as the Carthaginians. Comte de Volney, Chateaubriand, and Lamartine had given the contemporary Orient a bad press by depicting it as a drowsy region awaiting redemption through European imperialism. Moreover, despite their world-wide enterprises, in comparison with which Greek explorations pale, Michelet portrayed Phoenicians and Punics as the scum of the ancient peoples around the Mediterranean. To this assessment must be added Renan's anti-Semitic diatribes in *Système des langues sémitiques,* where the author presents his personal prejudices as scientific truths. Such prevalent notions led Martin Bernal to assume that Flaubert wrote *Salammbô* out of a "strong dislike" for the Carthaginians and hence identified them with the British.

Bernal's other principal contentions are just as questionable. He asserts, for example, that according to Flaubert, Carthage as a typical Oriental culture deserved to be annihilated by Rome in 146 B.C, so that the conquests of exotic countries by European powers in the nineteenth century were justified. The same goes for the claim that among European nations Flaubert considered only the English as being capable of emulating Punic cruelties, as they had demonstrated in the suppression of the Sepoy mutiny in India. While Bernal points out that "the France of the Second Empire was inflicting incredible outrages on the populations of China and Indo-China and, even more to the point, on those of Algeria,"[4] he implies that Flaubert was either not aware of these facts or ignored them. Yet the contrary is the case, for the novelist surely had the atrocities of the

Algerian situation between 1830 and 1847 in mind when he described the Mercenary War in *Salammbô*. In the Algerian War there was a steady acceleration of bloody retributions between the insurgent natives and the French occupation forces, which had its parallels in the confrontation of the Carthaginian mercenaries and the Punic state, as well as in the desperate uprising and suppression of the French workers by the French military in June 1848. Another reason supporting Flaubert's identification of the Punics with the Second Empire consists in his description of the Carthaginians treatment of the indigenous North African peoples in which he reflected the mistakes of French colonial adminstration in newly conquered Algeria.[5]

The main problem with Bernal is that concerning the Orient (including Algeria), he turns Flaubert into a representative Frenchman. Yet Flaubert was very fond of the Orient. To use an analogy, for him the Europeanization of the Orient would be comparable to raising the European working classes through education to the bourgeoisie's level of stupidity. The representative French view on Algeria was fully expressed in Louise Colet's poem "Le Marabout de Sidi-Brahim" (1845) that glorifies the heroism of 80 remaining soldiers of an Orléans batallion confronting 4,000 Arab-Berber insurgents. It is fitting that Colet received prizes four times from the Académie française, whereas Flaubert was never given any recognition. What saved the novelist from such honors were his genius and his so-called "perversities," for which Edward Said makes allowances. Far from applauding the conquest of Punic civilization on moral grounds—it was no more immoral than Rome or nineteenth-century France—he really appreciated Oriental licentiousness which, even more savory, was tied to religion in Carthage. Would Flaubert have considered Salammbô herself, that "divine virgin," lovely, smart, and determined, as the representative of a decadent civilization? Nor should one forget that he held Hamilcar, the ascending ancient tyrant in the highest esteem ("there is no more beautiful manifestation of man").

As to aesthetics, the decades following German Classicism and European Romanticism in the nineteenth century had a predilection for the symbol to the exclusion of allegory. This preference has been convincingly demonstrated by Hans-Georg Gadamer in *Wahrheit und Methode* (1960): in the age of Goethe the distinction between symbol and allegory was tantamount to that between art and non-art.[6] To be sure Walter Benjamin's *Ursprung des deutschen Trauerspiels* constituted a serious effort to rehabilitate the aesthetic qualities of allegory, but it was left to recent criticism to demonstrate the presence of allegory even in the lyric poetry and narratives of classical and Romantic literature. When Benjamin defines allegory as a void "that signifies precisely the non-being of what it represents," he provides a most appropriate characterization of the gist of Flaubert's labors and the imaginative tour-de-force of his Punic novel. For Flaubert had described his Carthage as a mixture of soap bubbles and the real, whereby the real consisted of the natural surroundings of the ancient capital which the author had inspected and observed, aspects of Oriental life and peculiarities of Oriental people he had experienced in Egypt and "Syria." All other ingredients for the composition of his image of the city and its characteristics were drawn from books or resulted from imaginative construction. Benjamin also asserts that allegory presents "the 'facies hippocratica' of history as a petrified primordeal landscape as history is depicted in the stages of its decay."[7] This understanding of allegory ties in with Paul de Man's claim that the trope is indissolubly linked to death as is, for instance, the last of William Wordsworth's "Lucy"-poems. The petrification of history which projects itself into landscape becomes manifest as soon as the meaning of allegory has been grasped. However, for de Man there only is allegory "if the allegorical sign refer[s] to another sign that precedes it. The meaning constituted by the allegorical sign can then consist only in the repetition [. . .] of a previous sign with which it can never coincide, since it is the essence of the previous sign to be pure anteriority."[8]

While *Salammbô* clearly displays a number of the aspects of allegory described above, it is distinguished for a more complex temporal structure than de Man's definition grants. The kind of temporality de Man ascribes to allegory evidently derives from the literary practices of medieval literature (in the sense of Erich Auerbach's "Figura"), Benjamin's conception of Baroque tragedy, and the Romantic longing for the supposed unity of pure origin. Yet what happens if a writer, especially a disillusioned romantic and professional demoralizer, does not believe in the purity and splendor of origins, but suspects that what constitutes the present derives from muddled or chaotic beginnings? In such a case the meaning of allegory can lie in the opposite temporal direction, the future, that is, the author's own time. This kind of allegory is found in historical novels which are not merely antiquarian or monumental.

Salammbô modifies Benjamin's and de Man's definitions of the trope "allegory" in yet another way. While the descriptive passages of the narrative portray nature at numerous instances in a seemingly petrified state,[9] and while the closure of the narrative conveys the transformation of the titular heroine into a statue and, ultimately, a corpse, the image of Carthage Flaubert evokes is not as transparent as that of traditional allegories. In other words, despite the author's soap-bubbles, the novel was read for too long as a love story set in ancient Carthage with the latter's sociopolitical paraphernalia. Thus the misprision of *Salammbô* must be attributed to the narrative and presentational skills of the Realist Flaubert, which created the illusion of a real city filled with real people and real life. Outside of proving his power as a conjurer, (for the author was well aware of the fact that he had evoked nothing but a "mirage"), Flaubert would have had no other compelling reason to devote six years of his life to such a purpose. Instead, the novel *Salammbô* should be perceived as an allegory of nineteenth-century France. It elucidates the rise of charismatic leaders from revolutionary chaos, seen against the backgound of a divided bourgeoisie and the restless lower classes. *Salammbô* reads like a retrospective prophecy and critique of Bonapartism.

Notes and References

1. This was also the time of St. Augustine, bishop of Hippo, whose native language was Punic or neo-Phoenician.

2. Thomas Mann, *Confessions of Felix Krull Confidence Man,* transl. Denver Lindley, Vintage Books (New York: Random House, 1969) 270–271.

3. Scholes/Kellogg, *The Nature of Narrative* (London, Oxford, New York: Oxford UP, 1966) 82–112.

4. Martin Bernal, *Black Athena,* eighth paperback printing (New Brunswick: Rutgers UP, 1994) 357.

5. Anne Green, *Flaubert and the Historical Novel: '"Salammbô" Reassessed* (Cambridge, London: Cambridge UP, 1982) 92. Green points out that two French studies published well before *Salammbô* demonstrated that Carthaginian methods of colonisation in North Africa were more benign to the natives than those adopted by France after 1830. See Simonde de Sismondi, *Les colonies des anciens comparées à celles des modernes* (Geneva, 1837) and Saint-Marc Girardin, "De la Domination des Carthaginois et des Romains en Afrique comparée avec la domination française," *Revue des Deux Mondes* (May 1, 1841) 413–14.

6. Hans-Georg Gadamer, *Wahrheit und Methode,* 4th ed. (Tübingen: Mohr, 1975) 70.

7. Walter Benjamin, "Ursprung des deutschen Trauerspiels," *Gesammelte Schriften,* ed. R. Tiedemann and H. Schweppenhäuser (Frankfurt a.M.: Suhrkamp, 1980), I, 1,1, 343.

8. Paul de Man, "The Rhetoric of Temporality," *Blindness and Insight* (Minneapolis: The University of Minnesota Press, 1983) 207. See also de Man, "Allegory (Julie)," *Allegories of Reading: Figural Language in Rousseau, Nietzsche, Rilke, and Proust* (New Haven and London: Yale UP, 1979) 188–220.

9. Victor Brombert, *The Novels of Flaubert* (Princeton: Princeton UP, 1966) 105–108.

Bibliography

My reading is based on Gustave Flaubert, *Oeuvres complètes,* 16 vols. (Paris: Club de l'Honnête Homme, 1971–75).

Vols. XlI to XVI contain his letters which follow *Correspondance,* ed. Louis Conard, 9 vols., fourth ed. (1926–33). The footnotes in my text concerning Flaubert's letters provide the dates of their composition. The translations are by and large my own. AlthoughI I am well aware of the fact that certain schools of contemporary criticism question the value of letters as an aid to interpreting literary works, I attach great significance to them. Flaubert, in particular, expressed his views on literature more freely in his correspondence than in any other medium. It is a matter of discretion how these epistolary views are applied.

In my text, citations from Flaubert's narratives are given in English. Those from *Salammbô* and from *Flaubert in Egypt* are followed by their page reference(s) in parentheses; quotations from other works are footnoted. All of them refer to the following editions:

Flaubert in Egypt, transl. and ed. Francis Steegmuller (New York: Penguin Books, 1996).

Madame Bovary, transl. Francis Steegmuller, Modern Library (New York: Random House, 1957).

Salammbô, transl. and intr. A.J. Krailsheimer (Harmondsworth, U.K.: Penguin, 1977).

Sentimental Education, transl. Robert Baldick (Harmondsworth, U.K.: Penguin, 1975).

The Temptation of Saint Antony, transl. Kitty Mrosovsky (London, etc.: Penguin, 1980).

Three Tales, transl. Robert Baldick (Harmondsworth, U.K.: Penguin, 1967).

Bouvard and Pécuchet, transl. A.J. Krailsheimer (Harmondsworth, U.K.: Penguin, 1978).

Other Primary and Seconday Works

Adert, Laurent. "Salammbô ou le roman barbare, in Riglio, Juan and Caruso, Carlo ed. and intr., *Poétiques barabares/Poetiche barbare* (Ravenna: Longo, 1998) 47–64.

Allem, Maurice. *La Vie quotidienne sous le Second Empire* (Paris: Librairie Hachette, 1948).

Aprile, Max. "Dureau de la Malle's *Carthage:* A Documentary Source for Flaubert's *Salammbô," French Studies,* XLIII (1989) 305–315.

―――. "Un Chapitre inédit de *Salammbô,"* in Flaubert, *Oeuvres complètes* (Paris: Club de l'Honnête Homme, 1971-75) XII, 263–303.

Aristotle. *Poetics,* transl. S. H. Butcher (New York: Hill and Wang, 1961).

Aristoteles. *Poetik,* Griechisch/Deutsch, transl. M. Fuhrmann (Stuttgart: Reclam, 1982).

Bakhtin, Mikhail M. *The Dialogic Imagination,* transl. C. Emerson and M. Holquist (Austin: University of Texas Press, 1990).

Balzac, Honoré de. *Les Chouans* (Paris: Librairie Génerale Française, 1983).

Bardèche, Maurice. *L'Oeuvres de Flaubert* (Paris: Les Sept Couleurs, 1974).

Bart, Benjamin F. *Flaubert* (Syracuse, N.Y.: Syracuse UP, 1967).

Barthes, Roland. *Writing Degree Zero,* transl. A. Lavers and C. Smith (New York: Hill and Wang/Farrar, Straus and Giroux, 1987).

Bem, Jeanne. "Modernité de 'Salammbô,'" *Littérature,* 40 (1980) 18–31.

Benjamin, Walter. "Literaturgeschichte und Literaturwissenschaft,"*Gesammelte Schriften,* ed. R. Tiedemann and

H. Schweppenhauser (Frankfurt a.M.: Suhrkamp, 1980), Werkausgabe III, 8, 283–290.

———. "Über den Begriff der Geschichte," *Gesammelte Schriften,* II, 1,2, 691–704.

———. "Ursprung des deutschen Trauerspiels," *Gesammelte Schriften,* I, 1,1 203–430.

Berckx, Ingrid. "Die romantische Form des historischen Romans," Diss. (Evanston, IL: Northwestern University, 1987).

Bergson, Henri. *Mélanges,* ed. A. Robinet (Paris: Presses Universitaires, 1972).

Bernal, Martin. *Black Athena: The Afroasiatic Roots of Classical Civilization,* I, eighth paperback printing (New Brunswick: Rutgers UP, 1994).

Bertl, Klaus D. *Gustave Flaubert—Die Zeitstruktur in seinen erzählenden Dichtungen* (Bonn: Bouvier/Grundmann, 1974).

Bevernis, Christa. "Vergangenheitsbewältigung und Gegenwartsbezug in Gustave Flauberts Roman *Salammbô,*" *Beiträge zur Romanischen Philologie* (1972) 22–38.

Bizer, Marc. "*Salammbô,* Polybe et la rhétorique de la violence," *Revue d'histoire littéraire de la France,* 95 (1995) 974–988.

Booth, Wayne C. *The Rhetoric of Fiction* (Chicago and London: The University of Chicago Press, 1963).

Bosse, Monika. *Metamorphosen des literarischen "Contre-pouvoir" im nachrevolutionären Frankreich: Mme de Staël, Saint-Simon, Balzac, Flaubert* (München: Fink, 1981).

Bosse, Monika and Stoll, André. "Die Agonie des archaischen Orients— Eine verschlüsselte Vision des Revolutionszeitalters," in Gustave Flaubert, *Salammbô,* transl. G. Brustgi (Frankfurt a.M.: Insel, 1979) 401–448.

Brady, Patrick. "Archetypes and the Historical Novel: The Case of *Salammbô,*" *Stanford French Review,* I, 3 (1977) 313–324.

Brée, Germaine, "Flaubert et la critique récente," in *Essais sur Flaubert en l'honneur du professeur Don Demorest,* ed. Charles Carlut (Paris: A.G. Nizet, 1979) 31–38.

Brombert, Victor. *The Novels of Flaubert* (Princeton: Princeton UP, 1966).

Bruhat, Jean. "Napoléon et sa légende: Le Mythe et sa réalité," *Europe,* April–May 47 (1969) 52–61.

Bruneau, Jean. *Le "Conte Oriental" de Flaubert* (Paris: Denoel, 1973).

Bruneau, Jean. *Les Débuts littéraires de Gustave Flaubert 1831–1845* (Paris: Armand Colin, 1962).

Butor, Michel. *Improvisations sur Flaubert* (Paris: Le Sphinx, 1984).

Carlut, Charles, ed. *Essais sur Flaubert en l'honneur du professeur Don Demorest* (Paris: A.G. Nizet, 1979).

Caven, Brian. *The Punic Wars* (New York: Barnes & Noble, 1992).

Charles-Picard, Gilbert and Colette. *Daily Life in Carthage at the Time of Hannibal,* transl. A.E. Foster (New York: Macmillan, 1961).

Chateaubriand, Francois-René de. "Études ou Discours historiques," in *Oeuvres de Chateaubriand,* 16 Vol. (Paris: Louis Vivès, 1878) VIII.

Chevalier, Louis. *Classes laborieuses et classes dangereuses à Paris pendant la première moitié du XIXe siècle* (Paris: Hachette, 1984).

Collingwood, R.G. *The Idea of History* (1946), (London, Oxford, New York: Oxford UP, 1968).

Croce, Benedetto. *History: Its Theory and Practice,* transl. Douglas Ainslie (New York: Harcourt, Brace and Co., 1921).

Croce, Benedetto. *Zur Theorie und Geschichte der Historiographie,* transl. E. Pizzo (Tübingen: J.C.B. Mohr, 1915).

Curry, Corrada Biazzo. *Description and Meaning in Three Novels by Gustave Flaubert* (New York, Washington, D.C., Baltimore, Bern, etc.: Peter Lang, 1994) 61–114.

Daspre, André. "Le Roman historique et l'histoire," *Revue d'histoire littéraire de la France,* LXXV (1975) 235–244.

De la Varende, Henri. *Flaubert in Selbstzeugnissen und Bilddokumenten,* transl. H.M. Enzensberger (Reinbek bei Hamburg: Rowohlt, 1958).

De Man, Paul. *Allegories of Reading: Figural Language in Rousseau, Nietzsche, Rilke, and Proust* (New Haven and London: Yale UP, 1979).

———. *Blindness and Insight*, second ed. (Minneapolis: University of Minnesota Press, 1983).

Demorest, Don L. *L'Expression figurée et symbolique dans l'oeuvre de Gustave Flaubert* (Paris: Les Presses modernes, 1931).

Dijkstra, Bram. *Idols of Perversity: Fantasies of Feminine Evil in fin-de-siècle Culture* (New York: Oxford UP, 1986).

Dilthey, Wilhelm. *Der Aufbau der geschichtlichen Welt in den Geisteswissenschaften* (Berlin: Königlich-Preußische Akademie, 1910).

———. *Pattern and Meaning in History*, ed. and intr. H.P. Rickman, Harper Torchbooks (New York: Harper and Row, 1962).

Diodorus Siculus. *Bibliothek der Geschichte,* transl. J.F. Kaltwasser, Vols. V and VI (Frankfurt a.M.: Hermann, 1786).

Donato, Eugenio. "Flaubert and the Question of History: Notes for a Critical Anthology," *MLN*, May–Dec. 91.2 (1976) 850–870.

———. *The Script of Decadence: Eassays on the Fictions of Flaubert and the Poetics of Romanticism* (New York and Oxford: Oxford UP, 1993).

Du Camp, Maxime. *Souvenirs littéraires* (Paris: Librairie Hachette, 1882).

Duquette, Jean Pierre. "Flaubert, l'histoire et le roman historique," *Revue d'histoire littéraire de la France*, LXXV (1975) 344–352.

———. "Flaubert politique," in *Essais en l'honneur du professeur Don Demorest*, 63–77.

———. *Flaubert ou l'architécture du vide* (Montreal: Les Presses de l'Université du Montreal, 1972).

Durr, Volker. "Hamilcar Barca and the Emergence of the Charismatic Leader: Flaubert's *Salammbô* and Nineteenth Century France," *Cincinnati Romance Review*, XI (1992) 34–42.

———. "Personal Identity and the Idea of the Novel: Hegel in Rilke," *Comparative Literature*, 39/2 (1987) 97–114.

———. "The Young Nietzsche: Historical Philosophizing, Historical Perspectivism, and the National Socialist Past," in *Nietzsche: Literature and Values*, ed. V. Dürr, R. Grimm, K. Harms (Madison: The University of Wisconsin Press, 1988) 29–40.

Eissfeldt, Otto. "Neue keilalphabetische Texte aus Ras Schamra-Ugarit," in *Sitzungsberichte der deutschen Akadamie der Wissenschaften*, 6 (1965) 1–49.

Elton, Geoffrey. *The Practice of History* (New York: Cornell UP, 1967).

Faguet, Émile. *Flaubert* (Paris: Librairie Hachette, 1913).

Fallowell, Duncan. "Sir Sacheverell Sitwell at Western Hall, A Conversation," in *Encounter*, LXX, No. 5 (1988) 12–20.

Fay, P.B. and Coleman, A. *Sources and Structure of Flaubert's Salammbô* (Baltimore/Paris: The Johns Hopkins Press/Librairie E. Champion, 1914).

Feuchtwanger, Lion. *Das Haus der Desdemona oder Größe und Grenzen der historischen Dichtung* (Frankfurt a.M.: Fischer Taschenbuch Verlag, 1986).

Forrest-Thomson, Veronica. "The Ritual of Reading *Salammbô*," *MLR*, 67 (1972) 787–798.

Foster, E.M. *Aspects of the Novel* (1927) (New York: Harcourt, Brace, and World, 1954).

France, Anatole. *La Vie littéraire*, III (Paris: Calman-Levy, n.d.).

Freud, Sigmund. "The Uncanny," *On Creativity and the Unconscious*, Harper Torchbooks (New York: Harper and Rowe, 1958) 122–161.

Gadamer, Hans-Georg. *Wahrheit und Methode*, 4th ed. (Tübingen: J.C.B. Mohr, 1975).

Gauger, Hans-Martin. *Der Autor und sein Stil* (Stuttgart: Deutsche Verlagsanstalt, 1988).

Gaultier, J. de. "Le Bovarisme de Salammbô," *Mercure de France*, CIII (1913) 31–40.

Gautier, Théophile. *Le Roman de la momie* (Paris: Garnier-Flammarion, 1966).

———. "Salammbô par Gustave Flaubert," *Le Moniteur universel*, December 2, 1862, 2–3.

Genette, Gérard. *Figures III* (Paris: Éditions du Seuil, 1972) 122–144.

———. *Narrative Discourse,* transl. J. E. Lewin, Fourth Printing (Ithaca, N.Y.: Cornell UP, 1990).

———. "Silences de Flaubert," *Figures I* (Paris: Éditions du Seuil, 1966), 223–242.

Gerhardi, Gerhard. "Romantic Love and the Prostitution of Politics," *Studies in the Novel,* 4 (1972) 402–415.

Ginsburg, Michal P. *Flaubert Writing* (Stanford: Stanford UP, 1986).

Godfrey, Sima. "The Fabrication of *Salammbô*: The Surface of the Veil," *MLN,* 95 (1980) 1005–1016.

Goethe, Johann Wolfgang. "Anhang" to his translation of *Das Leben des Benvenuto Cellini* (Frankfurt a.M.: Insel, 1981).

Goethe, *Werke,* 14 Vols, ed. Erich Trunz, Hamburger Ausgabe, 6th ed. (Hamburg: Wegener, 1965 ff.). The individual volumes were published in different years.

Goldmann, Lucien. *Pour une Sociologie du roman* (Paris: Gallimard, 1964).

Goncourt, Edmond et Jules de. *Journal,* Vols. I and II (Paris: Fasquelle-Flammarion, 1956).

Gooch, G.P. *History and Historians in the Nineteenth Century* (Boston: Beacon Press, 1959).

Gray, Eugene. "Flaubert's Esthetic and the Problem of Knowledge," *Nineteenth-Century French Studies,* 4 (1976) 295–302.

Gray, Francine du Plessix. *Rage and Fire: A Life of Louise Colet* (New York, etc.: Simon and Schuster, 1994).

Green, Anne. *Flaubert and the Historical Novel—Salammbô Reassessed* (Cambridge, London, U.K.: Cambridge UP, 1982).

Greenblatt, Stephen. *Marvellous Possessions: The Wonder of the New World* (Chicago: Chicago UP: 1991).

Griffin, Robert. *Rape of the Lock: Flaubert's Mythic Realism* (Lexington, KY: French Forum, 1988).

Haas, Eugen. *Flaubert und die Politik,* Diss. (Heidelberg, 1931).

Haig, Stirling. *Flaubert and the Gift of Speech: Dialogue and Discourse in Four Modern Novels* (Cambridge, U.K.: Cambridge UP, 1986).

Hamilton, Arthur. *Sources of the Religious Element in Flaubert's Salammbô* (Baltimore/Paris: The Johns Hopkins Press/Librairie E. Champion, 1917).

Hammer, Karl and Hartmann, Peter Claus, ed. *Le Bonapartisme * Der Bonapartismus* (Zürich and München: Artemis, 1977).

Hauser, Arnold. *The Social History of Art,* IV, transl. S. Goodman, Vintage Books (New York: Random House, n.d.).

Hebbel, Friedrich. *Sämtliche Werke,* hist. krit. Ausgabe, ed. Richard K. Werner, second ed. (Berlin: Behr, 1904).

Hegel, Georg Wilhelm Friedrich. "Vorlesungen über Ästhetik," *Theorie Werkausgabe,* 20 Vols., ed. E. Moldenhauer and K.M. Michel (Frankfurt a.M.: Suhrkamp, 1970) XIII–XV.

Hélein-Koss, Suzanne. "Discours ironique et ironie romantique dans *Salammbô* de Gustave Flaubert," *Symposium,* 40 (1986) 16–40.

Hendrycks, Anne-Sophie. "Flaubert et le paysage oriental, *Revue d'Histoire littéraire de la France,* 6 (1994) 996–1010.

Henry, Gilles. *L'Histoire du monde c'est une farce ou la vie de Gustave Flaubert* (Condé-sur-Noireau: Ch. Corlet, 1980).

Herder, Johann Gottfried. *Ideen zur Philosophie der Geschichte der Menschheit, Herders Werke,* IV (Berlin and Weimar: Aufbau, 1964).

Herm, Gerhard. *Die Phönizier: Das Purpurreich der Antike* (Reinbek bei Hamburg: Rowohlt, 1975).

Herodotus. *The Histories,* transl. A. Selincourt, revised A.R. Burn (Harmondsworth, U.K.: Penguin, 1978).

Holdheim, W. Wofgang. *Die Suche nach dem Epos: Der Geschichtsroman bei Hugo, Tolstoi und Flaubert* (Heidelberg: Carl Winter, 1978).

Hugo, Victor Marie. *Oeuvre de Victor Hugo,* 43 vols. (Paris: J. Lemonnyer, 1885–95) XXI–XXII.

———. *Quatrevingt-Treize* (Paris: Garnier-Flammarion, 1965).

Iser, Wolfgang. *Der implizierte Leser,* Uni-Taschenbücher, second ed. (München: Fink, 1979).

James, Henry. *The Future of the Novel,* intr. and ed. Leon Edel, Vintage Books (New York: Random House, 1956).

Jameson, Frederic. "Flaubert's Libidinal Historicism: Trois Contes," in *Flaubert and Politics* (Lincoln: University of Nebraska Press, 1984) 76–83.

Jauß, Hans Robert. *Literaturgeschichte als Provokation,* sixth ed. (Frankfurt a.M.: Suhrkamp, 1979).

Josephus ben Matthias. *The Jewish War,* transl. and intr. G.A. Williamson (Harmondsworth, U.K.: Penguin, 1959).

Kennard, Lindsay, C. "The Ideology of Violence in Flaubert's *Salammbô,*" *Trivium,* 13 (1978) 53–61.

Kinet, Dirk. *Ugarit: Geschichte und Kultur einer Stadt in der Umwelt des Alten Testamentes* (Stuttgart: Katholisches Bibelwerk, 1981).

Knight, Diana. *Flaubert's Characters—The Language of Illusion* (Cambridge: Cambridge UP, 1985).

König, Traugott, ed. *Sartres Flaubert lesen—Essays* (Reinbek bei Hamburg: Rowohlt, 1980).

A. Koselleck, W. Mommsen, J. Rüsen, H. Lutz, ed. *Theorie der Geschichte I: Parteilichkeit und Objektivität* (München: Deutscher Taschenbuchverlag, 1977).

Krailsheimer, A.J. "Introduction to *Salammbô*" in Flaubert, *Salammbô* (Harmondsworth, U.K.: Penguin, 1978) 7–16.

Laforge, Francois. "Salammbô: Les Mythes de la Révolution," *RHL,* 85 (1985) 26–40.

Lamartine, Alphonse de. *Voyage en Orient* (1835), 2 vols. (Paris: Hachette, 1887).

Lamb, Harold. *Hannibal: One Man against Rome* (New York: Bantam Books, 1963).

Leal, R.B. "Salammbô: An Aspect of Structure," *French Studies,* 27 (1973) 16–29.

Lévi-Strauss, Claude. *The Savage Mind,* transl. George Weidenfeld (Chicago: University of Chicago Press, 1967).

Livius, Titus, "The War with Hannibal," or Books XXI–XXX of *The History of Rom from its Foundation,* transl. A. de Selincourt (Baltimore: Penguin, 1965).

Llosa Vargas, Mario. *The Perpetual Orgy: Flaubert and Madame Bovary,* transl. Helen Lane (New York, NY: Farrar, Straus and Giroux, 1986).

Lottmann, Herbert. *Flaubert. A Biography* (Boston: Little, Brown, & Co., 1989).

Lowe, Catherine. Salammbô ou la question de l'autre de la parole," *L'Arc,* Nov. 58 (1974) 83–88.

Lowe, Lisa. *Critical Terrains: French and British Orientalisms* (Ithaka, N Y and London: Cornell UP, 1994).

———. "The Orient as Woman in Flaubert's *Salammbô* and 'Voyage en Orient'," *Comparative Literature Studies,* 23 (1986) 44–58.

Lowe, Margaret. *Towards the Real Flaubert* (Oxford, U.K.: Clarendon Press, 1984).

Lukács, Georg. "Erzählen oder Beschreiben? Zur Duiskussion über Naturalismus und Formalismus" (1936), in *Begriffsbestimmung des literarischen Realismus,* ed. R. Brinkmann (Darmstadt: Wissenschaftliche Buchgesellschaft, 1969) 33–85.

———. *Studies in European Realism,* (New York: Grosset & Dunlap, 1964).

———.*The Historical Novel* (1937), transl. H. & S. Mitchell (Boston: Beacon Press, 1963).

——— *The Theory of the Novel* (1906), transl. A. Bostock, sixth printing (Cambridge: The MIT Press, 1983).

Maigron, Louis. *Le Roman historique à l'époque romantique,* Nouvelle Édition (Paris: Librairie Ancienne H. Campion, 1912).

Malamat, Abraham. "Charismatische Führung im Buch der Richter," *Max Webers Studie über das antike Judentum,* ed. Wolfgang Schluchter (Frankfurt a.M.: Suhrkamp, 1981) 110–133.

Mann, Thomas. *Confessions of Felix Krull Confidence Man,* transl. Denver Lindley, Vintage (New York: Random House, 1969).

———. *"Death in Venice" and Seven Other Stories,* transl. H.T. Lowe-Porter, Vintage (New York: Random House, n.d.).

———. *Essays of Three Decades,* transl. H.T. Lowe-Porter (New York: Knopf, 1948).

Marrou, Henri-Irène. *The Meaning of History,* transl. R.J. Olsen (Baltimore, Dublin: Helicon, 1966).

Marx, Karl. *Der achtzehnte Brumaire des Louis Napoleon* (1852), (Berlin: Dietz, 1946).

———. *Die Klassenkämpfe in Frankreich 1848 bis 1850* (Berlin: Dietz, 1951).

Mayoux, Jean Jacques. "Flaubert et le réel," *Mercure de France,* February 15, 1934, 33–52.

Mehlman, Jeffrey. *Revolution and Repetition* (Berkeley, Los Angeles, London: University of California Press, 1977).

Meinecke, Friedrich. *Die Entstehung des Historismus,* ed. and intr. Carl Hinrichs, 4th ed. (München: R. Oldenbourg Verlag, 1965).

Michelet, Jules. "Histoire Romaine," in *Oeuvres complètes,* ed. P. Viallaneix (Paris: Flammarion, 1972) XI, 315–621.

Mink, Louis O. *Historical Understanding* (Ithaca and London: Cornell UP, 1987).

Molino, Jean. "Qu'est-ce que le roman historique?," *Revue d'histoire littéraire de la France,* LXXV (1975) 195–234.

Montesquieu, Charles de Secondat, Baron de. "Considerations sur les causes de la grandeur des Romains et de leur décadence," *Oeuvres completes,* 2 Vols., ed. R. Caillois (Paris: Gallimard, 1949–1951) II, 69–224.

Morson, Gary Saul and Emerson, Caryl. *Mikhail Bakhtin: Creation of a Prosaics* (Stanford: Stanford UP, 1990).

Myers, David. "The New Historicism in Literary Studies," in *Academic Questions,* 2 (1988–89) 27–36.

Nadeau, Maurice. *Gustave Flaubert, écrivain,* Nouvelle édition revue (Paris: Les Lettres nouvelles, 1980).

Neefs, Jacques. "Le parcours du zaïmph," in *La Production du sens chez Flaubert,* ed. Claudine Gothot-Mersch (Paris: Union générale d'editions, 1975) 227–241.

Nerval, Gérard de. *Oeuvres,* 2 vols., ed. Henri Lemaître (Paris: Garnier, 1958).

Nietzsche, Friedrich. *Werke in drei Bänden und einem Indexband,* ed. Karl Schlechta, 8th ed. (München: Hanser, 1977).

Picard, Gilbert. *Carthage,* transl. M. and L. Kochan (London: Elek Books, 1964).

Plautus, Marcus Accius. "Poenulus," in *Lustspiele,* transl. G.G.S. Kopke (Berlin: Nauck, 1820) II, 469–596.

Polybius. *The Histories,* six vols., transl. W.R. Paton, The Loeb Classical Library (London: W. Heinemann, 1922) I, 177–239.

Popper, Karl R. *The Poverty of Historicism* (1957), (New York and Evanston: Harper & Row, 1964).

Porter, Dennis. "Aestheticism versus the Novel: the example of Salammbô," *Novel,* IV (1971) 101–106.

Raleigh, John Henry. "*Waverly* as History; or 'Tis One Hundred and Fifty Six Years since," in *Novel,* III (1970) 14–29.

Ramanzani, Vaheed K. *The Free Indirect Mode: Flaubert and the Poetics of Irony* (Charlottesville: University of Virginia Press, 1988).

Renan, Ernest. *Histoire générale et système comparé des langues sémitiques, Oeuvres complètes,* ed. Henriette Psichari, Vol. 8 (Paris: Calmann-Lévy, 1947–61).

———. *The Life of Jesus,* intr. J.H. Holmes, The Modern Library (New York: Random House, 1955).

Rousset, Jean. "Positions, distances, perspectives dans Salammbô," *Poétique,* 6 (1971)145–154.

Sacy, Silvestre de. *Chrestomathie arabe, ou Extraits de divers écrivains arabes [. . .],* I [1826], reprint (Osnabrück: Biblio Verlag, 1973).

Said, Edward W. *Culture and Imperialism,* Vintage Books (New York: Random House, 1994).

———. *Orientalism* (New York: Pantheon Books, 1978).

Sallustius, Gaius C. *The Jugurthine War,* intr. and transl. S.A. Handford (Harmondsworth, U.K.: Penguin, 1963).

Sarraute, Natalie. "Flaubert le précurseur," *Preuves,* 168 (1965) 3–11.

Sartre, Jean-Paul. *L'Idiot de la famille: Gustave Flaubert de 1821 à 1857,* 3 vols. (Paris: Gallimard, 1971–72).

Schehr, Lawrence R. "Salammbô as the Novel of Alterity," *Nineteenth-Century French Studies,* 17 (1989) 326–341.

Scholes, Robert and Kellogg, Robert. *The Nature of Narrative* (London, Oxford, New York: Oxford UP, 1966).

Schor, Naomi and Majewski, Henry F. *Flaubert and Postmodernism* (Lincoln and London: University of Nebraska Press, 1984).

Schwab, Raymond. *The Oriental Renaissance—Europe's Rediscovery of India and the East, 1680–1880* [1950], transl. G. Patterson-Blackard and V. Reinking (New York: Columbia UP, 1984).

Scott, Walter. *The Standard Edition of the Novels and Poems of Sir Walter Scott,* ed. Estes and Lauriat (Boston: Dana Estes and Co., 1892 ff.).

Sherrington, R.J. *Three Novels by Flaubert: A Study of Techniques* (Oxford, U.K.: Clarendon Press, 1970).

Staiger, Emil. *Grundbegriffe der Poetik,* sixth printing (Zürich: Atlantis, 1963).

Starr, Peter. "Salammbô: The Politics of an Ending," *French Forum,* 10 (1985) 40–56

Steegmuller, Francis. "*Salammbô*: The Career of an Opera," *Grand Street,* 4 (1984) 103–127.

Taine, Hippolite Adolphe. *Balzac: A Critical Study,* transl. and intr. Lorenzo O'Rourke (New York and London: Funk & Wagnalls Co., 1906).

Tillet, Margaret. *On Reading Flaubert* (London: Oxford UP, 1961).

Todorov, Tzevetan. *Mikhail Bakhtin: The Dialogical Principle,* transl. W. Godzich (Minneapolis: University of Minnesota Press, 1984).

———. *The Poetics of Prose,* transl. R. Howard (Ithaca, NY: Cornell UP, 1977).

Troyat, Henri. *Flaubert,* transl. J. Pinkham (New York: Viking-Penguin, 1992).

Veeser, Aram H., ed. *The New Historicism* (New York and London: Routledge: 1989).

Vergil, Publius Maro. *The Aeneid,* transl. Jackson Knight (Harmondsworth, etc.: Penguin Books, 1966).

Vigny, Alfred de. *Le Journal d'un poète, Oeuvres complètes,* ed. F. Baldensperger (Paris: Gallimard, 1948) XI.

Volney, Constantin François Comte de. *Voyage en Egypte et en Syrie* (Paris: Bossange, 1821).

Weber, Max. "Die drei reinen Typen der legitimen Herrschaft," in *Gesammelte Aufsätze zur Wissenschaftslehre,* third ed. (Tübingen: J.C.B. Mohr, 1923).

———. *Gesammelte Aufsätze zur Religionssoziologie* (Tübingen: J.C.B. Mohr, 1923).

White, Hayden. *Metahistory: The Historical Imagination in Nineteenth-Century Europe* (Baltimore: The Johns Hopkins UP, 1973).

——— *Tropics of Discourse—Essays in Cultural Criticism* (Baltimore, London: The Johns Hopkins UP, 1978).

Subject Index

-A-

Abbas Pasha, 25
Account of the Manners and Customs of the Modern Egyptians (Lane), 22
Aesthetics (Hegel), 138
Aida, 5
Alexander the Great, 20
    destruction of Tyre, xi
Algeria, x
Algerian War, 158
Aprile, Max, 118
archeologism, 116
Aristotle, x
Arnim, Achim von 153
Auerbach, Erich, 159

-B-

Bakhtin, Mikhail, 127, 132, 133
Balzac, Honoré de, 59
Barante, Guillaume de 17, 154
Barca dynasty, viii
Bardèche, Maurice, 88
Barthes, Roland, 113, 119, 121, 122, 156
Baudelaire, Charles, 4, 31, 135
Belle Époque, 2
Bem, Jeanne, 89, 99
Benjamin, Walter, 7, 115, 154, 158, 159
Bergson, Henri, 140
Berlioz, Hector, 2
Bernal, Martin, ix, 52, 107, 158
Bernhardt, Sarah, 2
Betrachtungen eines Unpolitischen (Mann), 94
Bevernis, Christa, viii, 89
Birth of Tragedy, The (Nietzsche), 28
Black Athena (Bernal), ix,
Bonapartism, 91, 93, 95, 103, 115, 160
    compared to Bonapartisme, 96
    definition of, 96
Bonapartisme, 96, 98, 103
Bopp, Franz, 22
Bosse, Monika, viii, 89, 91, 95, 101
Bouilhet, Louis, 29
Bouvard et Pécuchet (Flaubert), vii, viii, 8, 92, 94, 123, 145
"Brakfast in the Grass" (Manet), 56
Brombert, Victor, 50, 88
Bruneau, M. Jean, 14
Brunetière, Ferdinand, 34
Butor, Michael, 5
Byron, Lord, 19

-C-

Canaanite mythology, 47
Carthage
    compared to nineteenth-century France, 89
    compared to Paris, 107
    destruction of, 40
    "otherness" of, 7
Carthaginians, ix,
    around the Mediterranean, ix
    Flaubert's description of, 46
    similarities to ancient Israel, 73
Cato the Elder, 49
Chateaubriand, François-René de, viii, 17, 19, 22, 154, 157
Cheruel, Adolphe, 14
Chouans, Les (Balzac), 59
Chrestomatie arabe (Sacy), 22
Cinq-Mars (Vigny), 19
Cloquet, Jules, 23, 35
Code Napoléon, 21

Colet, Louise, 31, 88, 92, 94, 158
Collingwood, R.G., 18, 139, 154
Colonies des anciens comparées à celle des modernes, Les (Sismondi), 108
Constantinople, 31
Cousin, Victor, 17
Crimean War, 97
Critical Terrains: French and British Orientalisms (Lowe), 47
Croce, Benedetto, 51, 115, 139, 154
Crosby, Henry, 2,
Culler, Jonathan, 53

-D-

Dahn, Felix, 113
Darwin, Charles, 114
Deans, Jeanie, 69
Débuts littéraires de Gustave Flaubert, Les (Bruneau), 14
Defile of the Axe, 81
De Man, Paul, 159
Dickens, Charles, 121
Dilthey, Wilhelm, 18, 51, 115, 139, 154
Donato, Eugenio, 7
Dostoevsky, Fyodor, 132
Du Camp, Maxime, 22, 24, 93, 107
  difficulties with Flaubert, 32
Dugazon, Gourgand, 14

-E-

Ebers, Georg, 113
"écriture," 119-25, 132
  imagery, 134
  of *Salammbô*, 119
Egypt
  prostitution in, 28
  slavery in, 28
Egyptian Institute, 21
Eliot, George, 121
Elton, Geoffrey, 139
Eschenbach, Wolfram von, 138
Essai sur l'inégalité des races humaines (Gobineau), 103
Études historiques (Chateaubriand), 17
European Romanticism, 158
Existentialist philosophy, 122

-F-

Falloux law, 101
fata morgana, 118
Flaubert, Gustave
  as Realist novelist, 14, 87
  as "scientific" novelist, 7
  attitude toward Napolean III, 106
  attitude toward racism, 104
  criticism of Revolution of 1848, viii
  description of Carthage, 5
  uncertainty about history of Carthage, 121
  description of Arabs, 23
  description of Egyptian landscapes, 48
  description of political events in the Orient, viii
  description of ruling class in *Salammbô*, 90
  doubts as a writer, 33
  fear of collapse of France, x
  historical struggles in racial terms, 15-16
  in Egypt, 24-30
  in the Orient, vii
  knowledge of the Orient in writing *Salammbô*, 19
  Oriental sexual licentiousness, x
  motivation for creating the character Salammbô, 69
  personality traits seen in plot of *Salammbô*, vii
  purpose of writing *Salammbô*, 14
  relationship with his mother, 33-4
  response to Sainte-Beuve's criticism, 62, 95
  travels in Syria, 30
  use of approximation, 121
  use of language in *Salammbô*, 125
  use of Mercenary War in *Salammbô*, 51-2
  uses of irony
    trope, 124
  writing of *Salammbô*
    landscape descriptions, 43
    researching Carthage, 41
Fleurs du mal, Les (Baudelaire), 31
Fontane, Theodor, 94
Forster, E.M., 70, 156

Index

France, Anatole, 93
Franco-Prussian War, 7, 17, 104
Free Indirect Mode, The (Ramazani), 131
Freud, Sigmund, 70
Friedrich, Hugo, 128
Froehner, Guillaume, 50, 121, 154
   archeology in *Salammbô*, 50

-G-

Gadamer, Hans-Georg, 158
Gallé, Émile, 44
Gates of Horn, The (Levin), 50
Gautier, Théophile, 2, 4, 51, 53, 70
   misreading *Salammbô*, 87
Genette, Gérard, 126
German Classicism, 158
"Geschichtsphilosophie," 16
Girardin, Saint-Marc, 108
Ginsburg, Michal, 102
Gobineau, Joseph-Arthur, comte de, 103
Goethe, Johann Wolfgang, 2, 54, 114, 117
Goncourt, Jules de, 145
Gounod, Charles, 2
Green, Anne, 18, 89, 90, 107
Grundbegriffe der Poetik (Staiger), 139
Guizot, François, 103
Gustave Flaubert (Thibaudet), 51

-H-

Hamilcar Barca, viii, xi, 63
   as charismatic hero of *Salammbô*, 70, 81, 93
     as "Realpolitiker," 82
     building of power base, 75, 77, 88
       development of army, 75
       use of religion, 101
     comparison to the Napoleans, 89, 99, 103, 146
     conflict with Carthaginian politics, 76
     death of, 79
     description of treasure vault, 44
     mytical attributes of, 71
     offering of his son Hannibal, 75
     political objectives of, 82
     rise of, x

Hannibal, 123
Hartim Bey, 24
Hauff, Wilhelm, 153
Heart of Midlothian, The (Deans), 69
Hebbel, Friedrich, 59
Hegel, Georg Wilhelm Friedrich, 17, 113, 119, 138, 143, 154
Hellenistic era, 39
Henry Esmond (Thackeray), 156
Herder, Johann Gottfried, 17, 18, 54, 114, 154
"Hérodias," vii
   setting of, vii
Histoire de France (Michelet), 15
Histoire de la conquète de l'Angleterre par les Normands (Thierry), 114
Histoire de la Révolution française (Michelet), 15
Histoire romaine (Michelet), 15, 104
Holdheim, W. Wolfgang, 51
Hugo, Victor, viii, 20, 153

-I-

imagery in *Salammbô*, 134-38
   reptile imagery, 134-5
"imaginative construction," 18
Isocrates, x
Ivanhoe (Scott), 125

-J-

Judith (Hebbel), 59
Jungfrau von Orleans (Schiller), 59

-K-

Keller, Gottfried, 121
Kleist, Heinrich von, 59
Kuchuk Hanem, 28, 53

-L-

Lamartine, Alphonse de, viii, 19, 154, 157
Lane, Edward William, 22
Leal, R.B., 1
L'Éducation sentimentale (Flaubert), vii, viii, 8, 91, 92, 94, 100, 123, 138
Levant, viii
Lévi-Strauss, Claude, 154

Levin, Harry, 50
Life of Jesus (Renan), 40
Llosa, Mario Vargas, 142
Lowe, Lisa, 47
Lucinde (Schlegel)
Lukács, Georg, 3, 6, 43, 50, 53, 62, 69, 88, 113, 141, 142
    historiography based on racial distinctions, 114
    "modernization" in *Salammbô*, 100
    objections to Naturalism, 3

-M-

Madame Bovary (Flaubert), vii, xi, 1, 4, 8, 13, 14, 58, 106, 118, 123, 145
Maghreb, vii
Malamat, Abraham, 72
Manet, Edouard, 56
Mann, Thomas, 9, 13, 28, 94, 117, 155
Marx, Karl, 8, 100, 102, 114, 146
    and Louis Napolean, 98
mare nostrum, 5
Mathilde, Princess, 93, 106
mechanistic conception of history, 123
Mercenary War, 3, 4, 7, 73, 88, 95, 100, 102, 103, 105, 116, 121, 124, 158
Mérimée, Prosper, 153
metaphors and similes in *Salammbô*, 46, 120
Meyer, Conrad Ferdinand, 113, 141
Michelet, Jules, x, 6, 15, 17, 23, 47, 48, 99, 104, 116, 154, 157
    elements of his narratives, 15
Mink, Louis, 154
Mohammed Ali, 24, 28, 31
"moira," 147
Momie, La (Gautier), 87
Mommsen, Theodor, 15
monotheism, x
Montesquieu, Charles de Secondat, 17, 154
Montijo, Eugénie, 101
Morris, William, 44
multiculturalism, 114
Mussorgsky, Modest, 2

-N-

Nadeau, Maurice, 88
Napoleon I, 89
    as a charismatic leader, 89
    and the bourgeoisie, 98
    defeat of the Mamluks, x
    expedition to Egypt and Syria, viii, 4
    and the Orient, 21
Napoleon III, Louis Napoleon, viii, ix, 89, 103
    compared to Hamilcar Barca, 103, 146
    use of religious sentiment, 101
Naturalism, 3
New Historicists, 114
Newton, Isaac, 140
Niebuhr, Barthold Georg, 15
Nietzsche, Friedrich, 17, 19, 28, 113, 127, 154
    "the will of power," 84

-O-

"Oriental crisis," 5
Oriental Renaissance, viii
Orientales, Les (Hugo), 20
Orientalism, 20
"other," 5
Ottoman Empire, 5, 21

-P-

Paris
    compared to Carthage, 107
    sexual mores in, 108
Parnasse, 50
Party of Order, 98
Parzival (Eschenbach), 138
pax romana, 5
Penthesilea (Kleist), 59
Phoenicians
    abominations, x
    as sea-farers, x
    development of political system, xi
    sexual mores, ix
    sexual reputation, 6
Poetics of Prose, The (Todorov), 129
Polybius, 41, 116, 140
Port-Royal (Sainte-Beuve), 113

Index

Pradier, James, 108
Publius Cornelius Scipio Aemilianus, ix
Punics, 6, 39
    description of culture, 40

-R-

Ramazani, Vaheed, 131
Ranke, Leopold von, 18, 114
Realist irony, 124
Realist novel
Realist school, 19
Red Skeletons, 2
Reforms of 1832, 105
Renan, Ernest, 22, 40, 73, 103, 154, 157
    and anti-Semitism, 22-3
repetition, 144
Reyer, Ernest, 2, 4
Rimsky-Korsakov, Barbe, 1
Ring des Nibelungen, Der (Wagner), 135
Rochegrosse, Georges, 2
Rodin, Auguste, 115
Roman de la Momie, Le (Gautier), 4
Roman History (Michelet), 23
Romans
    conquest of Jerusamel, 6
    destruction of Carthage and Corinth, 6
Roman slaves, 83
Romantic disillusionment, 138
Romantic irony, 123
Romanticism
    in the UK and German-speaking countries, 117
Rouge et le Noir, Le (Stendhal), 127

-S-

Sacy, Silvestre de, 22
Said, Edward, 8, 21, 47, 158
Sainte-Beuve, Charles-Augustin, 1, 3, 6, 62, 113
    judgment of *Salammbô*, 3
    misreading of *Salammbô*, 87
Salammbô (character)
    as a "femme fatale," 54
    death of, 72
        reason for death of, 102
    end of role in novel, 60
    patriotism of, 57
    wedding to Narr'havas, 61, 80

Salammbô (novel)
    allocation of narrative space in, 53
    archeology in (Froehner), 50
    as a counterstatement to *Madame Bovary*, 132
    as a historical novel, 1
    as a "Parnassian epic," 50
    as a political allegory, 8, 95
    as an allegory, 121, 160
    as an artists' novel, 2
    as narrative text, 8
    description of Carthage in, 42, 119
    description of Egypt in, 24-5
    description of landscapes in, 43-6
    double meaning of "revolution" in, xi
    elements of time in, 139-44
    "absolute time" (Newton), 140
    forms of speech in,
        free indirect discourse, 130
        indirect mode, 130
        psycho-narration, 130
        public addresses, 129, 133
    Hamilcar Barca as hero of, 70
    mechanistic form of argument in, 17
    Mercenary War in, 51-2
    narrative voice in, 131
    "dialogic problem," 132
    neglected by literary criticism, 1
    political themes of, 7
    as a political allegory, 87
    popular appeal to early readers, 1
    presentation of love in, 58
    presentation of time in, 9, 138-148
    principal flaw of, 69
    satire in, 123
    scenic representation, 126
    similes and metaphors in, 51
    traits of Flaubert's personality in
    plot of, vii
Salammbô (opera), 5
Sand, George, 70, 104
Sartre, Jean-Paul, 88, 106, 122, 153
Schehr, Lawrence, 51
Schiller, Friedrich, 59, 123
Schlegel, Friedrich, 20, 124
Schlesinger, Élisa, 53
schofet, 73
Schopenhauer, Arthur, 113
Schwab, Raymond, viii, 8, 20
Scienza Nuova, La (Vico), 16

Scott, Walter, 2, 50, 69, 125, 153
  narrative space, 3
Second French Empire, 7
Sherrington, R.J., 1, 53
similes and metaphors in *Salammbô*, 46, 120
Sismondi, Simonde de, 108
Smarh (Flaubert), 4
Soliman Pasha, 24
Souvenirs littéraires (Du Camp), 93
Staiger, Emil, 139
Stendhal, 4, 127
Stoll, André, viii, 89, 91, 95, 101
Strauss, Richard, 2
Suez Canal, 5
suffete, 73
Syssitia, 45
  lifestyles of, 45
Système des langues sémitiques (Renan), 157

-T-

tablets of Ugarit, 47
Taine, Hippolite Adolphe, 103
Tanit, 1, 126
  sacred veil of, 58-60
Tentation de Saint Antoine, La (Flaubert), vii, 4, 13, 19, 155
Thebaid of Saint Anthony, 26
Thebes, 25
Theory of the Novel (Lucáks), 138, 141
Thibaudet, Albert, 51, 88
Thierry, Augustin, 17, 18, 103, 154
Tiffany, L.C., 44
time
  presentation of time in *Salammbô*, 9, 137-148
Todorov, Tzevetan, 130
Tostes, 13
Trevelyan, George Macauley, 15
Tristan and Isolde (Wagner), 58
Trois Contes (Flaubert), 123
Tulard, Jean, 97
Tunisia, x, 43
typology of charismatic leadership, 74
Tyre
  destruction of, xi

-U-

Ursprung des deutschen Trauerspiels (Benjamin), 158
Uses of Uncertainty, The (Culler), 53

-V-

Verande, Jean de la, 25
Verdi, Giuseppe, 5
Vico, Giambattista, 16, 17, 18, 114, 123, 146, 154
Vigny, Alfred de, 19, 117, 153
Virgil, 46
Volney, Constatin, comte de, 21, 154, 157
Voltaire, 17, 154
Voyage en Orient (Volney), 21

-W-

Wagner, Richard, 28, 58, 115, 135
Weber, Max, x, 6, 8, 48, 71
  typology of charismatic leadership, 74, 95
Wahrheit und Methode (Gadamer), 158
Werner, Karl Ferdinand, 96
White, Hayden, 15, 17, 122, 154
Wilde, Oscar, 2
Winckelmann, Johann Joachim, 6
Wordsworth, William, 159

-Y-

Yonville, 13

-Z-

Zola, Émile, 115
"Zola Centenary," 3

Currents in Comparative Romance Languages and Literatures

This series was founded in 1987, and actively solicits book-length manuscripts (approximately 200–400 pages) that treat aspects of Romance languages and literatures. Originally established for works dealing with two or more Romance literatures, the series has broadened its horizons and now includes studies on themes within a single literature or between different literatures, civilizations, art, music, film and social movements, as well as comparative linguistics. Studies on individual writers with an influence on other literatures/civilizations are also welcome. We entertain a variety of approaches and formats, provided the scholarship and methodology are appropriate.

For additional information about the series or for the submission of manuscripts, please contact:

> Tamara Alvarez-Detrell and Michael G. Paulson
> c/o Dr. Heidi Burns
> Peter Lang Publishing, Inc.
> P.O. Box 1246
> Bel Air, MD 21014-1246

To order other books in this series, please contact our Customer Service Department:

> 800-770-LANG (within the U.S.)
> 212-647-7706 (outside the U.S.)
> 212-647-7707 FAX

or browse online by series at:

> www.peterlangusa.com